A PRACTICAL GUIDE TO WORLD-CLASS BUYING

A PRACTICAL GUIDE TO WORLD-CLASS BUYING

Brian Farrington PhD, MSc, BSc, FCIPS

Derek W. F. Waters FCIPS

CHAPMAN & HALL

London · Glasgow · Weinheim · New York · Tokyo · Melbourne · Madras

Published by Chapman & Hall, 2–6 Boundary Row, London SE1 8HN, UK

Chapman & Hall, 2–6 Boundary Row, London SE1 8HN, UK

Blackie Academic & Professional, Wester Cleddens Road, Bishopbriggs, Glasgow G64 2NZ, UK

Chapman & Hall GmbH, Pappelallee 3, 69469 Weinheim, Germany

Chapman & Hall USA, 115 Fifth Avenue, New York, NY 10003, USA

Chapman & Hall Japan, ITP-Japan, Kyowa Building, 3F, 2-2-1 Hirakawacho, Chiyoda-ku, Tokyo 102, Japan

Chapman & Hall Australia, 102 Dodds Street, South Melbourne, Victoria 3205, Australia

Chapman & Hall India, R. Seshadri, 32 Second Main Road, CIT East, Madras 600 035, India

First edition 1996

© 1996 Brian Farrington and Derek W. F. Waters

Typeset in 10/12pt Palatino by WestKey Ltd, Falmouth, Cornwall
Printed in England by Clays Ltd, St Ives plc

ISBN   0 412 72210 0

A catalogue record for this book is available from the British Library

Library of Congress Catalog Card Number: 95-70018

∞ Printed on permanent acid-free text paper, manufactured in accordance with ANSI/NISO Z39.48–1992 and ANSI/NISO Z39.48–1984 (Permanence of Paper).

CONTENTS

PREFACE

The beginning

The first buyer, from whom all buyers are descended, was the Stone Age hunter who was sent by his tribe to a distant Flint-Knapper to buy a supply of flint axe-heads and arrow-heads. He formulated the question all the subsequent buyers have asked, 'How much for twenty axe-heads and forty arrow-heads?' The Flint-Knapper thinking to himself, 'I've got a right one here,' replied, 'One mammoth please!' The Stone Age hunter's jaw set firmly and fingering his club menacingly said tersely, 'Too much! Try again!' So started the first negotiation.

Eventually the Hunter went back to the tribe well pleased with his purchases, having paid one small deer, which was still better than the Flint-Knapper had expected.

The early Norman Barons had thought about this buying business, so they looked round for the Knight that was the most cunning and the toughest for miles around and elected him Knight 'Pourchasser' which literally means the 'Hunting Knight'. The Baron gave him a bag of gold, and told him he was responsible for supplying the castle all its needs for the year from weapons and food, to horses and clothing. Anything left at the end of the year the Knight Pourchasser got to keep. If he ran out of gold before the year was out – well in those days people were executed for not meeting their job description. So the people in the Knight Pourchasser's area of influence found it advisable to quote **very** low prices indeed because quoting high was invariably fatal!

Now

The use of clubs and lances among buyers has more or less died out completely, although there may be the odd occasion when a buyer will long for the return of the old days, to be replaced with a battery of skills and techniques which today's buyers need to have at their fingertips.

This book has been written for the person studying purchasing or for new practitioners to improve their skills and for operating buyers perhaps to improve their performance, and also for those responsible for buying. With the book comes a useful set of aides memoire that you can keep on your desk for 'those difficult situations'. We've called them 'Memory joggers'.

The book traces the development of a buyer who starts off running a consumables and catalogue purchasing desk, and progresses through capital purchasing to production purchasing.

GLOSSARY

Advance payment A payment made to a supplier prior to work commencing on a project or prior to manufacturing starting.

Amortization A process under which a supplier recovers the cost of dies, tooling etc., over an agreed quantity of components. During this period the title to the dies, tooling etc. remains that of the supplier.

Annual saving The annualized result of costs saved by purchasing the same components, or services at a lower unit price than that paid the previous year.

Annual turnover The annualized spend which the supplier 'turns over' with the buyer.

Appropriation request A formal application (normally to the board of management) for the release of a specified capital sum for the purchase of requirements for project.

Arbitration An alternative process to the courts used to resolve contractual differences which arise during or after contract performance.

'Backing-out' the options A method to eliminate various options offered by suppliers in order to arrive at a comparable price between the various competitors.

Bank guarantee A legal document issued by a bank or insurance company which places an obligation upon them to pay the amount of the guarantee in the event of specified terms of default by the supplier; often required when advance payments are made.

Bankrupt A person, or company declared by a court of law to be unable to meet their debts in full, the estate therefore being administered by creditors, or their agents, often the official receivers.

Bid bond A financial undertaking given by the bidder, through a bank or insurance company, that is forfeited to the buying company in the event that a bid is withdrawn prior to the buyer's acceptance, always provided that such acceptance takes place within the bid validity period.

Blanket order An order placed for a period such as 'The life of the model (subject to continued buyer satisfaction)' which lists all the items and prices purchased from the supplier – but does not indicate volumes. The volume aspects are covered by the issue of delivery schedules which are the instrument of the order.

Bought out (BO) This describes items, services, processes etc. which are bought from outside suppliers, and may be sub-classified as BOF (bought out finished) or BOU (bought out unfinished).

BS 5750 The National Standard for Quality Management Systems which is harmonized with its European counterparts ISO 9000 and EN29000 Series.

BS 9000 The British Standards Institute is responsible for the operation of BS 9000, a quality assurance system specifically for electronic components, and is responsible in the UK for the operation of its Western European and international counterparts the CECC and IECQ systems.

Cartel An association of companies producing the same or similar commodities. While each one retains their independent existence the cartel formulates plans and policies to control and stabilize sales and prices, in their own interest.

Cashflow The rate at which a company uses cash to support its operations. If excessive inventory exists it requires funding through cash, as does its work in progress. It is to the benefit of a business if it can increase its use of cash.

Caveat emptor A Latin term meaning, 'Let the buyer beware'. In essence it points out the important role played by buying staff when a contract is being negotiated and awarded. The onus is on the buyer to ensure that the contract reflects the buyer's wishes.

Chartered Institute of Purchasing and Supply The Institute of Purchasing and Supply gained its Royal Charter in 1992. The Institute of Purchasing and Supply was formed in 1967 from the amalgamation of the Purchasing Officers Association (1932) and the Institute of Public Supplies (1949). Membership of the CIPS is normally gained by studying for the Diploma thus gaining membership of the profession.

Code of Ethics The Purchasing Code of Ethics was first formulated in 1976, based on much older ethical statements applied to the servant entrusted with the master's money, goods and chattels. An abridged version appears in Appendix 4. Failure to maintain the high standards required can, apart from any other penalty, result in expulsion from the CIPS.

Contract A written or spoken agreement, especially one enforceable by law; the document recording it.

Contract master file A comprehensive file that is maintained of all correspondence and contractual detail with regard to a particular transaction.

Contractual risk The degree of exposure that exists for the buyer in a contractual relationship with a supplier. If the supplier's terms and conditions of sale have been accepted the risk will be high for the buyer.

Copyright The exclusive legal right to print, publish, perform work normally vested in the creator of such work (see also *Intellectual property rights*).

Cost analysis A detailed approach to evaluating the seller's cost elements within a proposed price. This uses the data provided in a cost breakdown.

Cost breakdown A detailed explanation of the cost elements that have contributed to the supplier's proposed selling price. This would be usually detailed in materials, labour, overhead and profit.

Cost benefit analysis A process by which all aspects associated with a certain proposed course of action are costed in order to determine the lowest ultimate cost. This method is often employed when there is more than one possible course of action being considered.

Cost in use A summation of all costs that will be incurred in the long-term use of a product or component. This will include maintenance, servicing, repairs etc. All of these costs will need assessing at the time of purchasing the product or component. This term is sometimes referred to as the full life cost.

Critical path analysis A system of planning activities necessary for the completion on time of a project or manufacture of a complex product. When the activities are mapped out the critical path is revealed. Usually this system is referred to as CPA.

Current standard cost In order that accounting control can be maintained in internal cost processes a price/cost is determined as the standard for the financial year. In order that businesses using the standard costing system can achieve their profit forecast all costs must be held at or below the current standard cost.

Demurrage A charge paid for detaining a vehicle either collecting or delivering goods beyond the period of charter originally agreed, or for delaying a ship by failing to unload on time.

Delivery frequency The cadence of deliveries of supplies agreed between buyer and seller to suit the buyer's requirements with regard to inventory, supply and cash limitations.

Delivery schedule The planned requirements of the buyer from the supplier. The document detailing such requirements.

Depreciation A decline in value, especially that due to wear and tear; the allowance made for this.

Design engineering The person/persons responsible for the production of designs for future production.

Determination A legal expression which means to bring the contract to an end.

Direct production materials Those materials which can be directly attributed in cost terms to the completion of the finished product. These are distinct from indirect materials such as steel and other raw materials which may have a variety of applications, and consumable materials, such as lightbulbs which are not used in the end product.

Discount A reduction in the purchase price, usually a percentage of the price, offered by the supplier in return for specified quantity purchases or other contractual obligation.

Dutch auction This is an unprofessional practice which is not permitted in most buying companies, whereby one seller is played off against others. During this process the buyer reveals other sellers' prices and persistently calls meetings to seek further reductions in price.

Economic bulk (or batch) quantity (EBQ) The volume or quantity which the supplier can produce at the most economical price to the buyer while meeting the buyer's inventory limitations.

EC European Community.

Electronic data exchange Often using the designatory letters EDI, this is a system of electronic communication between buyer and seller which enables them quickly to respond to the needs of the buyer's business. It can mean accessing the supplier's inventory, with automatic ordering through linked computers.

Engineering changes Those changes imposed by design or production engineering during the life of a product which necessitate a negotiation taking place between buyer and seller to decide cost and time implications of the required change.

Engineering support A phrase normally employed where the buyer is acquiring a new machine/process where the manufacturers have greater operating expertise than has the buyer's personnel. The buyer seeks to have manufacturer's engineers on loan, and at no cost to the buyer to help the buyer through the 'teething troubles' which are likely to occur after the installation of the machine.

Escrow A legal term referring to a deed which becomes operative on the operation of a future event. Commonly used on computer software contracts to obtain source codes in the event that the supplier goes into liquidation.

Expediting A systematic approach by the buying company aimed at ensuring that the supplier will meet a contracted delivery date.

Feature analysis When enquiring for a piece of equipment the buyer may find that the quotes contain features which add to the cost of the product, but are less than essential. This is the supplier's way of obtaining added value. The buyer by isolating these features in a comparative study can decide whether or not the extra features have any value to the buyer and negotiate accordingly.

Firm price A price agreed at the time of contract placement which will remain unchanged throughout the contract period.

Fixed price A price which is fixed at the time of contract placement but which may change in the contract period in line with an agreed formula which involves pre-agreed indices.

Force majeure A contractual expression through which the supplier can have, within the contract, legitimate reasons for delayed delivery. It would include such events as strikes, lock-outs, acts of God, etc. All such reasons must be considered for legitimacy within a specified contract.

Ford Q 101 A comprehensive quality assurance system which has been in operation since the early 1960s and is applied to all Ford Motor Co. suppliers. Similar 'benchmarks' which define the capability of a supplier are AID Marks & Spencer Approval, BS 9000, BS 5750, etc.

Forecast Comprises a scenario which postulates a series of forthcoming events, and from this produces a set of plans to mitigate or evade or take advantage of, these events if they occur. If the scenario changes, the forecaster has the ability to modify the forecast without the necessity of returning to first principles.

Free issue This refers to materials which are the property of the buying company being supplied to the supplier for incorporation into their product prior to being returned to the buying company. It may also refer to items sent for machining which are owned by the buying company.

'Front of order conditions' These are clauses which apply specifically to the item/service being purchased. These are additional to the terms and conditions normally printed on the back of the order – hence 'front of order conditions'.

Fully absorbed cost In comparing a 'made-in' price with a 'bought-out' price the comparison is often made wrongly with the direct cost of the 'made-in' part which only embraces material and direct labour. This excludes the major part of the associated overhead.

The fully absorbed cost (FAC) takes into account the appropriate proportion of all costs born by the subject item from the managing director's salary down. This focuses the buyer's mind on the true cost of the 'made-in' item. However to enjoy the true saving 'buying-out' would confer, the contributors to the true overhead must either by redeployed or made redundant.

Handing-over certificate   A document used to cover the transfer of responsibility for newly installed plant and equipment from the seller to the buyer. It is not a contractual document but carries important legal significance.

Incoterms   An acronym for International Commercial Terms (see Appendix 3 for condensed version) used in contracts for sale of goods in international markets. It contains various terms which define the respective obligations upon buyer and seller. A booklet is available from the International Chamber of Commerce.

Inflation   A progressive increase in the general level of price brought about by an expansion in demand, or in the money supply. This has the effect of eroding purchasing power, and is a major obstruction to the buyer in driving to improve company profitability.

Instructions to proceed   A verbal or written instruction to a supplier to proceed with contractual work, issued prior to the formal contract. Often referred to as an ITP, it does create a legal relationship between the buyer and seller. It is the specific wording that will distinguish it from a *Letter of intent* (see below).

Intellectual property rights   Rights vested in the holder for intellectual effort in design, original thought, invention etc. which confer rights on the holder. If these rights are breached by the buyer the holder has remedies in law for infringement. (See also the entries under copyright and patent.)

Inventory   The amount or value of a firm's current assets that consist of raw materials, work in progress and finished goods. This ties up cash resources unnecessarily if it is more than the minimum judged to be safe, since apart from the actual purchased cost of the inventory, bank interest has to be paid (or forgone), heat, light, rent, rates, labour have to be paid for in order that the inventory is stored in good order.

Justification   A closely reasoned argument showing the movement in costs over a specified period supporting a supplier's request for a price increase. It should be looked upon solely as a 'first shot' in the supplier's campaign to increase prices, and should not overly influence any subsequent decision made on any price changes which may result from the ensuing negotiation.

Just in time   A contractual arrangement wherein the supplier makes deliveries to the buyer's premises at a precise time to match production or project needs. It avoids high levels of inventory and has cashflow benefits.

Lead time   The total elapsed time from identifying a need to having it available in the buying company. The accuracy of defining lead time will directly affect inventory levels and reliability in contracting for deliveries.

Learning curve   A technique for assessing the direct linkage between the time taken to undertake a task and the quantity produced. When high amounts of labour are required there will be reductions in time taken, hence there is an impact on price.

Liquidated damages   An agreed contractual remedy whereby typically the buyer deducts fixed percentages from the contract value for each defined period of time that the supplier is late on delivery. Such deductions must be genuine pre-estimates of loss.

Letter of intent A communication from the buyer to the seller informing the latter that it is the intention to place a contract for that which is the subject of a quotation. If correctly worded it does not create a legal relationship. (See reference under *Instructions to proceed*.)

Letting the order A phrase often used by lawyers – more often the alternative phrase 'awarding the order' is used by buyers.

Life of a product curve All products move through three phrases:

- infancy
- maturity
- age

Price will vary depending on the position of the item on the curve. It will be high at infancy due to desirability and scarcity, lower during the mature phase, and rising again at age due to reducing availability. The wise buyer waits until the maturity phase to buy, and moves on before the product becomes aged.

Management by objective Often referred to as MBO is a process whereby staff are tasked by management to achieve certain mutually agreed objectives. This allows both parties to have a clear view as to what is expected of the staff member. The tasks should be 'stretching' but within the capability of the staff member taking into account the level of development and skills the staff member should possess. Performance is regularly reviewed by management and performance assessed.

Material requirement planning (MRP) A process to plan the availability to satisfy the demands of products in a given period.

Material resource planning (MRP 2) A process to plan production and establish lead times based on consideration of available machine/production time and manufacturing cycle time.

Material labour and overhead ratios Often referred to as MLOs they are the ratios which exist between the three factors in the cost of a component.

Material segregation As part of the requirement for good quality the supplier must ensure that only material of the right specification is used. Many raw materials can be mistaken one for the other. After they have been correctly identified by laboratory check, or material certification procedures it is vital that they are stored in such a way that one cannot be mistaken for another. It is an integral part of a supplier's good housekeeping that a system is in place which prevents any possibility of wrong substitution taking place.

Metrology The study and practice of measurement.

Metallurgy The science of the properties of metals.

'Milestones' During the development of a project the buyer and supplier may agree that interim payments will be made on the satisfactory completion of defined stages. These stages are often referred to as 'milestones' signifying distance run and time and cost spent to reach the objective.

Neutral specification The description of a requirement for issue to potential suppliers which defines the buyer's requirements in terms which contain no reference open or implied to any manufacturer's product currently on the market. This process allows potential suppliers to quote 'unhandicapped' by a specification which insists/implies that they must follow an existing supplier's method.

Negotiation The process for resolving differences of opinion which arise in contract dealings between buyer and seller. The legitimate process of negotiation is not to be confused with the 'Dutch auction'.

Non-destruction testing Often referred to as NDT, the process can be x-ray, sonic testing etc., which allows the material to be tested without rendering the sample unfit for use as say, 'sectioning' would do.

Non-recurring cost Costs which are incurred by the seller in fulfilling a contractual obligation, but which only occur once, usually at the outset of a contract. Examples would be jigs, fixtures, design, software writing etc. These costs are negotiable and there is no obligation upon the buyer to pay them unless agreed in the contract.

Official Journal of the European Community This is usually abbreviated to OJEC. It is the official journal of the European Community in which potential contracts in excess of a defined value are advertised.

Organisation of Petroleum Exporting Countries Usually abbreviated to OPEC. It is an association of the 11 major oil producing countries who endeavour to fix oil prices to satisfy their objectives and to co-ordinate policies.

Order The commonest form of contractual document in use. It should contain the company's standard terms and conditions for doing business and where necessary appropriate 'front of order conditions'. After acceptance by the supplier it is a legal contract.

Penalty clause This is illegal in English Law. The buyer is not allowed to hold the supplier *in terrorem* (in terror). The term is often misused to signify liquidated damages. They do not mean the same thing.

Performance bond This is a contractual undertaking by either a bank or an insurance company to the buying company to pay a defined sum if the supplier does not meet a contractual obligation. A company standard document exists within most organizations to meet this purpose.

Pre-financial year planning A large proportion of a company's success depends on the effectiveness of its actions once it enters into a new financial year. In purchasing this planning has to define the strategy and decide the tactics which will be used during the financial year. Since in order to enjoy the benefits of tactical success, bearing in mind the lead times involved, the precautionary moves have to be planned well in advance of their planned implementation. Thus to ensure success plans have to be largely complete well before the commencement of the new financial year.

Price variation formulae A contractual mechanism which provides for the movement of price during the contract period, usually consisting of three cost elements, fixed, labour, and material expressed in a formula, the latter two being linked to defined indices.

Procurement cycle The phases that will be passed through by procurement specialists before, during and after contract formation to ensure that all aspects of a purchase will have been dealt with. These phases involve the lapse of time which must be considered within the product service or project lead time.

Progress payments   Agreed sums of money paid by the buyer to the seller during product manufacture or project work. These sums must be linked to demonstrable packages of work completed (see milestones) and title in the goods must pass to the buyer when such payments are made. The overall payment package is often called a payment schedule.

Purchase research   An activity undertaken by procurement to ensure that suppliers' organization, pricing, finances etc. are adequate prior to placing contracts or undertaking contract negotiation.

Quality assurance   The assurance by the seller to the buyer that the items supplied by the seller shall conform in all respects to the buyer's drawings, specifications, etc. The contract recording this agreement also contains the duties and responsibilities of suppliers should the materials, services etc. they have contracted to supply fall below the levels of performance recorded in the contract. The term can also refer to the department within the buyer's organization charged with the responsibility of supervising such suppliers to ensure their continued observance of best quality practices.

Quotation analysis   A process by which tool cost + unit price × annual usage are used as a comparison of quotations from competing suppliers. Often measured over an annual usage of either one year or three years, exceptionally over the projected model life.

Quote and select   A term often used to define both the process, and the time expended to complete the task.

Rationalization   The process by which the buyer sets up a competitive bidding environment amongst a group of suppliers who are already suppliers individually of part of the buyer's total demand. The buyer offers the total demand to all participating suppliers via the enquiry process. The supplier who quotes most competitively for the whole demand is awarded the order. Thus buyers are able to reduce their supplier portfolio down to one and enjoy the price benefits afforded by increased scale of purchase.

Rebate   An amount repaid by the seller, typically one year in arrears, to the buyer when purchases have reached a pre-agreed sum of money or number of units. The amount and method of payment is negotiable.

Receiving inspection   A process by which when goods are received by the buyer they are inspected at point of receipt and goods of unsatisfactory quality are returned to the supplier.

Retention monies   A sum retained by the buyer against the satisfactory completion of the contract.

Return on capital employed   A measure of company profitability which relates profits to the amount of capital utilized in a business.

Ring pricing   Where a group of suppliers who have each received the same enquiry from the buyer combine to ensure that they will all submit quotations such that only one will appear satisfactory to the buyer. This 'most competitive' quotation is over-priced. On the buyer's acceptance of the quote the excess paid is shared between the 'unsuccessful quoters'.

Shelf life   Some items will deteriorate in storage after a certain time lapse. This is known as shelf life and must be identified. It requires that stock rotation is properly managed and that there is agreed responsibility for identifying goods with restricted shelf life.

'Silence means consent'   If after a reasonable interval the supplier who has received an order from a buyer and has not either acknowledged it or sent in his own conflicting terms and conditions then his silence is deemed as consent to produce the requirement on the buyer's terms.

Supplier appraisal   A methodology used at the pre-contract award phase to assess the supplier's capabilities to undertake defined work. It will involve quality, safety, commercial and financial evaluation of a potential supplier.

Supplier partnerships   A relationship between a buying company and a supplier whereby both parties agree to develop a long term, often exclusive, relationship to the mutual benefit of both parties.

Supplier quality assurance   A systematic approach to evaluating a supplier's capability to manage quality through all phases of purchase, handling manufacture etc. The system should be independent of procurement. (See also *Quality assurance*.)

Supplier rationalization   A strategic approach used by the buyer with the express purpose of reducing the existing number of suppliers to move manageable proportions, from which various contractual benefits will be obtained.

Tenders   Formal requests or invitations, issued by the buyer for the seller to make an offer to sell (the tender) against strict conditions regarding submission dates, opening, negotiation, validity periods, etc. The unqualified acceptance by the buyer of a tender will create a contract.

Transfer machine transfer line   A capital machine which performs a series of operations moving the workpiece automatically from one machining station to the next. Customarily an item of raw material is fed in at the beginning and a finished component emerges at the other.

Unit cost   Is the representative cost of one unit in a batch, of which all the other units in the batch have the same cost.

Unit price   The selling price of one unit of production within a batch which is representative of the price of all the other members of the batch.

Unliquidated damages   These are the amounts of monies paid by the seller to the buyer which reflect the actual losses sustained by the buyer in the event of a contract default by the seller. These are more commonly referred to as consequential loss.

Validity period   The time specified by the bidder during which the offer will remain valid, in other words open for acceptance by the buyer. At the end of this specified period the offer lapses unless it is extended by the seller.

Value analysis   A systematic approach to investigating all aspects of cost and eliminating unnecessary cost in a manufactured product after production has commenced.

Value engineering   A systematic review of all projected costs within a product, conducted at the design and engineering phase of product life.

Value for money   The situation that exists when the buyer has obtained from the supplier optimum cost in respect of the total features of a purchase. It avoids a fixation with price and requires that all aspects of cost are studied with care.

Variation order   An amendment to a contract instructing the supplier to undertake additional work or to omit some work already authorized and stating the impact on price and other contract terms.

Vendor rating   A systematic approach to monitoring and measuring aspects of a supplier's contractual performance, including delivery, quantity, quality, service support etc.

Without prejudice   A legal term meaning without dismissing or detracting from an existing right or claim. It can refer to informal discussions which are seeking to resolve a contractual dispute.

Works cost   The costs of labour, material and overhead, prior to the addition of costs of sales, transport and profit.

Zero defects   This refers to the supply of goods by a supplier where there are no faulty items within a delivery. The onus is upon the supplier for quality management and associated control of quality when delivering.

1 AN INTRODUCTION TO THE TOOLS OF THE TRADE

This chapter starts by looking at buyers' and sellers' rights and at buyers' motivation. It explains the basic relationship between works cost and the selling price and then goes on to demonstrate the role and importance of key tasks such as buying records, enquiries, orders, order amendments, policies and procedures and terms and conditions.

The seven buyer's rights

Well, here you are at the buyer's desk and now you've got to perform! Before you do anything, consider what you are at the desk to do, and what your boss and your company expect of you. The most important objective they will expect you to achieve is that you will buy:

1. The right material
2. At the right time
3. At the right quantity   to satisfy the company's manufacturing needs
4. At the right place

5. At the right price   to satisfy the cost competitive requirement

6. At the right quality   to avoid production problems and eliminate after-sales warranty problems

7. At the lowest feasible inventory level   to avoid tying up cash unnecessarily in stock

These seven points are called the 'buyer's rights' and the whole of this book is designed to help you to obtain them and to satisfy your boss, and the company's expectation of you.

Motivation

Your company is in competition with others as far apart as Japan and Australia, or the US and Norway. The size of any market is finite, and besides the overseas competitors there are those in your own country to recognize. They all have buyers competing with you to obtain their buyer's rights. Now unless you're better at it than they are, then somebody is going out of business – and it could be you!

Your suppliers are also in competition with each other, and they, like you are in the business to make money. This means that they are looking to find customers who will buy their product at a price that will give them the highest possible profit. They too have 'rights' – the seller's rights.

The seller's rights

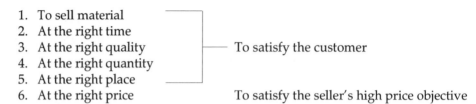

1. To sell material
2. At the right time
3. At the right quality — To satisfy the customer
4. At the right quantity
5. At the right place
6. At the right price   To satisfy the seller's high price objective

But remember!

The seller's idea of right price and yours will differ, and every time the supplier achieves the top price objective you have failed in your objective!

So the buyer's motivation is to be a successful agent of competitive buying.

Cost v. price

So far we have been discussing price, often confused with cost, which is a dangerous error!

cost = money deployed to make a product
price = money the seller aims to be paid for the product

A phrase you will become very familiar with in your buying life will be 'works cost'. This section of the cost accountant's reports always refers to purchasing activities and is universal in all manufacturing activities only the percentages change:

Works cost

This equals

cost of materials   say 60%
cost of labour   say 20%
cost of overhead   say 20%

Full cost

This equals cost of the three factors plus cost of sales/advertising and transport.

Selling price

This equals full cost plus profit.

In your own company the purchasing element of which you the buyer are a part will cover:

1. Cost of all direct materials used in production, plus say half the cost of overhead in indirect materials. So you, the buyer, influence at least 70% of the works cost in the prices you pay your suppliers. And that's not all.
2. If you select a supplier who does not deliver at the right time, right quality, right place and the right quantity, production is adversely affected and the labour cost goes up.
3. It must not be forgotten that if you allow inventory to rise above the minimum necessary to support production the company have to borrow the money **at penal rates of interest** to pay for the extra stock, tying up money that could be used for something else, and necessitating extra expense in labour to look after the material, and extra heating and lighting in the storage area.

If the buyers working for your competition are better at their job than you are at yours – then the final result is inevitable!

So where do you start to compete successfully?

The first six questions

1. What commodity groups am I responsible for?
2. Where are they used in production?
3. How are they made?
4. What are the company's requirements in terms of quantity and timing?
5. How do I get informed of the company's requirements?
6. How are the company's requirements expressed to the supplier?

The first three questions come under the generic heading of: **know your items**. The second three: **know your systems**.

It is vital that you have the answers to these questions buttoned up as fast as you can and to remember that self-help is often the best help.

Find the time to relate part numbers and descriptions and **handle** the items. The checklist following should become second nature to you every time a new component or item or material crosses your horizon.

Know your items

What are they?

castings	forgings
plastics	pressings
turned parts	bearings

assemblies	consumables
chemicals	paper products
packaging	other

Generic description?

part numbers	operation numbers
family descriptions	other
drawing numbers	

How are they made?

pressed	moulded
turned	cast
forged	flame cut
milled	drilled
woven	extruded
other	

What is the raw material?

steel	aluminium
copper	brass
iron	nylon
paper	polypropylene
other	

Where are they used?

assembly	machine shops
stores	other
packing	

You should also look at the drawings, specifications, quality requirements to see how the design department tolerance items, and how quality is obtained. At the same time you must know your systems, and the checklist below will help you get a grip.

Know your systems

How is material requisitioned for you to buy?

- production control releases;
- design department releases;
- sales/marketing releases;
- requisitions;
- memo;
- verbal instructions;
- unplanned panics;
- other.

Who are the individuals authorized to requisition material on you?

- manager of production;
- manager of production control;
- manager of sales;
- memos from named persons only;
- computer-based releases;
- other.

How are quantities, duration of order, delivery point, identified to you?

- single quantity to be delivered at a specified time;
- multiple quantities to be delivered at stipulated times;
- scheduled requirements;
- other.

What type of documentation is used to advise the supplier?

- firm order (fixed quantity);
- blanket order (scheduled quantities);
- electronic transfer (electronic data interchange);
- fax/letter/phone;
- other.

Raising an order

What method is used to record the following:
- supplier;
- price and quantity;
- delivery dates (for progress action);
- competitive quotations;
- part no., description, specifications;
- rebates, discounts, etc.;
- computer/typed/faxed;
- other.

Approval level

At what expenditure level does the buyer have to submit the order to a senior manager prior to dispatch of the order?

How are orders progressed?

- computer due date report;
- manual follow-up record;
- progress department responsibility;
- requisitioner responsibility.

Circulation of the order

There are several departments who need to know that you have placed the order for various actions which are now triggered off to take place.

The first copy clearly goes to the supplier, normally to his or her sales department, who record the order and allocate a works order reference and are usually the progress contact. They in turn pass it to the production department in order that your requirement is put into production.

The second copy of your order goes to accounts. Firstly they need it to establish a forward commitment figure. The forward commitment figure adds all the sums due month by month to ensure that future commitments are not greater than income from sales for the same period. If outgoings are greater than income, even temporarily, there is a cashflow problem which can be a crisis if the company is up to its limit on its bank borrowings. Secondly, the order is used by accounts to pass payment to the supplier when the goods are received and the invoice and statement are received. The invoice travels with the goods and will read: 500 brackets @ £1.00 each. Total £500. The statement which the supplier sends in monthly lists all the deliveries the supplier has made in the month, and presents a total sum required as payment. Accounts compare the statement with the list of invoices received and if the two figures agree they authorize payment.

If they don't agree, it's the buyer's responsibility to resolve the discrepancy.

The third copy goes to production control to allow them to plan production based on the 'due date' given on your order.

The fourth copy goes to inform the expediter responsible for ensuring delivery at the required date.

The fifth copy goes to the receiving department so that they will be able to verify that the goods being delivered are what was ordered.

This system is often computerized when all departments are informed electronically, but many companies still carry out this vital circulation by distributing copies of the order. Figure 1.1 is a copy of a completed order form.

PURCHASE ORDER

TO: THE SUPPLIER

DATE:...............

PURCHASE ORDER No 1500

FROM: THE COMPANY

CONTACT........................

TELEPHONE....................

FACSIMILE......................

DESCRIPTION

A-165588 BRACKET

QUANTITY:

PACKING:

DELIVERY POINT:

DELIVERY REQUIRED BY 21.09.95

TO CONFORM TO SPECIFICATION 99-409/341. COPY ATTACHED.

£1.00 EACH.

500

NON RETURNABLE

NO 6 STORES

....

SIGNATURE

....

COUNTER SIGNATURE

CONFIRMATION SLIP

PURCHASE ORDER No 1500

We confirm that we accept the order subject to the terms and conditions overleaf and that delivery will be as requested.

....(Authorized signature) for supplier.

Figure 1.1 Purchase order form

Your most frequently used tools

Enquiry form (Figure 1.2)

The importance of this document (sometimes called an RFQ – request for quotation) is to seek quotations from potential suppliers, by providing them with the following information in order to provide you with a quotation:

- part number description and engineering level;
- quantity required;
- delivery date for samples;
- delivery date for first production;
- delivery point;
- appropriate drawings and specifications;
- terms and conditions of contract;
- latest date by which quotations must be received in order to be considered.
- the length of time the quotation must remain open for acceptance (validity period).

These are the minimum requirements of an enquiry form, and later chapters will amplify the detail an enquiry form can be used to elicit.

Normally not less than three enquiries or more than six should be launched but there are occasions when this procedure has to be varied. These too will be discussed in later chapters.

Quotation analysis (Figure 1.3)

This is a form that you will find invaluable in arriving at the correct purchasing decision. Despite the fact that you have sent all the enquiry details listed above the suppliers will produce quotations which differ in detail, both from each other, and in certain cases will not necessarily conform to your terms and conditions. This is often called a non-compliant quotation.

Purchase order amendment (Figure 1.4)

This document is used when the purchase order has to be modified in some details but does not change the rest of the order. It is quicker to produce than an order and has the same circulation as the order. It can be used to:

- change delivery requirements;
- record and update engineering level;
- record price increase or reduction and operative date;
- vary order quantities.

ENQUIRY

TO: THE SUPPLIER

DATE: ....

FROM: THE COMPANY

CONTACT: ....

TEL NO: ....

WOULD YOU PLEASE PROVIDE YOUR QUOTATION FOR THE ITEM/S, MATERIAL/S, GOODS OR SERVICES LISTED BELOW:–

3049 Pressing

2741 Casting

9024 Clamp

1000 per annum

5000 per annum

500 per annum

These items are the components for the assembly 304–6150 widget, and are shown on the assembly drawings and specs enclosed. Do not quote for assembly, in line with operation sheets no. 715/137/22 enclosed.

....

SIGNATURE

Notes:

1. Please quote 'DELIVERED OUR WORKS' (Incoterms, 1990).
2. Tool costs are to be shown separate from unit cost and whether part or full tool cost.
3. Samples must be provided off production tools.
4. VAT to be shown separately.
5. Packaging costs must be included in unit cost.
6. Quotation should observe terms and conditions printed overleaf.
7. Period of price stability should be shown.
8. Quotations to be considered must be received not later than four weeks from date of enquiry and remain open for acceptance for a period of 90 days.

Figure 1.2 Enquiry form

Part no.	Current price	Supplier price A	Supplier price B	Supplier price C	Current vol.	Supplier A Vol. × price	Supplier B Vol. × price	Supplier C Vol. × price	Current Vol. × price
Totals									

Recommended source

Supplier Code: A = Romeo-Papa; B = Zebra-Foxtrot; C = Lima-Tango.

Component sets to produce 304–6150 widget

EXAMPLE

Part no.	Current price	Supplier price A	Supplier price B	Supplier price C	Current vol.	Supplier A Vol. × price	Supplier B Vol. × price	Supplier C Vol. × price	Current Vol. × price
3049	£0.75	£0.64	£0.79	£0.73	1000	£640	£790	£730	£750
2741	£1.00	£1.05	£1.01	£1.04	5000	£5250	£5050	£5200	£5000
9024	£3.12	£2.95	£3.05	£2.75	500	£1475	£1525	£1375	£1560
Totals						£7365	£7365	£7305	£7310

Recommended source: Supplier C

Figure 1.3 Quotation analysis

PURCHASE ORDER AMENDMENT

TO: THE SUPPLIER   FROM: THE COMPANY

DATE: ....   CONTACT: ....

NO 307   TEL NO: ....

WITH EFFECT FROM   .... (DATE) WOULD YOU PLEASE AMEND ORDER
NO.   .... FOR THE UNDERMENTIONED ITEM/S, MATERIAL/S, GOODS OR
SERVICES AS SHOWN BELOW:–

....
SIGNATURE

CONFIRMATION SLIP

We confirm receipt of Purchase Order Amendment no.   .... to Order No.   ....
and confirm that the Purchase Order Amendment will be implemented as requested. Any costs
associated with this change will be advised separately.

.... SIGNATURE (for Supplier)

Figure 1.4 Purchase order amendment

Policies and procedures

It is probable that your purchasing department has both aspects covered and you will find two books at the desk which contain policies and procedures. If they exist read them and operate in line with what you read. If not then consider what has been discussed so far and see what policies and procedures you could write for yourself.

Policy no. 1

Your prime role is to obtain the 'buyer's rights' on your company's behalf.

This has several implications which stem from this first policy statement. As the agent of competition you must give all potential suppliers equal opportunity in your enquiries, so that they have a level playing field on which to quote.

If you are applying fair competition then you must be above suspicion yourself. This includes not accepting a gift from a supplier that could be construed as a bribe. The best line to take is that simple hospitality is acceptable provided that your company would permit you to reciprocate to the same degree. For example if a supplier pays for your lunch on one occasion you will return the gesture on another.

Because you are operating in a competitive environment then anything you learn from a supplier is confidential and must not be revealed to competitors. They will be grateful for what you tell them, but they will never trust you with their confidence in the future, and you will be labelled as a 'leaker'!

So we now have three more policies.

Policy no. 2

All suppliers must be treated in the same scrupulous and even-handed manner.

Policy no. 3

The buyer's position must not be used for personal gain of any description, which includes acceptance of any gift which might be construed as a bribe.

Policy no. 4

Confidential information obtained by the buyer in the course of business is to be kept confidential. The buyer has the same right to demand that information given in the course of business is kept confidential. In some situations the buyer may ask potential suppliers to sign a 'confidentiality agreement'.

As we delve deeper into the buyer's role more policies will emerge which taken together will provide a map by which the buyer, feeling at sea on an uncharted ocean, will be able to navigate successfully.

A policy states a bed-rock principle; the procedure explains what is to be done to ensure that the policy is adhered to.

Policy no. 1

States that even handed fairness is paramount in competitive enquiry.

Procedure no. 1

Explains that to ensure this policy is always carried out you must ensure that you have got the best up to date information on:

- engineering release information (specifications, drawings etc.);
- required volumes;
- start-up dates required;
- not forgetting to verify that you've got the suppliers correct addresses! This procedure may well give detailed instructions as to how forms are to be laid out, etc.

All aimed at producing uniform enquiries providing identical information.

Policy no. 2

Continues the concept of even-handed treatment of suppliers, and your prime tool in assessing the competitive situation with regard to the quotations you have received in response to your enquiry is the quotation analysis.

Procedure no. 2

Instructs that in all cases a quotation analysis must be prepared as the basis for producing a justified sourcing decision.

Additionally, there will be some precautionary guidelines:

(a) If the lowest quote appears ridiculously low it should be checked out before discarding it – it could be the only one that's right!
(b) Normally, with the exception of the case in (a) the lowest quote gets the business.

There will be later policies with attendant procedures which will result in refinements to the source selection processes as the story of the buyer's role unfolds but for the moment this basic procedure will suffice.

Policy no. 3

Probably the only policy which does not have an attendant procedure. Sufficient to say that buyers who disregard this policy have very short careers!

Policy no. 4

The procedure which is driven by this policy covers a wide range of aspects of confidentiality issues:

(a) The buyer does not reveal to one competitor another's price. (This automatically rules out the risk of starting a 'Dutch auction'. The Dutch auction starts by revealing to potential supplier A the price supplier B has quoted, and inviting A to requote at a price lower than B's. When the revised quotation from A is received, then going back to B telling him or her that A's quote is lower than B's and inviting B to requote at an even lower price, and so on until one supplier can go no further. This is unethical practice, and brings the buyer and his or her company into disrepute.)

(b)   If a design is patented and the buyer obtains drawings of the patented item, it is a breach of confidentiality to pass these drawings to another potential supplier. In the retail trade this is known as 'copy action'.

(c)   Copyright and intellectual property. Even if the design has not been patented the copyright and the intellectual property rights rest with the originator. As with a patented item the test for infringement is 'That if a lay person can see that the copy is inspired by the original then the copier is guilty of infringement of the originator's rights.' Woe betide the buyer who involves his/her company in an expensive lawsuit over encouraging infringement of another's rights in law.

It will be seen that the procedure on confidentiality consists of a lot of don'ts.

The buyer having read so far will be perhaps feeling that the buyer's desk is surrounded by rules which prevent anyone from functioning in a competitive role. The truth is that the buyer's job combines a wide range of activities which require a knowledge of legal and fiscal matters, engineering and design knowledge and market knowledge. Only then can the buyer be truly effective. The buyer has another 'policy/procedural' matter, to take on board quickly, and that is the 'terms and conditions', which are the definition of the way the buyer's company trades.

The T&Cs, as they are affectionately known, have been drawn up by the company's lawyers and senior purchasing personnel as a protection to the buyer, and you should know yours off by heart. Unfortunately many buyers will fail this test.

The first thing to remember is that a purchase order when accepted is a legally binding contract which commits your company to certain courses of action and equally commits the supplier to perform in the way specified in the order.

If you refer to the example enquiry for 304–6150 Widget (Figure 1.2) you will see that the supplier, Lima-Tango came out as most competitive on the quotation analysis (Figure 1.3). The T&Cs sent out with the enquiry will have included some 20+ clauses which your company wants the supplier to adhere to as part of the contract/order you are processing.

The terms and conditions of order

1. Terms of payment

As already mentioned, the supplier will send an invoice with each delivery, and also if required a monthly statement. Normally the statement is used by accounts to agree total monies owed monthly, but will pay the supplier against invoices for goods received and accepted up to a cut-off date in the month. For example, in order that accounts can complete each month's work on time they will not consider invoices rendered after the 26th of the month. These invoices will be included in the following month's remittance.

Now, in order to conserve cashflow the first consideration is to decide if the goods can be received, incorporated in the company's product, sold to the end customer, with payment received before it becomes necessary to pay the supplier.

In the past the function of cash paid out prior to cash coming in via sales was to some extent ignored, resulting in companies having too much month left at the end of their money. This is tough on an individual but it can mean bankruptcy to a company. So often for cash conservancy reasons clause 1 may read:

Terms of payment net 60 days from receipt of invoice

This means to the supplier that any deliveries he makes from the 27th of the month 1 up till the 25th of month 2 will not be paid until the end of month 4.

This of course necessitates the supplier having to borrow money from the bank to cover the purchases of raw material and pay labour etc. The cost of borrowing will be incorporated in the overhead section of the price.

Knowledge of the buyer's payment terms allows the supplier to take this into account when preparing the quotation.

2. Quality

(a)   Rejected materials found on receipt will be returned to supplier at supplier's cost.
(b)   All items supplied must conform to customer's drawings, specifications, and such other written instructions the customer may give.
(c)   We reserve the right to rework material which is rejected at your cost if our requirement is urgent.

3. Confidentiality

Confidentiality must be maintained by the supplier on all drawings, patterns, design or other detail, and must not be divulged to any third party.

4. Intellectual property

All intellectual property provided to the supplier in the course of preparation of quotations or in the commissioning of orders remains the property of the company.

5. Quotations

Quotations must include all packaging and delivery costs, and be presented as separate components of unit cost.

6. Tooling payment

The supplier must indicate on the quotation the tool cost, and indicate if this sum is full or part cost, in the event that the figure represents part cost only, the full cost must also be indicated.

7. Tool costs

Special tooling, special jigs and fixtures only should be quoted. The company does not make contributions to capital tooling.

8. Samples

All first off samples must be submitted off production tooling.

9. Sub-contract

Work awarded to the supplier will not normally be permitted to be sub-contracted unless approval is obtained beforehand from purchasing.

10. Quantity variation

Quantities on the order will not be varied except by agreement of both parties.

11. Flexible deliveries

The supplier is to endeavour at all times to be capable of responding to unscheduled requests and provide their best endeavours to meet these changed requirements.

12. Price variation

Price cannot be varied except by submission to the buyer (one month prior to the date the new price is required to be effective) of a properly constructed justification which the buyer reserves the right to vary, dispute or reject depending on circumstances.

13. Packaging

All packaging must be non-returnable. No packaging supplied will be returned.

14. VAT

Value Added Tax is to be shown as a separate item on all quotations, invoices etc.

15. Letting the order

The terms and conditions of this order are the only ones on which the order will be let.

16. Force majeure

Actions to be taken by both parties in the event of force majeure, e.g. supplier not delivering on time, or the company cannot take the materials in although delivered on time. Examples of events which may cause either party to declare force majeure include fire, flood, earthquake, act of war and strike. If this event occurs at the supplier's premises the buyer reserves the right to buy his or her requirements from elsewhere, if the supplier cannot deliver; although where possible he or she will attempt to give the supplier an extension of time. If the buyer cannot take the material he or she will request the supplier's help in not insisting on delivery or payment until the buyer is able to accept delivery.

17. Invoices

Suppliers are to submit invoices showing quantities, part numbers and extended prices with each delivery. Monthly statements are to be received not later than the 26th of each month to the accounts department.

18. Invoice discrepancies

If invoices are submitted with prices which differ from those on the order they will not be paid.

19. Purchase order amendments

When an order price is agreed by both parties to be changed the invoices must bear the old price until the purchase order amendment is in the supplier's possession.

20. Time is of the essence

Delivery (where the supplier has been notified of a requirement, either by scheduled requirements, or by dates shown on this order) time is considered to be 'the essence of the order' and failure to meet these dates may result in cancellation of the order.

Consequential losses will be claimed by the buyer in the event that losses have been incurred as a result of the supplier's failure to deliver on time.

21. Material delivery

All goods are to be invoiced 'delivered our works', imported materials are to be delivered 'our works' under Incoterms 1990 (DDP).

22. Supplier's responsibility for buyer's tools, materials etc. at the supplier's works

All tooling laid down by the buyer and drawings, patterns etc. provided by the buyer shall be maintained in good order and properly insured against 'all risks' until the buyer informs the supplier in writing that the materials are no longer required, at which time the supplier may dispose of them.

23. Cancellation

In the event that the supplier fails after adequate warning and counselling to achieve the standards embodied in this order and the accompanying specifications the buyer reserves the right to cancel the order and to withhold payment for work undertaken.

24. Applicable law

The applicable law is English law. In the event of a dispute between the buyer and the supplier, arbitration can be applied by mutually agreed arbitrators.

The 24 terms and conditions listed in the foregoing are standard (there may be more) but each company varies them according to their legal advice and the business that they are in.

If you refer to the example order (Figure 1.5) you will see that special conditions apply to the supply of shafts. These are called front of order conditions as distinct from the T&Cs that apply to all purchases and all enquiries.

ORDER

TO: **THE SUPPLIER**

DATE: **20.10.95**

ORDER: **2140**

FROM: **THE COMPANY**

CONTACT:

TEL NO:

7613 Shaft.   £30.00 ea

Price stability until 1/10/96.
Samples submission date 10/1/96.
Quantity p.a. 30 000. Delivery to Schedule.

Finish: Lightly oiled.
Engineering level 30451/22/1.
Specification: 9345/93.

PACKING INSTRUCTIONS.

Both ends are to be protected by plastic caps.

Shafts are to be delivered in 'A' stillages in four layers of 10. Each layer is to be separated from the
layers above and below with corrugated cardboard.

SEE PACKING SPEC M 167.

DELIVERY TO NO 10 STORES.

....

SIGNATURE   COUNTER SIGNATURE

....

CONFIRMATION SLIP   ORDER NO 2140

We confirm we accept the order and delivery will be as required.

....   Signature (for supplier).

Figure 1.5 Purchase order (completed)

Summing up

To sum up the main features of this first chapter we have shown that you are the front line in obtaining the most competitive purchases for your company in a very global environment.

We've highlighted:

- the buyer's rights;
- the seller's rights;
- works cost breakdown;
- relation between cost and price;
- the buyer's influence on company cost;
- know your items;
- know your systems;
- the information aspects of the order;
- your most frequently used tools;
- purchase enquiry;
- quotation analysis;
- purchase order amendment;
- purchasing policies;
- purchasing procedures;
- front of order conditions;
- draft standard terms and conditions.

These are the maps you will have at the buyer's desk. In the following chapters we will show how to be able to sail on those uncharted seas of competitive purchasing and become a world-class buyer.

MEMORY JOGGERS

1 **The buyer's rights**
- Purchase the right material
- At the right time
- At the right quantity
- At the right place
- At the right price
- At the right quality
- At the lowest feasible inventory

REMEMBER – These are essentials and cannot be compromised ever!

2 **The buyer's motivation**
- Buy better than anyone else
- Make my company competitive
- To be a world-class buyer
- To keep production moving
- To hit deadlines

REMEMBER – If other buyers are better than you, guess who goes out of business – You!

3 **Cost v. Price**
- Seek competitive quotations
- Know your markets
- Challenge prices
- Establish the basis of cost
- Do the bid analysis

REMEMBER – You should create and control the competition – use your skills!

4 **Know your items**
- What is the raw material?
- How are they made?
- Where are they used?
- Are they standard or a special?
- What is the lead time?

REMEMBER – If you don't know your items you will surely pay too much!

5 **Terms and conditions of contract**
- Know them inside out
- Make sure they apply to your purchases
- Know what they are for
- Know what they protect
- Have a good reason to change them

REMEMBER – They are to protect your company's interests – use them!

6 **Policies and procedures**
- Develop key policies
- Define the procedures
- Make them work
- Tell others what they are
- Change them when they can be improved

REMEMBER – Policies and procedures give you direction – without that you are lost!

2 THE REQUISITIONER IS NOT ALWAYS RIGHT!

In this chapter we begin to quantify supplier performance, and to examine various methods of inventory control. Potential problems such as 'resistant' colleagues and 'amateur' buyers are also dealt with. The chapter concludes with some competitive cost reduction exercises and an explanation of budgetary control.

It's Monday morning and you've just sat down at the buyer's desk and you see that there's a batch of requisitions in your in-basket. Now don't panic, read them carefully and look particularly at the dates the requisitioners want delivery. As a new buyer beware of the joker. When the writer started buying he was put on lubricants of which he knew less than nothing. The first requisition he picked up was for a lubricant supplied by Shell, BP, Mobil etc., according to the requisition. He rang each of the suppliers in turn. Each said they didn't stock it. Beginning to panic now he went back to the Shell contact and said plaintively, 'Haven't you got a substitute we could use?'

The Shell man laughed and said, 'We've got some feline (what you want) and I guess we could drum up some bovine, but we've got no canine – there's very little call for it!'

Thinking the world had gone mad he looked again at the material he'd been turning the oil world upside down for. It was a requisition for 'K.9.P'. He said it over to himself a couple of times and suddenly the penny dropped! He'd fallen for a variant of the black and white striped paint gag!

The writer read requisitions very carefully after that.

On the perhaps unsound assumption that there's no-one in your organization with that sense of humour, you should prioritize in order of date of requirement.

Assuming item A is wanted in 1 week, B in 2 weeks, C in 3 weeks, and D in 4 weeks.

Then item A is the one to start with. The questions to ask are:

- Does the buying record show if it's been bought before?
- When was it last bought?
- Who was the supplier?
- How much did we pay for it?
- What was the lead time?

Part no 236–002		Description 3″ × 1/8″ bolt 'S' quality steel		Engineering E.I. release no 47493		First release 1/1/93	
Release date	Quantity	Requisition no.	Delivery required	Received	Supplier	Competition	Price delivered
1/1/93	2000	971	7/1/93	9/1/93	Tree Ltd	Smith Ltd Green Inc.	50p each
3/3/93	4000	1050	10/3/93	14/3/93	Smith Ltd	Tree Ltd Green Inc.	45p each
6/6/93	3000	1120	12/6/93	11/6/93	Tree Ltd	Smith Ltd Green Inc.	48p each
9/8/93	4000	1300	19/8/93	21/8/93	Tree Ltd	Smith Ltd Green Inc.	48p each
11/10/93	5000	1720	28/10/93	28/10/93	Green Inc.	Smith Ltd Tree Ltd	43p each
1/2/94	2000	3100	7/2/94	6/2/94	Tree Ltd	Smith Ltd Green Inc.	50p each
1/4/94	5000	3700	20/4/94	18/4/94	Green Inc.	Smith Ltd Tree Ltd	43p each
1/6/94	2000	3800	15/6/94	15/6/94	Smith Ltd	Green Inc. Tree Ltd	45p each
1/8/94	1000	4020	14/8/94	13/8/94	Tree Ltd	Smith Ltd Green Inc.	50p each

Figure 2.1 Draft buying card (completed)

The buying record

This is often known as the buying card (see Figure 2.1) and it should be able to answer these questions. It may be held in the computer system or maintained manually. It is another of your tools and it should be kept up meticulously.

Analysis of suppliers' performance

Clearly there are three suppliers who are capable of delivering this bolt, and previous buyers have been in the habit of enquiring from Tree Ltd, Smith Ltd, and Green Inc. and selecting the best price and delivery and equally clearly they have (rightly!) placed the highest priority on delivery.

The requisition in front of you is for delivery in seven days. The quick way to place the order is to phone or fax the three suppliers and ask for price and delivery for 3000 bolts (not forgetting to ask them to confirm their quote in writing) then place the order on the best quote.

It's obviously what your predecessors have done but it's hardly world-class buying!

There were 18 000 purchased in 1993, and it appears that three-quarters of the way through 1994, including the latest requisition 13 000 have been required so far in 1994, the probability is that the 1994 total will also reach 18 000.

So what did we pay for our bolts in 1993? (See Table 2.1.)

Table 2.1 Expenditure on bolts, 1993

Release date	Volume	Total price
1.1.93	2000 @ 50p	£1000
3.3.93	4000 @ 45p	£1800
6.6.93	3000 @ 48p	£1440
9.8.93	4000 @ 48p	£1920
11.10.93	5000 @ 43p	£2150

Total expenditure for 1993 = £8310 for 18 000 bolts giving an average unit price of £0.462 ea.

Now let's look at 1994 to date (see Table 2.2).

Table 2.2 Expenditure on bolts, 1994

Release date	Volume	Total price
1.2.94	2000 @ 50p	£1000
1.4.94	5000 @ 43p	£2150
1.6.94	2000 @ 45p	£900
1.8.94	1000 @ 50p	£500

Expenditure to date in 1994 = £4550 for 10 000 bolts giving an average unit price of £0.455 ea.

From the analysis several points emerge:

1. Tree are normally the fastest off the ground – but they are the most expensive.
2. Tree reduce their price for higher volumes – so there must be price breaks for higher volumes. What are they?
3. Green is 14% cheaper than Tree, but only are successful when the lead time is a little longer, and the volume requirement is at 5000. Does this mean that their price break is at 5000?
4. Smith have also quoted successfully twice, once at a high volume and once at a lower volume, once at a short lead time and once at a longer. The reason needs some investigation.

Several points which the world-class buyer will recognize straight away emerge.

1. Short leadtimes and small volumes promote higher prices because the buyer is desperate to obtain supplies and doesn't want to risk putting production in jeopardy by spending valuable time on negotiation. It savours of fiddling while Rome burns!
2. In the case of this bolt the effect of the random requisitions caused the average unit price to be $0.32 \times 18\,000$ more than it need have been if all purchases could have been made from Green Inc. So £576 was effectively wasted.
3. The year of 1994 is not yet over, but already the average unit price for the first 10 000 is £0.455 when the material might have been had for £0.43p ea. Which would have been a saving of £250. Assuming you follow your predecessors then the most probable end-year result will be that another £500 odd pounds will be thrown away!
4. This means that if all the bolts alone are purchased this way, and there's possibly a hundred different types in regular use, then there may be more than £50 000 per annum just being wasted!

This is where you look back at the **buyer's rights** which are:

- the right material;
- at the right time;
- at the right quantity;
- at the right place;
- at the right price;
- at the right quality;
- at the lowest feasible inventory level.

And **know your items**.

You know they are turned, you know their generic description, you know they are steel. What you don't know is where they are used. The requisition came from stores, so that's your next step. Your questions are:

- Where are they used?
- Why are they requisitioned with such a short-notice period? Surely they must know more than a couple of weeks ahead that they are becoming short?
- What do they believe the annual volume to be and what stock do they want to hold?

The Chief Storekeeper, Fred Pink, tells you that the bolt 236-002 is used on one of the company's products which would be one of the volume products for some years to come. He also says that production will be run at about 400 per week.

He explains the min-max stock holding process that was used for standard parts such as nuts, bolts, washers, seals, bearings, paint, oil and grease. There are also similar methods employed for light bulbs, toilet paper, cleaning materials and a wide range of other consumables.

The min-max system

Consumption equals 400 per week.

Lead time for the acquisition of new materials equals 1 week.

Minimum stock to allow for replacement process before stock-out is therefore two weeks.

For safety he allows another week making a total of three weeks which in the case of 236–002 amounted to 1200 pieces in stock and when stock falls to this number he raises another requisition.

This means that in effect his minimum stock holding is at least two weeks; at average unit cost he likes to hold £0.455 × 800 = £364 in stock. So why do requisition quantities vary?

'Well,' he says, 'with all the items I have to look after on the low value items I like to raise a requisition of a higher quantity to build up some stock, otherwise I'd be doing nothing else but raising requisitions.'

'So what actual stock do you actually hold of this bolt?' you ask.

'Oh, a couple of thousand at least,' he says.

'How many different bolts do you carry in stores that you stock on a min-max basis?'

'Eighty-five types,' he replies, 'and that's not counting washers and nuts.'

Thanking him for the information you return to the buyer's desk deep in thought, having learned another truth.

The requisitioner is not always the authority when it comes to price, delivery and stocking policy – the buyer usually knows best!

Starting from really reading one buying card and performing a simple analysis you have uncovered a way to save the company a considerable sum, with practically no effort, and with a reduction of paperwork on both your part and that of the storekeeper.

The operation can be carried out in several different ways.

1. Since you have discovered that 4000 lots from Smith are priced at £0.45p each, and 5000 lots from Green are obtainable at £0.43p each, then the Economic Batch Quantity (EBQ) would appear to be 4000 in Smith's case and 5000 in Green's case.

The buying price could be reduced at an annual saving of £500 + per annum if the storekeeper would order in 5000 lots; always by buying from Green, provided stores gave two weeks' time for Green to react.

The minimum stock and re-order quantity would remain the same, needing only four requisitions a year but instead of holding an unofficial maximum of 2000 valued at the average price of $2000 \times £0.455 = £910$ he would be holding a max stock of 5000 at $£0.43 \times 5000 = £2150$.

Even taking the buying saving of £500 into account the cost of buying in 5000 lots would mean that a loss of $(£2150 - £500) = £1650$ loss.

So in this case the EBQ solution is not the answer.

It is clear that the value of inventory is the 'problem' in obtaining the benefit of buying bolts at higher volume breaks.

2. So how can the higher volume break be purchased and the inventory cost be reduced?

Clearly the time has come to involve the suppliers, and to look at the various ways in which the proposals can be put to them.

(a)   If one of the suppliers would accept an order for a year's requirement of 18 000 could they provide a lower price than the £0.43 that is the lowest that has been achieved so far?

(b)   If the answer to (a) is affirmative, would the supplier hold stock until it was called off?

(c)   Would the supplier deliver regular quantities?

(d)   How about a bond stock arrangement? (This is where a stock is held on the buyer's premises at the supplier's cost as an emergency stock which the buyer does not pay for until bond is broken by using the stock.)

At this stage an enquiry should be formulated to the three suppliers bearing in mind policy nos 1 and 2 relating to the necessity of providing all competing suppliers with identical information. The terms and conditions are an essential piece of information which you must ensure is either printed on the back of the enquiry, or otherwise included in the pack together with the relevant drawings and specifications.

If the reader refers to the example enquiry form you will see that the largest box is for the enquiry details to be printed. The following should appear in this box.

Part no.   *Description*
236–002   3″ × ⅛th bolt, 'S' quality steel

Please quote for the supply of 18 000 p.a. to be delivered weekly at the rate of 400 per week.

Then mail the three enquiries to the three potential suppliers.

If the suppliers are willing and able to deliver weekly the storekeeper could reduce stockholding to say one week's stock when the next weekly delivery is made so that minimum stock would be 400, and maximum is 800. In which case at the current average unit cost of £0.455 the inventory cost would not exceed $800 \times £0.455 = £364$, leave aside maximum stock which seems to be around 2000 bolts costing $2000 \times £0.455 = £910$.

In view of the fact that the requisition for the bolt only gives you a week you've probably phoned the three suppliers, placed the order and are now looking at the second priority item with a requirement for two weeks' time. The requirement is for two 45 gallon drums of a special cutting oil supplied, according to the buying card, only available from Mobil.

The buying card shows that every month for the last two years someone in production meticulously raises a requisition for delivery on the third week of each month.

Are there opportunities to reduce the cost of the purchase?

Obviously if there is available competition that's a good lever, and the place to find out is production engineering who specify the oils required to be used on the various capital machines used in the machine shop.

Having found the production engineer who is in charge of specifying cutting oils, to your surprise the engineer provides you with equivalent specifications supplied by each of the big five, and several others as well. It's perhaps the first time you've heard the phrase, 'it's only bog standard – nothing special about it at all!'

So now you know it's 'nothing special', it's advisable to go to the requisitioner and find out where the oil is held, how it's used and what happens to the drums when they're empty.

A production superintendent gives an opinion

The 'requisitioner' is one of the production superintendents, Mr Wilson. 'We have always used Mobil on this section, and I don't want any front office "Fancy Dans" telling me that other producers can do as well, and if you don't like what I'm telling you, take it up with the general factory manager!' He does have the grace to tell you that the supplier collects the empty drums when the next delivery is made.

Back at the buyer's desk you make a note to survey all the oil purchases before testing the market – clearly Mr Wilson won't be shaken out of his allegiance to a supplier, in which he has faith, on a cost argument – but his boss would surely be persuaded if it were possible to reduce the costs of the oil purchases.

Requisition no. 3 is for a laptop computer. Not only are the make and type specified but also the name of the stockist and the price. The 'requisitioner' is the sales director's secretary. You check the book of authorized signatories and find that she is allowed to sign for purchases up to £2000 but why has she specified the stockist? There are dozens around and there's an outside chance you might even be able to get it from the manufacturer at a much better price than a stockist could supply it. Out of curiosity you phone her to ask if this stockist is something special.

The affair of the laptop computer

'Oh, yes,' she says, 'all the secretaries have our own pet stationery suppliers. I think mine is the best, he comes to see me every day to see if there's any little thing I need and he's so obliging. In fact I've already told him he's got the order and to drop the computer in later this week, so be a dear and send him the order quickly!'

You put the phone down, seething.

The price shown on the sales director's secretary's requisition was £972. After four phone calls you have discovered that three stockists can supply the same laptop computer at prices below £900 and the manufacturer will supply at £850. Delivery in all cases is from stock.

Procedure no. 2 tells you that normally the lowest quote – all other things being equal – should be accepted and a quick check of the Policy and Procedures Manual states that requisitioners must be informed if their action will influence the company adversely. This is under Policy no. 5.

Since you are responsible for purchase of stationery then you have no alternative but to go back to the sales director's secretary and tell her that she is being over-charged; one might even say being ripped off, by her 'pet' stockist. You can offer to tell the 'pet' stockist that if he can supply the laptop at £850 he can have the order, otherwise the order will go elsewhere. Hopefully she will be pleased with your recommendation and agree to your plan. If not, then the best advice is to ring the 'pet' stockist yourself and tell them they have lost the business and you're going elsewhere. You will have made two enemies – but that's life at the buyer's desk!

There are three important points to remember here:

1. That if each secretary is buying from her own 'pet' stockist, the company budget on stationery must be a complete shambles, with all kinds of prices being paid for the same goods, and the opportunity for bulk buying and cost reduction had been lost, and must be regained.
2. Requisitioners should be encouraged not to specify by brand name but by description and in no case commit the company to a supplier.
3. Many people believe that the right to raise a requisition makes them buyers. The requisition is only a request for supply. So the third point is: **beware of amateur buyers – they are death to a company which seeks to be world-class!**

A supervisor has a problem

The fourth requisition was to establish a new contract for the supply of laundry services for the overalls worn by the workers on the assembly line, the buying card showed that the current contract was held by a company called Purity Services and appeared to be costing £1000 per month. The supervisor who had signed the requisition was a Mrs E. Ferguson. Clearly there was more in this than just a laundry service and again **know your items** is the first prerequisite in placing an enquiry, so a visit to Mrs Ferguson to find out what service she actually needs is the first step.

She explains that she has been told that she has to reduce her budget by 10% for the new financial year and she's looking to purchasing to help her do it. The present routine is that, as a company directive, all her workforce must have three clean overalls per week. There are two reasons for this:

1. The MD and the sales staff often bring customers on to the shop floor to show how clean the environment is as part of their selling pitch.
2. Cleanliness is an important factor in preventing contamination of the products being produced in her area.

Also in discussion she tells you that there are three sizes of overall supplied by the company for male operatives and three for the female operatives. This means that she has to ensure that there are sufficient overalls in stock to cover all eventualities plus a provision for new starts. The average life of an overall is two years. She employs one operator to control this aspect and to collect the dirty overalls and to issue clean overalls to each employee every other day.

The cost of the operative who looks after the overalls to Mrs Ferguson's budget is £12 000.

She has been told unofficially that Purity Services are proposing to ask for a 7% price increase in the next few months, which would make her budget reduction even more difficult to achieve.

She explains that Purity Services collect Monday's dirty overalls and return them on Wednesdays when they collect the next load of dirty overalls and they perform the same service again on Fridays. This ensures that each operator has one overall on, one at the wash, and a clean one in his or her locker.

The value of this discussion in formulating the enquiry is clear and it appears that you must carry out a survey of laundries specializing in the cleaning of industrial clothing, and discuss the possibilities with Mrs Ferguson and the potential suppliers to decide the best and most effective solution to her problem of reducing laundry costs by 10% by the beginning of the new financial year. There were 50 operators on the assembly line in question and the cost of laundering an individual garment was £1.66p.

Back at the buyer's desk you refer to *Kompass*, *Kelly's Directory* and the *Buyer's Guide* and select four laundries that would appear to be possibles. A telephone call to each of the laundries sales sections and appointments are made for them to visit you in the next couple of days.

Budgets: their use and abuse

Mrs Ferguson told you that she had been told that she had to reduce her budget by 10% for the next financial year, and its worth while at this stage spending a little time to understand the principles of budgeting.

Consider the costs that you, sitting at your desk working, actually cost to employ; of course, there's some obvious ones like:

* salary;
* overtime payments;
* travel and expenses;
* NHI and pension contributions;
* training courses.

But how about the cost of pens, pencils, order forms etc?

* depreciation on your desk and chairs, VDUs, fax system, phone system, and office decoration;
* heat, light, water rates;

- replacement equipment;
- office and window cleaners;
- canteen services;
- publications;
- memberships to professional bodies.

The pre-financial year process is when each manager is required to forecast all the costs of his/her department for the new financial year and present the forecast to accounting who add them all up and decide if the sum can be afforded as part of the company's overhead. Your purchasing manager has had to do a forecast for purchasing.

You can expect two reactions from your 'customers' at this stage. Some like Mrs Ferguson will be asking for your help. Others may well take a line that you as a buyer will feel is reprehensible. Towards the end of the financial year you may be flooded with requisitions for items you know they don't need. Policy 5 says that you must advise the requisitioner if they are adding unnecessary cost to what they have used in the past. Following this policy you should tell the requisitioner, 'You had three chemical balances this year what on earth do you want a fourth one for?' It's likely that they will reply, 'Well, I don't need another actually, but if I don't spend this year's budget up to the hilt my budget may be cut next year in line with what I spent in the current year.' (This tells you two things about them, and this is an occasion where you ask your boss to talk to the laboratory's boss. Your boss may have had to cut purchase's budget as Mrs Ferguson has had to do, because the laboratory is throwing money away.)

Budgets should be an accurate forecast of projected expenditure and not a method to camouflage ineptitude. So your boss will advise the head of laboratory that there is a problem to solve!

In this chapter there are several points to remember:

The requisitioner is not always right

The chief storekeeper believes **he** is the sole arbiter of stock management.

The production superintendent tries to exclude the buyer from any involvement in his domain.

The sales director's secretary believes that raising a requisition confers on her the position of amateur buyer.

The assembly shop supervisor has shared her problem with you and is hoping you can solve part of her problem.

These four examples have one thing in common:

Buyers can only function effectively when they have got the confidence of their customers.

In the next chapter we will see how to build that confidence by the use of buying skills.

MEMORY JOGGERS

7 **Beware the amateur buyer**
- Buying is second priority to them
- You know the market
- You have the knowledge and skills
- Buying is your job
- You have the contacts

REMEMBER – You are trained with special skills. That's why you are a pro!

8 **The min-max system**
- It's not always the best way
- Stock less than mean improves profit
- Bonded stock may be possible
- Savings on stock add to profit

REMEMBER – Excessive stock is a drain on working capital!

9 **Competitive enquiry**
- All suppliers to have the same information
- Provide a good specification
- Ask for supplier's suggestions
- Create competition
- Create level playing field

REMEMBER – Good purchase enquiries lead to an effective purchase!

10 **Manage your in-tray**
- Check it daily
- Don't ignore tough purchases
- Don't let it manage you!
- Set priorities
- Stick to them

REMEMBER – You should be the master of the in-tray – it's good practice!

3 USING BUYING SKILLS

This chapter explains the effective application of some of the fundamental tools of buying such as quotation analysis, cost benefit analysis, signature authority levels, Dun & Bradstreet and the 'lowest ultimate cost'. We also reveal some psychological insights and show the role of buyer as the prime motivator for cost improvement. This chapter introduces the basic structure of the contract before going on to greater detail in later chapters.

The quotation analysis in use

A few days later you receive quotations from Tree Ltd, Green Inc. and Smith Ltd and you prepare the quotation analysis as shown in Figure 3.1 (over).

It is most important that the quality department are asked to comment from their statistical surveillance reports. The full range of the quality department activities are discussed in Chapter 4.

With regard to Dun & Bradstreet reports it is normal for the company to have an account with D&B who can normally provide a report in a day or two on virtually any company, and can give good indications as to their financial reliability. It should be noted that there are other agencies offering the same service.

Basic negotiation tips

It goes without saying that no buyer should put any dependence for regular supply on to a supplier who could go bankrupt at any time.

The value of the quotation analysis can be seen clearly in this example. Without going through the routine Smith would appear the most attractive source, since they have the lowest price, they are offering a pack which has the smallest quantity; both of which are plus points in their favour. Unfortunately for them their quality rating is low and the D&B report is signalling caution.

Tree is fine from a quality, and D&B standpoint, but their unit cost is the highest and despite the request in your terms and conditions that payment is 60 days – they have quoted 30 days.

Green has submitted a reasonable price, their quality and D&B ratings are satisfactory – but there's a problem: they've quoted for delivery in 1000 lots, not at 400 per week, and a question: if Smith can quote at £0.365, why can't Green?

So you must negotiate with Green to see if you can get deliveries of 400 per week

PART NUMBER	DESCRIPTION	WHERE USED
236–002	3″ × ⅛ bolt S. Qual	Stores/Product XP

Quantity required		Delivery frequency
18 000 p.a.		400/week

Supplier	Unit price	Payment terms
Tree	£0.39	30 days nett
Green	£0.37	60 days nett
Smith	£0.365	60 days nett

Quality report

Tree	100% quality
Green	100% quality
Smith	98% quality

Financial status

Dun & Bradstreet Reports.
Tree. No adverse reports. Trading satisfactorily.
Green. No adverse reports. Trading satisfactorily.
Smith. Three recent actions on non-payment of bills. £200 credit maximum allowed.

Supplier comments in quotation letters

Tree. Packed in 500 lots.
Green. Packed in 1000 lots.
Smith. Packed in 250 lots.
All three sources state delivery as required.

Figure 3.1 Quotation analysis

and a price reduction to the level of Smith's price. The sales representative for Green agrees to come in later on in the day.

Although Green looks most attractive so far – you must be careful not to give the Green rep any clues to the fact that they have been most successful in the enquiry – because if you do, they won't move on price and they may demand a higher price for smaller deliveries. If they do then you might end up having to try to persuade Tree to reduce their price and to accept 60 days' payment. The time that a representative is most likely to make concessions is when they guess that they are close to getting the order – but have still got to give a little more so as to secure the order!

When the Green representative sits down at your desk – relax; never mind how tense you feel – don't show it. Most representatives have training in reading body language and they are often uncannily accurate in reading your thoughts, if you fiddle nervously with your wrist watch strap or keep adjusting your necktie. **Be cool!** No matter how difficult it seems.

Remember the salesperson's rights in Chapter 1. They will go along with all the buyer's rights except price!

So be pleasant – but one thing – don't let them get control of the meeting. They will if they can!

The sales representative opens a briefcase, takes a brochure out and invites you to look at it while telling you about the company. This is ploy one. You know all you need to know for the moment. It would be useful to look at later. So just tell them that you'd like to look at it later. Then thank them for their prompt reply to your enquiry and say that's what you want to discuss. **You get control**.

Longer term orders v. spot buys

'Firstly,' you say, 'I was surprised that after I had asked for a quote in 400 lots you chose to quote in 1000 lots. We are aiming at a closer control on inventory, and I have to say that I was most unimpressed by what appeared to be ignoring our wishes.'

The sales representative will probably see that the best line is to be apologetic and reply, 'Well, we could, of course, deliver in 400 lots on a weekly basis, if that's what you want, but it will mean that we may have to increase our price to cover weekly deliveries, and of course, it will mean changing our packing arrangements.'

'I would have thought,' you say, 'that those are costs well worth paying in return for getting a year's order; pretty well doubling our year's offtake from you. In fact I'm surprised that you hadn't quoted a lower unit price considering the volume involved.'

While this is being absorbed, hit again. 'Look,' you say, 'I've soon got to carry out this exercise on some 80 odd bolts, and their associated nuts and washers, and I'm looking for a supplier who is prepared to be competitive on delivery by helping us to control our inventory, and provide competitive prices to help us remain competitive in our world markets!'

'Well, I didn't know that you were in the market for that amount of business, look, let me go back to the office and speak to my boss, and I'll phone you first thing tomorrow.'

It looks as though the penny's dropped and that they will decide to re-quote at 400/wk and do something about price. Be careful not to show any signs of pleasure or relief.

Simply say pleasantly, 'Fine, make it before 10.30 am please, as I have a meeting to go to then.'

If your body language has shown cool confidence, and you've not betrayed your extreme interest in their product, you've done your best.

So you must keep your patience until tomorrow.

Looking through the brochure the Green sales representative left for you, there is a price list. There are pages and pages of it! Surprisingly, 236–002 isn't in the list, but many very similar bolts are listed and the price breaks are clearly shown.

Quantities		
	500–2000	53p ea.
	2001–4000	49p ea.
	4001–6000	43p ea.
	6001–8000	41p ea.
	8001–10 000	38p ea.

Delivery inclusive.

These prices are for delivery in single lots.

Tree and Smith presumably have similar literature which to the unwary are a snare and a delusion. They are designed for the one-off sale, not for a longer term contract. Suppliers are nearly always willing to go the extra mile for long-term continuity of business as the three quotes demonstrate.

So here's another lesson: never go for a one-off/periodic buy if you can, with some thought, offer longer term continuity of business.

Speaking of which, the value of this order, provided you can settle the supply details with the chief storekeeper, will be in the order of £6500 per annum so you'd better check your signature authority list. This tells you the level that you can sign off an order and at what level a superior has to countersign and authorize.

Buyer's signature authority list

Value of order

£500 – £10 000	No authorizing signature except buyer required
£10 000 – £50 000	Chief buyer approval mandatory
£50 000 – £1 000 000	Purchasing manager approval mandatory
£1 000 000 and above	MD approval mandatory

There are several reasons for having such a rule:

1. Somebody senior to you may well know something you don't. For example that despite your information, the XP product is being cancelled in six months' time, although the decision is still secret at this time.
2. Someone may be sourcing all bolts to China in some global deal.

3. To ensure that you haven't made some fearful blunder.
4. To ensure that you have followed all necessary procedures. The higher the sum involved the greater the risk and the higher the authorizer needs to be.

In this particular case there is no need to seek authorization.

The laundry problem is next on the agenda. In the end you decided to see three new laundries first and save Purity until last.

The new suppliers are:

Baker Charlie Industrial Cleaners
Alpha-Foxtrot Industrials
Delta Laundries Inc.

The Dun & Bradstreet reports on all three are favourable, as is the D&B on Purity, and *Kompass* shows that they are all of reasonable size. The one thing that you need to find out is if they deal with other companies of similar size. You can then phone the buyer and ask if they get good service from the laundry they use. Most buyers are 'cagey' when a buyer from a possible competitor phones them but on a straightforward question like, 'How do they perform?' they are usually very helpful.

Reception tells you that Mr English of Baker Charlie Industrial Cleaners is in reception. You have already planned to see him with Mrs Ferguson so the meeting takes place in her office.

Specifying requirements

This is an occasion where you take a back seat, and copious notes, while Mrs Ferguson explains her requirements.

Briefly she wants three overall changes per week with her staff, collecting dirty laundry, and distributing the clean. There are 50 staff male and female on the section that require this service and because there are three sizes for males and three for females it is imperative that if she sends a list such as:

5 large male
10 medium male
2 small male
10 large female
3 medium female
10 small female

she gets back exactly what she sent. Also Mrs Ferguson requires early morning delivery so that her staff member can inspect the overalls, make small repairs if appropriate and if not repairable draw a new replacement from stock.

(This then necessitates a new order, and the last price according to the buying card was £12.00.)

Mr English listens carefully to what Mrs Ferguson has to say, then says, 'There's another way to handle your overall cleaning, you know. We have a scheme that works like this. We supply the overalls at no cost to you provided you give us a two-year contract. We recover the cost of the overalls in the cost of laundering. We maintain a stock of sizes because we carry out this service to a wide range of companies so we can bulk-buy overalls at a much lower price than I expect you pay, so new starts are no problem. Also in the event that a damaged one is received in a dirty laundry basket we can replace it from stock if it's not repairable. We only bill you if the damage appears to be not attributable to wear and tear. Provided you can ensure that all dirty coats are dumped in a laundry basket that our employee can access easily they will collect them and leave the clean ones at an agreed place within your unit. Provided your laundry list will show the sizes and male or female overalls we undertake to return exactly the same mix, at the intervals you have specified.'

'What would the price be for the whole service?' you ask.

'I will have to check it and send you a formal quote tomorrow – but "roughly-roughly" about £1.80 per clean overall,' he replies.

After he leaves Mrs Ferguson looks at you and says disappointedly, 'Well, that was a blow-out!'

But you are not so sure.

'How many overalls do we have in circulation?' you ask.

'There's 150 in use and I have to maintain a stock of three of each size, say another 12.'

'So our stock value at launch would be 150 × £12.00 = £1 800.00 and with a life of two years they would all have to be replaced. Also the operator who looks after the overalls earns £12 000 per annum which makes £24 000 over two years. We also know that currently we pay £1.66 × 150 washes per week = £249.00; over 40 working weeks = £10 000 approx per annum, so over two years that makes £20 000. So the total cost over two years = (£1800 + £24 000 + £20 000) = £45 800. This compares with (£1.80 × 150 × 80) = £21 600.'

'That's incredible,' says Mrs Ferguson. 'That would halve my costs!'

'Frankly,' you remark, 'it's unbelievable – so let's try and see if we can see how the costs can break down.'

Lowest ultimate cost

'This looks like a lowest ultimate cost exercise,' you mutter to yourself.

'What is that?' she asks.

'**Lowest ultimate cost: is where the buyer not only takes into account the cost of the purchase but the cost of spares, maintenance, use of energy obsolesence, life of product, etc.**

'If his estimate of £1.80 per cleaning is right, then if we deduct the current price we are paying of £1.66 he is making (£1.80 – £1.66) = £0.14 per wash. Multiply that by 150 × 80 = £1 680.00.

'Even if you assume he's buying his overalls at half the price we are paying that would mean his two-year cost would be £900.00 leaving £780 to pay the operator that would actually handle the work making his labour allocation £390 p.a. Well I suppose it's possible but I'm going to question his costs very closely.'

'You know what,' says Mrs Ferguson, 'in lowest ultimate cost terms there's two things we've not put into the cost equation. If we decided to go for English's proposal first there's the obsolescence problem. We could end up with 150 overalls of different ages and an employee too many, and second if we decided to make her redundant we'd have to add the costs to the price of going to Baker Charlie Industrial Cleaners.' So you draw up an analysis (shown in Table 3.1).

Table 3.1   Analysis: Purity v. Baker Charlie

	Purity	Baker Charlie
Cost of 2 yrs laundry	£20 000	£21 600
Cost of 2 yrs overalls	£1800	Inclusive
Cost of labour (2 yrs)	£24 000	Inclusive
Redundancy cost		£10 000 (est)
Cost of redundant overalls at written off level (50%)		£900
TOTALS	£45 800	£32 500

'It still looks very promising,' observes Mrs Ferguson, 'and come to think of it, one of my girls is leaving soon, so I could transfer the overall caretaker into her job and we wouldn't have the redundancy to consider.'

'Yes,' you say, 'but what happens at the end of the two year contract? – There's a lot I still need to know!'

As you leave her office en route for the buyer's desk you say over your shoulder, 'We've still got three more to see before we can come to a decision!'

The following morning you list on your desk pad four things that must be done today and they are:

1. Get the revised quotation from Green for 236-002.
2. Talk to the chief storekeeper about the supply method.
3. Get a list for all the nuts, bolts, and washers and annual usages.
4. Meet Alpha-Foxtrot Cleaners with Mrs Ferguson.

Then down to the in-tray. Hmm, there's quite a lot today – lightbulbs, some more oils, some more stationery, 400 ft of copper conduit, some oil seals and gaskets, some office chairs, a plastic bucket, and a load of toilet paper. There's a good long lead time for all of the requisitions except the toilet paper which is wanted in a week. **Something to remember – on most things a buyer will in time be forgiven, if very occasionally he is late on delivery – but he will never ever be forgiven if the factory runs out of toilet paper. A shortage of that commodity and the factory will strike!**

So whatever else crosses your desk there's your absolutely top priority. So get it placed now!

A price reduction negotiation

Just as you've finished placing the toilet paper order, the phone rings. It's the Green representative. 'You'll be pleased to know that we've considered your proposal to deliver in 400 lots on a weekly basis, and we will do it at no extra cost. Does that give you what you wanted?'

'I'm sorry to say it doesn't,' you reply. 'I had also asked you to consider again the price you are offering in view of the size of the order we're discussing.'

'When will you be raising the major nut, bolt and washer enquiry you told me about when I was with you?'

'By the end of the week, I hope.'

'Will Green be getting an enquiry?'

'Yes,' you growl, 'I could do with a laugh!'

The Green representative's laugh floats down the phone. 'OK, how does £0.36 grab you?'

'Well, if that's the best you can do,' you smile, 'I suppose I'd better tell you I'm going to award you the order.'

'Thanks very much,' responds the Green representative. 'I'll give you written confirmation later today.'

'Yes and I'll come back to you in a day or two, to confirm delivery arrangements.'

Now it's off to talk to the chief storekeeper.

Review of the negotiation

But just reflect for a moment on your discussion with the Green representative. He tested you three times in that brief conversation.

1. He tested your determination to get the price reduction by offering the 400 per week delivery concession first. He hoped you would thank him for conforming to your delivery request.
2. He was still reluctant to concede the price reduction until he felt that you'd been telling the truth about your intending to launch the big enquiry and that they were on your list of potential suppliers. You convinced him that he could be in with a chance on a really big order.
3. When he offered you a small reduction you pronounced yourself satisfied. He stopped selling because you had stopped buying!

Remember this: a supplier will not sell you anything at a price lower than can be afforded so always keep pushing until you get a response which tells you they are not prepared to go any further!

The chief storekeeper is quite impressed when you show him how it is possible to reduce not only the unit price and both the size and cost of inventory which will produce the cost benefits shown in Table 3.2 (opposite).

You jointly decide that you will raise an order for 12 months for delivery at the rate of 400 per week. The chief storekeeper will be named as the progress contact with the right to moderate volumes in accordance with the company requirements.

Table 3.2   Cost benefit analysis

Old method	*New method*
Av. unit cost £0.455	Unit price £0.36
Min. stock £364.00	Min. stock (1 wk) £144.00
Max. stock £910.00	Max. stock (2 wks) £288.00
Forecast annual cost	Forecast annual cost
(18 000 × £0.455) = £8190	(18 000 × £0.36) = £6480

Annual saving: £8190 – £6480 = £1710.

Min. stock reduced by 40%
Max. stock reduced by 315%

He will not have to raise requisitions, but an extra copy of the invoice should be marked for his attention for record purposes. In the event of any supply difficulty the chief storekeeper will inform you immediately. As you leave the office you hear him telling his staff to list all nuts, bolts and washers with annual volumes and 'where used' information as he is involved with the buyer on a major cost-saving exercise. And he wants it done quickly!

You've gained his confidence: make sure you keep it!

A basic contract

You now have to write a series of instructions to Green which amplifies the terms and conditions on the order; because you want to incorporate extra information on the order to stores, accounting and of course the supplier.

Clause 1   **Packaging**
The goods are to be supplied in non-returnable packs of 400.

Clause 2   **Delivery**
Weekly

Clause 3   **Co-ordination**
Mr Pink. Chief Storekeeper

Clause 4
Each weekly delivery is to be accompanied by the original and one copy of the invoice. The copy invoice is to be addressed for the attention of Mr Pink.

When you receive the revised quotation from Green you must also ensure that you obtain the period of price stability that you require – say 12 months minimum from the date of issuance of the order. Then clause 5 will read 'price as revised quote dated. . . ., price stability to date. . . .'

These five clauses can be typed on the order, or a continuation sheet carrying the order number. This is a basic contract and is underpinned by the terms and conditions, in certain cases you will find it necessary to write special conditions which differ from the terms and conditions. In which case another condition must define which condition rules. An example might be, 'where these conditions are at variance with the standard conditions then these special conditions take precedence'.

Chapter 8 on contracts will discuss the construction of a contract in more detail – but the important point to remember at this stage is that every contract is an order and vice versa. It is the buyer's responsibility to specify in as clear and detailed a way as possible the rules that must be adhered to.

It is now time to meet Alpha-Foxtrot Cleaners with Mrs Ferguson.

The meeting starts with Mrs Ferguson **specifying** her requirements. After some discussion they offer the same service as the current source but they offer price stability for the year of the order, if they are awarded it, of £1.50 per wash. The benefit analysis in this case is shown in Table 3.3.

Table 3.3   Cost/benefit analysis: Purity v. Alpha-Foxtrot

Purity		Alpha-Foxtrot
Cost of 1 yr's laundry	£10 000	£9036
Cost of overalls	£900	£900
Cost of labour	£12 000	£12 000
Potential price increase	7%	Firm price for 12 months

Another aspect of cost has been raised in this benefit analysis. Mrs Ferguson has already heard a whisper that Purity is threatening to put their price up by 7% if they can. It's probable that the prices of overalls may be uplifted and the cost of the operative who looks after the overalls may also have a wage increase. Even with low national inflation the likely cost increases will be say:

Purity:
Cost of 1 year's laundry   £10 000 + 7% = £10 700
Cost of overalls   £900 + 3% = £927.00
Cost of labour   £12 000 + 3% = £12 360

Which means that if no action is taken prices will rise to £23 987 from £22 900, being a growth of £1087. Alpha-Foxtrot producing a saving of £964.00 would not provide the reduction Mrs Ferguson has been instructed to obtain, e.g.:

Reduction of 10% on **current** cost. This means that if she is going to achieve her objective she must try to reduce the price of overalls from a purchased cost of £900 to £810, laundry cost from £10 000 to £9000 and reduce labour cost by £1200.

This now demonstrates that nothing short of a lowest ultimate cost solution will meet the target.

Very often buyers will do the equivalent of buying from Alpha-Foxtrot and congratulate themselves on having made a saving and prevented the increase planned by Purity taking place – but unless they have considered the lowest ultimate cost potential they will have only done part of their job.

So you'd better see if you can find a cheaper source for overalls, but without reducing the quality or service that you are getting at present. Clearly the cost of labour rests with Mrs Ferguson but the proposal to sub-contract the whole operation is the only one that really offers the certainty of achieving the objective she has been set.

After having seen the other sources you prepare the quotation analysis and cost benefit analysis (see Figure 3.2, over).

Purity produced a re-quote to try to hold the business, Delta quoted for both options. Your current overall supplier offered a 10% reduction. All with a price firm for the next 12 months.

A lowest ultimate cost solution

You decide not to look for a third source who will offer you a full contract service, now you can see that the costs of actual washing is so close in all cases. The big variable is in the cost of the overalls where the laundry's buying power is so much greater than yours – and finally there is the difference in administration costs.

So now two quotation analyses must be prepared A and B. A is continuing with the present method, and B is sub-contracting all activities.

A definitive cost benefit analysis

Cost of contract with Baker Charlie =	£21 600
To which must be added contra-costs of:	
1. redundancy of employee =	£10 000
2. written off cost of overalls =	£900
Total cost to company =	£32 500

Subsequent discussions with Baker Charlie result in their agreement to purchase the company stock of written off overalls at a 50% rate of their bought-out price of £6.00 per overall, thereby reducing their price of £21 600 – (150 × £3.00 = £450) to £21 150.

Assuming that management accept that the employee can be redeployed to replace a 'leaver' then the final cost benefit analysis to be presented to management becomes two documents:

1. The quotation analysis;
2. cost benefit analysis as below.

Cost benefit analysis

Cost of contract with Baker Charlie = £21 600

To which must be added contra-costs of £450 being the residual cost of sale of company stock of overalls.

Total cost to company = £22 050 being a saving against current price of 49.86%.

A *Continuing with present method one-year costs*

1 year	Current Purity	Alpha-Foxtrot	Delta	Purity requote
Cost of laundry	£10 000	£9036	£9000	£8900
Cost of overalls	£900	£850	£850	£850
Cost of labour	£12 000	£12 000	£12 000	£12 000
Labour increase		+ 3% (£360)	+ 3% (£360)	+ 3% (£360)
Totals	£22 900	£22 246	£22 210	£22 110

Saving 3%, recommendation – stay with Purity

B *Contracting out labour and overall supply two-year contract*

	New Purity	Baker Charlie	Delta
Cost of 2 yrs' laundry	£17 800	£21 600	£23 000
2 yrs' overalls	£1700	Incl.	Incl.
2 yrs' labour	£24 720	Incl.	Incl.
Totals	£44 220	£21 600	£23 000

Notes: (a) possibility of selling overalls to Baker Charlie; (b) redundancy cost avoidable if redeployment possible.

See cost benefit analysis on p. 46.

Figure 3.2 Quotation analysis: comparison of two systems

Writing a contract

Assuming that management accept the proposal, which, because of the order value will have to be approved by your chief buyer, there is the contract to write. Mrs Ferguson and you have made clear to all the potential sources what it is you require as a service.

This is easy to do because the requirements are obvious to you.

The supplier is to supply clean, undamaged overalls every Monday, Wednesday and Friday and collect from a pre-assigned point the dirty overalls accompanied by a laundry list and to return the same 'mix' on the next delivery.

The laundry lists will be approved by Mrs Ferguson and in the event of a new start requiring a set of three she will fax her requirement to the supplier who will deliver them with the next delivery.

The cost for this will be compensated for by the applied laundry cost but if the contract is not renewed after the initial period of two years then the supplier will be allowed to charge the written-down cost of overalls less than two years old.

What if things go wrong?

This is not obvious to you. For example what if 'the one on, one at the wash, and one in each operator's locker' breaks down, leaving the operators without clean overalls to put on? If it's a case of force majeure then the terms and conditions tell you what action to take – but say it was supplier incompetence?

The minimum would have to be a clause stating that in the event of the operator's being left without clean overalls you reserve the right to get them cleaned elsewhere and bill the supplier with the cost. The terms and conditions state that as 'time is of the essence' cancellation is a possibility.

In this way you build up your protection clauses which the supplier must agree to.

This exercise started as a request to find a cheaper laundry supplier and finished as a make v. buy study. The buyer should always keep in mind that in many cases buying rather than making is the preferred solution.

The buyer sits at the centre of most factory activities. Just look at the activities the buyer can motivate to make their company more profitable and more competitive.

The buyer as motivator

The aims
Factory requirements
Competitively priced
Minimum inventory
Good quality

The tools
Efficient source selection
Efficient record keeping
Efficient market research
Supply on time
Negotiation skills
Good communication skills
Good motivation skills
Good liaison skills

Sister depts
Production control
Finance/accounting
Design
Engineering
Sales
Contracts
Quality control
Manufacturing
Stores
Costing/estimating

The knowledge
Raw materials
Manufacturing methods
Costing/estimating
Law
Economics
Inventory control
Tactics/strategy
Overseas opportunities
Human nature
Sales techniques
Finance

The aims are clear, always drive to achieve the lowest ultimate cost.

In order to play your part effectively you must become a motivator of your colleagues in other departments. If you are not playing a full part in leading them you run the risk of becoming their slave rather than their equal, and decisions get made that are not in the best company interest.

Your professional knowledge will come from studying for and gaining your Chartered Institute of Purchasing Diploma (for study subjects see Appendix E). The effective use of your tools will come from your own drive and application.

There is always a way to reduce cost and obtain company benefit and it's your job to find it!

MEMORY JOGGERS

11 **Quotation analysis**

This is designed to compare the various bids for:

- Price
- Delivery
- Tool cost
- Other non-recurring items
- Payment terms
- Quality information
- Financial status
- Contractual compliance or otherwise

REMEMBER – this is an organized way to ensure that all factors are evaluated.

12 **Dealing with the supplier no. 1**

- Don't lie
- Be fair
- Be businesslike
- Give due consideration to what has been said
- Specify what you want

REMEMBER – it's your job to test and check what you are told.

13 **Dealing with the supplier no. 2**

- Listen to what is said.
- Don't let the seller control the meeting
- Listen for negotiating signals
- Don't be afraid to ask for what you want

REMEMBER – the more the seller controls you the less chance there is to negotiate. Why do you think they want control?

14 **Dealing with the supplier no. 3**

- They want the maximum price
- You want the lowest cost
- You must find the 'bottom line'
- Use competition
- Maintain enough pressure to get what you want

REMEMBER – the seller is at the most vulnerable when it is realized you are looking for one last concession and then the order is theirs.

15 The one-off buy
- Don't buy off the price list
- Ask for a discount
- Check if there are any price breaks for quantity
- Are there future orders in the pipeline which could be used as a lever?

REMEMBER – sellers make good profit from one-offs, therefore the price can be challenged.

16 Lowest ultimate cost
The lowest ultimate cost will involve many factors depending on the nature of the purchase but will probably take into account:
- Unit price
- Storage costs
- Maintenance costs
- Warranty provision costs
- Energy costs
- Life of product spares support costs
- Likely technology change costs, i.e., computer software replacement/enhancement

REMEMBER – all these costs must be quantified for make v. buy studies and for a major purchase. They must be proven by a cost benefit analysis.

4 RATIONALIZATION, QUALITY AND SPECIFICATION

This chapter builds on the basic skills and tools covered in earlier chapters and looks at rationalization, the quality function, 'speeds and feeds', blanket order/scheduling process, combining 'front of order' conditions with standard terms and conditions to formulate basic contracts. We then go on to show how to develop specifications, evaluate supply options and construct a contract preparation checklist. 'Political persuasion' is also introduced as a practical consideration.

The chief storekeeper was as good as his word, and within a week he presented you with his list of nuts, bolts and washers with their annual usages. There were various types and sizes of all three items, but, what was noticeable was that there were ranges of bolts of the same diameter, thread size and diameter conforming to the same specification, but of different lengths. When listed in order of the length they were seen to go up in steps of 2 mm.

Now 13 mm is approximately equivalent to ½″ so that in this particular family there were no less than six bolts with annual usages varying from 4000 to 50 000 using the same nut and washer.

A rationalization opportunity

Clearly if the mean length, or indeed the maximum length, could be used in all applications then only one length of bolt need be bought, and with a combined volume of some 250 000.

The advantages from taking this action would not only produce a unit cost saving but would reduce administration costs. Once started on this train of thought, other families emerge from the list, and if other rationalization exercises could be implemented across the 85 bolts listed they could be perhaps condensed to only 20 different types. But where to start? The departments with an involvement in change are:

design engineering
quality

manufacturing
production engineering
production control
stores

What will convince them to change?

- price savings;
- cost savings in handling and administration;
- facilitating easier assembly;
- reduced inventory.

Getting your ducks in a row

You are probably aware of the old duck-hunter's advice, 'Before you shoot, get your ducks in a row!' Each of the departments you have to motivate in order to persuade them, or at best ensure that they stay neutral, believe that they are doing a good job. Often they see change as either tiresome interference, or even downright sabotage, threatening to disturb their nice comfortable existence.

This is not to say that you should take counsel of your fears but rather that you should plan carefully how you will motivate these sister departments in the most efficacious way.

The steps to successful persuasion are as follows:

1. research;
2. divide the group of departments you seek to persuade into gainers and losers;
3. gain the support of the gainers (this is sometimes called picking off the easy ones first); this has the effect of isolating the possibly/probably/certainly 'antis'.
4. it's usual that one department, probably the one who has to do most work to implement your change, is the one who will try to throw up every conceivable obstacle. If however they know that everyone else is for the change they will be persuaded, because nobody likes to be labelled as 'stick in the mud'.

Research

This follows two distinct lines.

1. Raising enquiries for the 20 representative bolts, nuts and washers you have selected, asking for weekly deliveries at the volumes which emerge from amalgamating all the volumes into their family groups.

On receipt of the quotes prepare a quotation analysis and a cost benefit analysis based on reduced stockholdings, instead of the min-max process.

Let us imagine that the potential savings are £50 000 reduction per annum in unit cost, and £70 000 in inventory cost. This is certainly worth going for!

2. Knowing your items is again the first prerequisite.

Firstly, you need to assess if reducing the number of bolts used in assembly could facilitate production. Fortunately your friend Mrs Ferguson is able to show you just what a nuisance the different lengths of bolt are. 'In fact,' she confides, 'the operators if they're short of the specified size, will often fit a bolt several sizes longer with no deleterious effect at all!'

This proves there is scope to reduce the range of lengths brought in.

The Quality Department agree that in most cases the range of bolts supplied are overspecified and this overspecification causes them problems in two areas:

(a)   In receiving inspection. Because they have to maintain records on so many different types, and if this number could be significantly reduced it would allow more time to be spent on higher priorities.

(b)   Outgoing inspection requires that the bolted assemblies have to be inspected on a percentage basis because of the assembly operators' tendency to fit an unspecified length of bolt in an incorrect location. Although in 99.9% of cases it makes no difference to the product at all, assemblies with wrong fittings have to be returned to production for rectification before dispatch. Quality control state that if design engineering could be persuaded to reduce the number of different lengths of bolt used they would be wholly in support.

Production control are also supportive of the project, stores comes under production control, and they feel that min-max stock systems promote surplus stocks at all times and particularly when a length of bolt is phased out. If there were, say, only 20 types they could be carried as a production supply and fed direct to production without having to 'dwell' in stores at all! This would mean that you would be relieved of having to respond to requisitions every so often. All you would have to do would be to raise a blanket order listing all the items and prices, and production control would schedule their requirements directly on the supplier.

Production engineering are quite neutral, although they agree that what you have been told by the other departments is broadly true. Then you divine that their reason is that they should have thought of it themselves. They do say however that provided design engineering will support the change they have no objection.

In this instance you have researched the supplier market and your internal customers and to a greater or lesser degree they are all gainers, so that your meeting with design engineers will be as well prepared as possible.

Before you meet the design engineer it is worth while trying to see things from their point of view, since this presentation of your proposal will in fact be a kind of negotiation since they have to admit that due to the way they have designed this range of products they have been causing the company to waste an inordinate amount of time and money for some years. If the force of your argument persuades them, they will have to dig out hundreds of drawings (unless they have CAD/CAM) and modify them. They may also have to modify spares handbooks and sales promotion literature, which causes them a lot of work, when probably like everyone else in the company they are already under pressure.

When you meet the designer, perhaps you can open your discussion by saying, 'There's a potential saving of at least £120 000 per annum that can be made in facilitating production – but it needs your help to implement it.' This should excite their curiosity at least, and if you then explain your idea, and don't dwell on the point that everyone agrees the design was overspecified, the design engineer will promise to look at your proposal.

They may have said that just to get rid of you, so don't say 'Thanks very much,' and walk out of the drawing office smiling and swinging your arms. Remember **you're** selling and the engineer is **buying**.

Ask what the Engineer has to do; when he/she tells you that all the drawings have to be reviewed and various graphs prepared before the engineer can say yea or nay, you ask, 'How long will this take?'

Political persuasion

Then get a commitment as to when this will be. Assuming the answer is 'two weeks' then say, 'OK, I'll be back then.'

If after a fortnight the engineer has done nothing, find out why you're getting the run-around. Often the answer is, 'I've been too busy!'

In that case you can offer to get your boss to write to his opposite number saying that since the engineer is so overloaded as to be too busy to help save the company £120 000 perhaps the chief engineer could employ a temporary engineer to do the necessary; funding the extra head out of the saving!

If that still doesn't generate activity you've no alternative but to see the chief engineer yourself or inform your boss and let them take it up.

The learning point here is to avoid politics if you can, but to remember the use of politics is a good 50% of motivating others.

While you are waiting for the design engineer to come up with recommendations it's time to learn some more about the way the company assures itself that incoming materials conform to the drawings and specifications.

The reason is that although you've been buying bolts as an indirect material, or consumable, you are now going to convert the bolt 'buy' to a direct production material. In most companies different rules apply to the quality control of direct materials (used directly in production) compared to indirect materials, such as paint, oil, grease, etc. or consumables which are consumed in the process of manufacture. Your nuts and bolts are changing from consumables to direct materials.

The distinction is sometimes rather arbitrary, but the definition is a management convenience, defining workflows and responsibilities. At present you are working as a consumables buyer with no responsibility for buying production materials. This allows you a measure of specialization and the sister departments are similarly channelled.

In this case you will be passing the nut bolt and washer buy to a production buyer, and you must now set up the 'buy' in line with production buying practices. So you must talk to the quality manager.

The quality department's role

Typically the quality department will be organized with the following responsibilities:

1. laboratory;
2. metrology;
3. metallurgy;
4. dimensional;
5. receiving inspection;
6. in-line inspection;
7. quality assurance;
8. warranty.

Some inspection departments do not have their own facilities in all eight areas but make use of public test houses and commercial laboratories. This doesn't reduce their responsibilities, however, and you as a buyer must have a good working knowledge of what goes on in the various areas.

Very often the bolts you buy are specified to have a protective coating, such as cadmium plate, passivated, or phosphate coat and oiled etc. These coatings are to protect the bolt against adverse conditions which could degrade the bolt while in service.

The laboratory will be able to check that the coating deposit is of the right composition according to specification. The bolts are specified to be of a certain steel which the laboratory by analysis can report on, and also by various mechanical methods can test for hardness, tensility, and other physical properties. Metrology deals in fine measurements and dimensional inspection deals with the dimensional checks against the drawing.

All samples must pass through these processes prior to being given approval for production, receiving inspection checks of representative deliveries as received and from time to time quarantine deliveries in order that they can be thoroughly checked. In-line inspection sets out to ensure that production and assembly operations are conforming to the processes laid down by design and production Engineering. Final inspection is to ensure that the final product goes to the customer in a satisfactory saleable condition, and warranty inspection has the duty to inspect items returned under warranty to establish why the subject component failed and to recommend changes to prevent such a failure re-occuring.

All these processes should be available to the supplier in the same way as they are to the buyer. Since all these processes are expensive and are there to protect the company it follows that if buyers could find suppliers capable of assuring the company that they will undertake to ensure all their materials conform in all ways to the company's requirements there would be no need for this expensive resource to be maintained and this is where quality assurance comes in.

If you order 100 bolts you have the right to expect that they will all be to 'print' and to specification, but how can you be sure that the supplier you have chosen will be capable of meeting this requirement?

This means that each potential supplier must be submitted to an inspection to see that the supplier has the equipment to ensure that their products will all conform to requirement and do not need to be inspected on receipt at your works.

Suppliers who hold AID, BS 5750, Ford Q101, or similar certification already state that they quality assure their products.

Many potential suppliers however do not have these qualifications and the quality assurance team have to check them out to see if they are quality orientated.

The quality survey

The quality survey covers every process at the supplier from the receipt of their raw materials to shop floor practices, inspection processes etc. When raw materials are received the quality assurance inspector will look either for the supplier taking a sample for laboratory checks or material certification from the raw material supplier. He or she will also look for material segregation in stores which ensures that operators cannot take the wrong material to work on because one steel bar looks very much like another. Then the quality assurance inspector will look at the machine shops, looking for a tidy environment normally referred to as 'good housekeeping', proper maintenance of tools and gauges and operator responsibility for quality. This is because no inspector can inspect a bad piece of work into a good piece, but if the operators have the responsibility for checking their own work then the shop floor practice aspect is favourable.

It is also important to note that a very high percentage of high quality comes from the design of the machines and tooling in use; also to a great extent the age of the machines. The best maintenance in the world cannot prevent a machine, due to wear and tear, becoming less accurate as the years go by. This is usually noticeable in for example a turning machine which cannot hold tight tolerances. So the quality assurance inspector will ask to look at the supplier's records on machine performance and overhaul statistics.

Your selected bolt supplier will have to undergo such an inspection, and subject to satisfying the quality assurance inspector you will have to agree with the supplier a 'quality assured clause' which imposes certain duties and clauses defining the action you will take in the event of a failure to deliver OK material.

It is advisable that you go round with the quality assurance inspector and learn how the job is done. Often you will find as your career develops that you will be at a supplier's premises and you will need to form an impression of the work when there is no quality inspector around. So you must learn as much as you can whenever the opportunity presents itself.

In Chapter 2 the Dun & Bradstreet check on a supplier's financial state was outlined, and beside the quality assurance survey there are two other aspects which need to be covered in order to be assured that a company is **commercially** suitable. These are covered in Chapter 9 on negotiation. In the particular example of the bolt supplier, since the company has long and satisfactory experience of working with them, it is not so necessary that these checks are carried out as a prerequisite of placing further business with them.

Speeds and feeds

On your visit with the quality inspector to the bolt supplier it is useful to take a watch with a second hand with you. This may seem unusual but it will be an opportunity to do some elementary timing studies. Bolt-making machines spit out bolts like bullets out of a machine gun but just as there are slow and fast firing machine guns there are slow and fast bolt-makers. Without letting anyone see what you are doing (the operators might think you were some efficiency expert hired by the management and strike because they'd not been forewarned!) time the rate at which bolts are coming off the machine, say 100 per minute. All machines have the manufacturer's name on them somewhere. The machine might be a Bloggs 900. When you get back to the buyer's desk, open a file called 'speeds and feeds'. The speed you have established with your watch, the 'feed' will be the raw material which is fed into the machine. You should also ask what specification the steel is, the length of the bar material which is loaded onto the machine, and what wastage occurs. For example, if the machine was set up to make 12″ long bolts, and 6′ bars were being loaded you would not get six bolts off the machine, you would only get five! The reason? Firstly because the machine needs an allowance to hold the workpiece and secondly because each 12″ length cut off causes some material to be wasted in the cutting process. Thus you have to pay for waste! Later on we will discuss ways and means by which the buyer can reduce the scrap content, and your notes on 'feeds and speeds' will help you to compare the various efficiencies of machines, suppliers and raw materials usage techniques.

After a while your record of 'speeds and feeds' will tell you which machines are best for your particular requirement and you will be able to select suppliers who are best equipped to serve your particular purpose.

Once back at the buyer's desk you find a memo from the design engineer who tells you that the range of 85 bolts can be cut down, not as far as you proposed but can be reduced to 40. The 40 types are listed and where some bolts can be phased out and which ones replace them are also given. By analysis you are able to calculate new usages and re-enquire. Because some volumes are lower than your first estimate, unit costs may be a little higher, but still the savings are very good and of course the saving on inventory by going from min-max to direct supply remains the same.

There are just two jobs left to do:

1. Raise a blanket order and write the special extra clauses needed.
2. Agree the phase out of the bolts which are being replaced in order to ensure minimum obsolesence with production control, and discuss the scheduling procedure that should be employed.

Well, as is often the case at the buyer's desk, getting your ducks in a row means that (2) must be tackled before (1).

Constructing a delivery schedule

You have already agreed with the supplier that weekly delivery is required and your knowledge of how they acquire their raw material demands two months lead time. This means that if they are to supply on a continuous process they need to know **three** months ahead what raw material to order. This is a minimum. If they could be given a reasonably accurate forecast allowing them three months' visibility for ordering raw material they could buy in larger quantities and get volume discounts from their supplier and so keep your prices down, so that the best schedule pattern would be a call off of requirement for a weekly delivery of all bolts plus three months' forecast of requirements.

On discussion with production control you find that they can give two months' firm requirements of bolts on a weekly basis, and they can provide a three-month forecast by month which will tentatively match their forecast requirements.

But they warn you that these latter requirements are only tentative and they would not expect to be held liable for material bought against their tentative schedule.

So between you and production control you draw up the schedule for deliveries shown in Figure 4.1 (opposite).

It will be seen from this schedule that item (ghi) is being phased in as stocks of its predecessor must be used first and that (ghi) is forecast to have reduced usage after the end of March.

It will also be noted that the standard schedule form advises the supplier that the tentative section is for information only; but you have the choice of amending this clause both on the schedule and as a special condition on the blanket order too. The tentative bloc may be used for the acquisition of raw material, but the company does not hold itself responsible for components made beyond the firm commitment given in this schedule.

Construction of the blanket order

Based on the agreement you have with production control, and the supplier you are now in a position to raise the blanket order. The first essential is to take a copy of the terms and conditions listed in Chapter 1, and see what variations to them you need to make to form the front of order conditions for the new blanket order.

1. Terms of payment

You've agreed 60 days – so no change there.

2. Quality

The supplier is **quality assured**. Therefore you need to have an extra 'front of order condition' here. The supplier warrants that all materials will be in line with the company's specifications, drawings and such other instructions as may be given by the company from time to time. Failure to achieve a statistical level of less than 99%

	Firm									Tentative		
Part no.	w/c 1/2	w/c 7/2	w/c 14/2	w/c 21/2	w/c 1/3	w/c 7/3	w/c 14/3	w/c 21/3		Apr	May	Jun
abc	400	400	400	400	400	400	400	400		1600	1600	1600
def	1000	1000	1000	1000	1000	1000	1000	1000		4000	4000	4000
ghi	nil	nil	nil	600	600	600	600	600		600	600	600
klm	300	300	nil	nil	nil	nil	300	300		1200	1200	1200
nop	5000	5000	5000	5000	5000	5000	5000	5000		20 000	20 000	20 000

Delivery schedule

Last delivery date considered ....

Notes to supplier:

1. The tentative months shown on this schedule are for information only.
2. The Firm commitment for the second month may be varied when next month's schedule is issued.
3. The last date considered shown above may/not be the last dispatch you have made, in which any later deliveries are to be deducted from this schedule.
4. In the event that for any reason you are unable to make a delivery your contact (shown below) is to be immediately informed.
5. All deliveries are to be made in non-returnable packing.
6. Schedules are issued on the 25th of each month.

Your contact is Mr J Smith, Ext. 304.

Figure 4.1 Delivery schedule

quality may result after adequate notice in cancellation of the order. In the event of such failure the company may at its discretion apply for liquidated damages.

3–9. These clauses stand and do not require modification.

10. Quantity variation

The enquiry and the order are based on the premise that the annual volumes will be broadly speaking what will be required, and we have no reason to believe that this is not so. However volume requirements do change as the draft schedule shows. So the clause that must be inserted here is, 'The monthly generated schedules are the Instrument of the Order.'

11. Flexible deliveries.

This does not need amplification.

12. Price variation

In your negotiations you will have agreed a period of price stability, say two years from placing the order. So an extra 'front of order' condition needs to be added here. 'Price to remain stable until January 1st 1996 as agreed with Mr P Grey'.

No other 'front of order' conditions need to be added as all the other clauses seem to cover the situation without extra amplification, so now all that has to be done is to list all the bolts, their prices, the extra conditions and to add, 'This order will remain active for the life of the requirements embodied within it provided all Terms and Conditions are obeyed and the supplier remains competitive.'

So apart from cancelling the old orders for these parts if any are not being run out, just pass the order to the boss for approval, and then dispatch it to the supplier.

The writers have several times made the point that prioritization is vital in the daily life of the buyer seeking to be world-class and with the experience gained in setting out to achieve lowest ultimate cost in standard parts and in laundry costs, two quite unglamorous commodities, it's time to decide where other areas can be found to reduce cost.

Probably your chief buyer, and your purchasing manager call for a savings report each month in which you list the commodity, the previous price paid, the current price paid, both then annualized, and the difference between them presented as a saving. In the two cases tackled so far, savings were made which extended far beyond just the unit cost differentials achieved. But these savings can be forgotten unless you the buyer stress the whole effect of your work.

Savings opportunities

The way to get the biggest savings is of course by tackling the biggest turnover commodity groups. These can be identified by supplier, or by commodity or sub-commodity, for example stationery could be the commodity title, but it could all be being bought from one supplier, or you might decide to select photocopying paper as a sub-commodity or you might decide to tackle the whole subject of stationery aiming at not only unit costs but factory savings too.

Let us imagine that your list of commodities look like this:

(a)	paint, oil and grease	£70 000 p.a.
(b)	cutting tools	£100 000
(c)	stationery	£40 000
(d)	electrical requirements	£60 000
(e)	window cleaning	£15 000

Which will only represent a small proportion of the consumable buyer's range of purchases but they total £285 000 p.a. and are currently all bought off requisitions, from people in areas all over the factory, who don't know what other requisitioners are using.

You must ask yourself, 'Could I save 10% of current costs if I set these buys up as projects and analysed each one to obtain the best company benefit by whatever buying and supply method was most appropriate?'

The world-class buyer would answer an emphatic, 'yes' and probably more than 10% too!

There is a saying that you often see on calendars which is very true when applied to buyers of all ranks, 'Footprints in the sands of time were not made by sitting down,' and the buyers who spend more time at their desk than is strictly necessary are not making the right prints!

In fact two projects almost prioritized themselves. There was the brush with the sales director's secretary who told you that stationery is ordered by the secretaries from their own pet stockists, and the shopfloor superintendent who told you that **he** decides what oil supplier he will use, despite the fact that the production engineer told you the oil in question was 'bog standard' and could be obtained from many different suppliers.

Centralizing the stationery buy

Where a commodity is requisitioned by users who are calling off materials like the secretaries specifying pencils, paper, post-it notes, files, binders, paper clips and the rest from different stockists or various shopfloor personnel requisitioning a lubricant under different brand names the ability to make savings is very high. Savings of over 20% or more are often obtainable.

The process of finding out who is entitled to raise requisitions and what commodities they call off is where your research starts. One way to start is to list all the items in a commodity and then ask all the requisitioners to tick off on the list the ones they personally requisition. Using stationery as an example your list could be:

paper clips	erasers
A4 copying paper	typing ribbons
spring back files	computer disks
rulers	pencils
correcting fluid	in-trays
envelopes	calendars
manilla folders	wastebins
Pritt	notebooks
filing cabinet separators	

The list may well be longer than this but however long the list you also need to ask how many the requisitioners call off, and which stockist they use. Accounts can tell you how much was spent over the last 12 months and also you can inspect the invoices to verify the materials that have been called off to cross check the results of your questionnaire (see Figure 4.2, over).

The stationery questionnaire shows that each of the requisitioners sticks to a stockist different to the others. The buying card will show last prices paid, and these prices can be listed on the questionnaire and the amount spent by the requisitioners over the last year computed. Then an enquiry should be sent to each of the stockists enquiring for the total quantities, not forgetting to apply for a Dun & Bradstreet report on each stockist.

	Miss A.	Qty.	Miss B.	Qty.	Mrs M.	Qty.	Mr X.	Qty.	Mrs W.	Qty.	Totals
Paper clips	1	70	2	30	3	45	6	48	4	74	267
A4 paper	1	60	2	25	3	19	6	91	4	48	243
Biros	1	50	2	91	3	16	6	48	4	36	241
S/B files	1	48	2	24	3	60		96	4	72	300
Rulers	1	6	2	18	3	12	6	36	4	48	120
Corr. fluid	1	6	2	24	3	12	6	18	4	36	96
Envelopes	1	120	2	60	3	120	6	400	4	240	940
Manilla folders	1	96	2	200	3	68	6	72	4	84	520
Pritt	1	60	2	30	3	12	6	9	4	12	123
F/C seps.	1	24	2	36	3	48	6	12	4	50	170
Erasers	1	12	2	24	3	12	6	11	4	16	75
Typing ribbons	1	24	2	48	3	36	6	48	4	36	192
Comp. discs	1	20	2	30	3	15	6	23	4	21	109
Pencils	1	36	2	96	3	36	6	28	4	24	220
In-trays	1	4	2	8	3	7	6	11	4	3	33
Calendars	1	6	2	8	3	2	6	13	4	5	34
W/bins	1	0	2	3	3	4	6	4	4	1	12
Note-books	1	3	2	5	3	7	6	11	4	6	32

Paper clips: boxes of 100; paper: quires.

Code 1. Alpha Stationers; 2. Orange Stationers; 3. Victor Stationers; 6. Bravo Stationers; 4. Easy Stationers.

Figure 4.2 Stationery questionnaire

The quotations will be very keen since each stockist will be quoting for approximately five times the volume they have previously supplied. By comparing the prices paid last year with the best of the quotes received you will almost certainly be reducing the purchasing price of the materials by a sum in excess of the 10% figure.

Assuming that Victor Stationers have presented the best prices you won't have any trouble convincing Mrs M. but the other four will need to be persuaded to accept that they can no longer use their pet stockist.

The advantages you can offer is first of all the saving, then you have a choice of other benefits you can show. Naturally you will negotiate a fixed price for a year. Normally on 'spot orders' the price moves up at six monthly intervals, so this stability will help them with their budgets. You can also give them a less labour-intensive way of obtaining their requirements by taking the burden of seeing stockists, and raising requisitions off their backs.

Stationery supply options

Now you have selected one source only you can arrange one of the following routines:

1. They can phone you with their requirements, you raise one requisition, phone the requirement to the stockist who delivers next day, you associate the invoice with the requisition and pass it to accounts who pay against the blanket order you have raised. It saves the requisitioners' time (as well as you) and you've taken on the responsibility of chasing their requirements.
2. If you can allocate a lockable store room you can establish a model stock, from which the requisitioners who have a key can draw their requirements. Then every Friday the stockist comes to the store room and replaces the material which has been drawn thus restoring the model stock, and presents an invoice for the material used in the past week. This is also supported by the blanket order.
3. You can also allow your requisitioners to phone the stockist direct to call off requirements **provided** the items requested are already on the blanket order, in which case they must each be given a copy of the blanket order. If items are required which were not on the blanket order when it was first raised they can be added to the blanket order via a purchasing order amendment. When after 12 months you go out on enquiry to do a market test, you have a centralized list which contains all the items likely to be ordered, which eliminates the previous need for extensive research.

The routines employed to produce savings, and eliminate unnecessary paperwork, and even more importantly still reducing the efforts of the **amateur buyers** can be carried out on oils, greases, paints, cutting tools, electrical requirements, etc.

The window cleaning 'buy' will serve as an example for a range of services the consumables buyer has to organize which include gardening, office cleaning, canteen services, waste disposal, etc.

Very often the requirement for such a service will come to purchasing via the personnel department (poshly known as human resources) who are instructed by top management to 'just lay on a window cleaning service as quickly as you can!'

Of course personnel come to the consumables buyer in a terrible flap asking for help. Possibly the job is a new one because the employee who used to do the job has been made redundant, and personnel forgot to allocate his work to someone else – or perhaps there wasn't anyone to take the job over. Anyhow you've got to start from scratch. The one question you **must** ask is: whose budget will the charge be allocated to?

Define task.	
Clean all windows, inside and out, on the Company's site at 24–36 Binns Road, Everytown	
Where to be carried out	Office block (single-storey) 48 windows Manufacturing Block (two-storey) 60 windows Store 11 (two-storey) 16 windows Store 12 (single-storey) 24 windows
When to be carried out	Office block: once weekly All other blocks every other week
How to be carried out	Wash leather/squee-gee with clean water, polished with a clean duster (or approved alternative)
Time to be carried out	During working hours, Mon–Fri (Schedule of planned days and times on site to be submitted by Contractor)
Equipment required	To be supplied by Contractor
Satisfaction criteria	1. Schedule maintained, except in the event of inclement weather, when revised schedule must be agreed with Company Representative 2. Windows to be completely clean including corners 3. No dirty stains on windows, sills, blinds, carpets, curtains, etc.
COMPANY REPRESENTATIVE TO ENSURE SATISFACTION. Mr J. Smith. Security Manager	
The Contractor must show insurance indemnity with regard to damage, injury to Company Property and Employees to a value of £2m.	

Figure 4.3 Checklist to develop a specification

Writing a specification

Then before you can go out on enquiry you must write a specification. It's not only engineers who write specifications. Buyers very often do. Figure 4.3 is a checklist which will help formulate the questions you must obtain answers to in order to write the specification which will form the basis of the enquiry.

The specification can then be issued to appropriate potential suppliers, and the best source selected. The security manager, because he and his staff are permanently patrolling the site and all visitors have to report to security on arrival on the site, is best equipped to ensure that the window cleaners are keeping to their programme.

In many cases, when specifying a service, purchasing are not the best people to ensure that the agreed routines are carried out. It is usually better that the service is overseen against agreed criteria by people who are closer to the job. Nevertheless however well the spec. is written there will be hiccups!

The writer on one occasion negotiated a cleaning contract where the receptionist was given the part of the specification relating to reception and asked to ensure that the spec. was followed by the contract cleaner.

One part of the spec. said, 'The radiators are to be dusted off daily.' After a few days the receptionist came back to the writer saying, 'The cleaner is not dusting the radiators properly!'

A check with the cleaner's supervisor showed that the radiators were being dusted off religiously every day – so what was the problem?

'Ah,' said the receptionist, 'when I dust my radiators at home I dust the back and underneath, not just the top and the front!'

The cleaner said it would take an extra five minutes a day to do the radiators, and since times were tight it would require extra payment! In the end the writer found himself having to rewrite the spec. as follows, 'The radiators will be dusted front and top, daily, and once weekly back and underneath must be dusted,' which the cleaner agreed to do without extra charge. It was far from the easiest negotiation the writer has ever undertaken, because the writer had a budget to protect, and the matter of how to dust a radiator had become an affair of professional honour between the cleaner and the receptionist. The learning point for the writer was to involve the company rep. in writing the specification!

MEMORY JOGGERS

17 **Product rationalization**
- Get your ducks in a row before firing
- Who will resist your efforts?
- What reasons for change will you give them?
- Can you obtain high level support for your actions?
- Start with something that looks readily achievable
- Make sure you find credible sources of supply.

REMEMBER – product rationalization is an excellent way to lower costs but it needs an organized approach as you select the commodity groups for action.

18 **Supplier quality assurance**
- Make sure your quality standards are appropriate
- Check the supplier's level of approval, e.g. BS 5750.
- Send them a QA questionnaire.
- Make a visit with QC personnel.
- You want defect free deliveries.
- Get samples of workmanship – take up references.

REMEMBER – SQA is a total approach involving you and the Supplier. Standards cannot ever be compromised. If they are take immediate action.

19 **Speeds and feeds**
- Take into account cycle times
- Check the level of bar stock wastage.
- What type and specification of raw material is being used?
- Use your eyes when observing the process.
- Keep a record of your observations.

REMEMBER – You don't need a PhD in space age engineering to check key events at a supplier – good observation should be developed.

20 **The blanket order**
- It isn't used for ordering blankets for a hospital!
- It can be used for the life of the item/model.
- The schedule is the instrument of the Purchase Order.
- It provides a single record for all items purchased from a supplier.
- Additions can be made simply.
- It is an administrative mechanism which reduces work.

REMEMBER – these blanket orders can be introduced and maintained very easily and they will reduce workload, letting the time be used for other things.

21 Front of purchase order conditions

- They are no substitute for the main terms and conditions.
- They supplement the main terms and conditions.
- Define the detail precisely!
- If in doubt seek a senior manager's advice.
- Make sure they accurately reflect what has been agreed.

REMEMBER – the complete package of purchase order terms and conditions of contract are a critical feature of the deal – make sure you get them right!

22 Savings

- They can always be found!
- The buyer must take the initiative.
- The lowest ultimate cost is a moving target.
- Know your costs through the supply chain.
- Tell someone when you have a success.

REMEMBER – a continuous programme of savings must be a key performance indicator for every buyer!

5 PAYING A FAIR PRICE

This chapter looks at some of the problems associated with paying a fair price and establishing what is a fair profit. It exposes some of the dirty tricks used against buyers and gives suggestions as to how to counter these tricksters. There is also a clear explanation of the important laws with which buyers should be familiar.

We have shown how lowest ultimate cost savings can be made principally by eliminating inefficiencies, and concentrating purchases in order to maximize buying power and how the systems and organizational techniques can be applied in order to support these activities.

But despite the fact that the processes employed have (probably) earned you some praise from your chief buyer, and perhaps the odd grunted, 'Well done!' from the purchasing manager you're still a long way from reaching the status of the world-class buyer.

The policy guides

Policy states a set of principles concerning the envelope in which a buyer buys.

1. The buyer should pay a fair price for the commodities, items, services etc. that are required.
2. The buyer should be ethical, and not take unfair advantage of a weak supplier (sometimes called 'screwing').
3. The buyer should comply with both the law and the spirit of the law.
4. The buyer should declare any personal interest which could cause the buyer to make decisions which might not be in the best company interest.
5. The buyer's integrity, both inside and outside the workplace, must be unimpeachable.
6. Attempt to foster good community relations wherever possible.

These are company policies which have been laid down to guide you.

The Code of Ethics published by the Chartered Institute of Purchasing and Supply originally in 1976 is published in Appendix D and is a guide which is invaluable to the buyer in pursuit of world class.

However policy does present some problems.

Paying a fair price

What is a fair price?

Buyers have been asking themselves that question since the year dot. One definition we have already referred to is the saying, 'A seller won't sell the product for a lower price than they are willing to sell it for.' But is the lowest price fair?

A fair profit

Every penny spent by the buyer eventually ends up as a component of the selling price of the buyer's product. The buyer's company needs to make an adequate profit in order to stay in business, and if this profit margin is say 10%, is it fair that some suppliers make more than 10% on their sales to the company?

In many cases the buyer's company make a product for a competitive market where the risk they take is that they will be unable to sell all their output, in which case the profit per unit has to be sufficiently high to offset this risk. The supplier on the other hand is protected against loss of sales, because of schedules and orders which give a far greater security of business. This argues that the unit profit should be less than the buyer's.

In the case where the buyer is able by analysis to establish the supplier's manufacturing costs, a fair price could perhaps be established by suggesting that their risk is only 50% of the buyer's risk, then the profit the buyer pays on top of the supplier's manufacturing cost is only half what the buyer is hoping to make.

The world-class buyer will have developed a range of skills to enable assessment of the manufacturing cost of the supplier's product as a basis for negotiation purposes, and also to determine whether the supplier's manufacturing costs themselves are justified. Provision is made for this aspect of the buyer's work in the terms and conditions (Chapter 1) which states:

12. Price variation

Price cannot be varied except by submission to Purchasing (one month prior to the date the new price is required to be effective) a properly constructed justification which Purchasing reserve the right to vary, dispute or reject depending on circumstances.

But unless the buyer is equipped to examine and critique from strength of knowledge this clause is not worth the paper it was written on!

Sadly many buyers will say to themselves, 'Oh well, national inflation is 3% the supplier has only asked for 2½% so I'll approve the price increase!' This of course is a world-class blunder!

A basic estimate

The cost structure of any manufactured item consists of only five components:

material (raw or semi-finished)
labour
overhead
profit
transport.

It can be modified by:

economic effects;
changes in efficiencies;
changes in volumes;
scarcity or surplus;
pricing 'rings';
patented items;
'life of product curves';
marketing policies.

There are relatively few categories of raw materials, if any, that cannot be placed in one of the following categories:

metals
plastics
chemicals
natural fibres
foodstuffs.

Of course each one of these headings can be sub-divided into many hundreds of more specific categories for example metals can be broken down into:

ferrous
non-ferrous
noble
precious.

Then again into steel, aluminium, platinum, gold etc.

There are many references in journals, newspapers etc. which will tell you the market price of these materials and it is part of the practice of the world-class buyer to keep a graph of the price movement of the materials which form the special interests of the buyer.

Labour costs vary from town to town and country to country and industry to industry; again the buyers should know the average hourly rate of the workers in their special areas of interest. This is best recorded as an hourly rate. This is not so easy to establish but judicious questioning of suppliers, reading the newspapers etc. will soon allow a graph to be built up in a similar way to the raw materials graph. Labour is determined by the speed and efficiency of the machines/processes that staffing is required for. This is why in Chapter 4 you were advised to start a 'speeds and feeds' record. For example you might learn that in Taiwan operators were only earning £2.00 per hour, and in Italy operators making the same product were earning £5.00 per hour. If they were operating the same type of machine at the same level of efficiency, then provided raw material prices were equivalent you'd be right to expect a lower price from Taiwan, but if the Italian machine was three times faster then the alternative would seem likely.

This leaves the question of overhead.

Every supplier operates their overhead account differently. There are as many ways of costing as there are accountants; for example, one company may include inspection as an overhead, another may include the inspectors into direct cost of production, etc. It is however in exceptional cases only that you need to get into this level of detail, because your main interest is in the result of externally applied overhead movements which again you can follow via the press and record. The basic headings are:

> rent
> rates
> heating
> lighting
> gas
> water
> NHI contributions
> telephone
> staff.

In order to use this information the world-class buyer at minimum before placing an order makes it a condition of placing the order that the supplier tells the buyer the material, labour and overhead content of the item under discussion. The seller may say, 'It's 60% material, 20% labour and 20% overhead.' The supplier is concealing profit by this answer because there is a profit content in each of the three factors, but what you have obtained is the supplier's MLO ratios.

These should be recorded on the buying record.

Analysis of a supplier's price increase justification

Let us imagine that 12 months after placing the order the supplier, in line with section 12 of the terms and conditions, submits a justification for the price increase of 6%. The justification may read as follows:

> | Raw material | 5% |
> |---|---|
> | Labour | 3% |
> | Overhead | 4% |

The increases we have incurred over the last 12 months are recorded above. However in view of our business relationship we are willing to contain our increase to 6% provided that you can settle our increase swiftly.

You would be surprised to know how many buyers would **add** the three cost components to a total of 12% and think the supplier is being gracious in only asking for 50% of a justifiable increase!

Firstly you would check your data to see if indeed the price of the raw material had moved by 5%. If you agree that is has increased by 5% then since material is only 60% of the price then the justifiable increase is $(60\% \times 5\%) = 3\%$ of selling price, on labour, the supplier has claimed a movement of 3%, $(20\% \times 3\%) = 0.6\%$ similarly on the claim of 4% on overhead $(20\% \times 4\%) = 0.8\%$. Therefore on the supplier's figures they have actually 'justified' a price increase of only $3\% + 0.6\% + 0.8\% = 4.4\%$.

Secondly, it is more than likely that the figures are high against your own records. You may have recorded a general **reduction** of 4% in overhead over the period, in which case the only price increase that could be considered is $(3\% + 0.6\% - 0.8\%)$ $= 2.8\%$.

Thirdly, you should check to see if any changes in your efficiencies or theirs have taken place which could reduce cost. For example they may have quoted for two deliveries per week, and this has been reduced to one. This is (to the supplier) a cost reduction, which should be passed on to you.

If quantities have been increased these should result in lower prices to you, since the supplier should be able to get better volume output and thereby lower unit cost. The supplier may also have bought new machines which increase efficiencies thereby increasing profit margin, which unless you revise your 'feeds and speeds' record you will never learn about.

As a point to remember here you could have **forecast** what the supplier would be likely to claim from the data you have collected, and gone out to the market and obtained competitive quotations prior to the supplier submitting his claim.

In which case you can advise that if they want to move the price at all they will cease to be competitive which leaves you no option but to resource! We will be returning to the subject of forecasting again in a later chapter, but it is another of the tools of the world-class buyer which sits on top of the other techniques the buyer needs to use.

But, you will say, we selected this supplier against competition, we've paralleled the costs but we still don't know what profit is being made and if it is a fair profit. This requires another piece of information. This is the supplier's annual report which you should collect from all your suppliers annually. If for some reason you cannot obtain one from the supplier you can always obtain one for a small fee from Companies House.

Also by the type of price discussion you can have with a supplier given the appropriate data you can certainly contain his ambitions towards making an increasing profit.

However, armed with the supplier's annual report you should look at the figure, 'Profit before tax' and compare it to his figure of 'Total sales', express the profit as a percentage of sales and the resulting figure will give you a fair indication of the profit he is making on what he is selling to you.

With reasonably thorough research which can be done either at the buyer's desk or visiting suppliers it has been shown that it is possible often to arrive at a 'fair price'.

Short supply

Buying demands different skills when items are in short supply. The rules of the market will argue that price goes up in conditions of shortage, just as it comes down in periods of surplus. The world-class buyer will be able to foresee by appropriate reading that a material will be moving into a period of shortage. Also Newton with his Laws of Motion has something to say in the matter, 'What goes up must come down!'

An example that one of the writers was involved in came to light with a world shortage of molybdenum which is used in the order of 2% molybdenum to a tonne of steel to improve its freecutting properties. The reason was that copper which was heavily used in electric and electronic applications was suddenly being replaced by printed circuits and micro-chips. So copper mines all over the world were closed – but there was a snag!

Molybdenum is found with copper deposits, and mined together, and so molybdenum became very difficult to obtain. At the beginning of the period a tonne of steel cost say £300 per tonne and molybdenum cost £200 per tonne, so that the addition of 2% molybdenum put the price of steel with the molybdenum addition up to £304 per tonne which was a tiny price to pay, in order to increase the speed of cutting steel and prolonging the life of cutting tools. In no time at all the price of molybdenum was topping £5000 per tonne making the price of a tonne of steel with 2% molybdenum £400 per tonne which was prohibitive. Since the writer had realized that this was liable to happen, his company had taken the following steps:

1. The laboratory were looking for other alternative steels that could be obtained using different additives which had the same or nearly the same free-cutting properties.
2. The machine shops were experimenting with steels that were not free-cutting in order to see if tool wear and tear could be reduced by running the machines more slowly.
3. Purchasing were ordering sample batches of steel with 1% and ½% molybdenum additives to see if these could help the machine shops problem.

As producers saw the price that molybdenum was fetching they re-opened mines; and with the increased volume on the market prices started to come down. In our own case we found another additive instead of molybdenum. If we hadn't we would have been in considerable difficulties before the price of molybdenum came down again.

During a period of scarcity suppliers are liable to renege on contracts to supply at low prices when the cost of the material becomes such that they are having to buy materials dearer than the price of your contract. The world-class buyer watches the forward raw material markets and alerts the company in time to take evasive action.

Clearly if a period of surplus is on the horizon the buyer must keep re-negotiating reduced prices, and suggest that the company takes all the advantage possible to maximize the windfall because just like the shortage – it's only temporary!

The molybdenum shortage was a genuine shortage unlike some of the 'rigging' which various marketing techniques create which are described below.

Why marketing exists

Marketing is a function which is set up to frustrate the buyer's aim of trying to pay a fair price for a product. Their aim is to try to 'differentiate their product' from those of competitors and by virtue of it's 'difference' to charge a grossly inflated price for it.

A case study for people wishing to enter marketing was for many years the following:

Your company have obtained the rights to market a pocket telephone the size of a matchbox. The material cost is £5.00, the labour cost is £2.00 and overhead is £2.00. Total £9.00. Tool costs £50 000. There are 20 000 000 telephone users in the UK. How would you market the product?

The buyer would think along the lines of selling say 1 000 000 in the first year, and amortizing the cost of the tooling over the first million so that each pocket telephone bore a burden of £0.05 + £9.00 + 10% profit + transport and packing + an element for advertising – say generously £11.00 each.

The answer was in fact along these lines:

1. The first 5000 should be sold only to the top people, only discreetly advertised in say *The Times* and *The Director* at £2000 each.
2. The next 10 000 (gold-flashed) sold through *Vogue* and the top women's magazines as 'The One Thing the Woman-About-Town Cannot be Without' – the improved Model A Handbag telephone, at £1750 each.
3. The next ploy would be to trim the same model with a piece of **real** mink fur, and advertise say a further 10 000 in women's magazines as 'the vital accessory for evening wear', at say £1000 each.
4. The same model next launched as the 'Sportsman's Essential' – the rugged pocket phone (actually the same model, but with a decal on the side SPORTSMAN) at £300.
5. Finally, the popular version – 'as used by top people and sportsmen everywhere' at £65.57 each.

You will note that the conditioning of the public mind has made the average customer think that at £65.57 the pocket phone is a real snip!

The test for the world-class buyer is to buy the 200 required for the company's sales staff at £11.00 each.

A very great number of products are sold this way, from motor cars, machine tools, common household medicaments to name but a few. There are ways in many cases of paying a fair price which will be discussed later on, but it takes time, patience and a lot of determination!

Which are all attributes of the world-class buyer.

Patents

Another frustration to paying the right price is where the component nominated by engineering for incorporation in a new product is patented. The writers have even come across cases where the design team discussed an idea with a supplier, and who patented it before the designers had time to patent it themselves! Either way it means that you cannot buy the item in its existing form, and from any other source but the patent holder who can charge any price they like because they have got you over a barrel.

Normally when you find yourself in this position time is against the obvious solution of researching the patent and getting your design team to design round it, although you do get them on this task immediately. Clearly you will aim to pay the right price at which you will arrive, plus a percentage for using their patent, but the wise buyer will insist that all suppliers who come to visit engineering are requested to sign a document which repeats Clause 4 of the terms and conditions in Chapter 1 which states:

> 4. Intellectual property
> All intellectual property provided to the supplier (or potential supplier) in the course of preparation of quotations or in the commissioning of orders remains the property of the company.

'Ring' pricing

The next obstacle to obtaining a fair price is strictly against the law but is much more common than one might think. This for want of a better word is 'ring pricing'. It is also difficult to prove.

The simplest form is when you are launching enquiries for some fairly extensive building work, and you launch your enquiry to a group of reasonably local builders. Enquiring within a radius of your factory makes good sense because if you go outside that area the builders have quite severe transport and storage problems to face which add to the cost of the job.

Suppose that in the area you have made enquiries to five firms, and from their quotes you prepare the quotation analysis (see Figure 5.1).

It's almost too simple isn't it? Bulky is out – too expensive! Ample's price is a bit high, anyhow they couldn't complete on time. So they're out. Dosser's price and Craft's price are close, but only Craft could complete on time, and Easy can't quote. So the only choice is Craft which is just what the 'ring' want you to think.

What happened was that as soon as they received your enquiry they met down at the local and on a 'Buggin's Turn' basis decided that it was Craft's turn to have this business; and so they agreed the prices they would quote, and when Craft got the business he would split the 10% overcharge you were paying among the others.

They then moved along to another enquiry they had received from another local manufacturer to get Ample the business this time.

Proving this fiddle has taken place is of course pretty well impossible, so the wise

Project:	To construct Bay 5 on Store No 11 in line with architect's drawings enclosed. Building work must be completed in order that occupation can be complete not later than 1 August.	
Supplier	*Price*	*Completion date*
Ample	£150 000	November. Too busy to complete earlier
Bulky	£200 000	End July
Craft	£129 000	Mid June
Dosser	£130 000	End August
Easy	No quote	Order book full

Figure 5.1 Quotation analysis

buyer decides to send enquiries to the major national builders, and makes a decision based on their quotes.

This fairly petty fiddle pales into insignificance when compared to major multinationals who set out to price, based on the market share they want to dominate. Their interest is based on an aspect of marketing thinking that if Company A is selling product at £10.00 each to get 40% of the market, then Company B which is happy with 20% of the market can charge £10.50. The fact that in the buyer's view the product is only worth £5.00 maximum anyhow is nothing to do with it.

The buyer will see a similar pattern in quotations when enquiries are issued to these suppliers to the building quotation analysis; but there is a difference. When companies are playing the market share game they also want to improve their market share without letting their competitors know how it's being done – and this is their Achilles heel. By careful questioning you can find out which of the companies is in this position. If to offer your total requirement to one supplier means that you will remove work from their competitors it reduces the competitor's market share and increases theirs at one fell swoop. Now you have a lever to get either reduced list prices or unofficial (or official) rebates which will help you get nearer to the 'fair price' you are seeking. It will not be the absolute lowest ultimate cost but perhaps there are other cost benefits you can go for which might include just-in-time supply, or increased warranty coverage to name but two. Then maybe the next year you can interest another of the companies interested in increasing **their** market share and excite a competitive situation. Eventually you might even get the price down to the £5.00 which was the figure you first thought of!

Unfair tactics

It will be seen that there are a large number of obstacles to the search for the lowest ultimate cost, or even obtaining a 'fair price'. The world-class buyer knowing that these practices exist doesn't employ unfair tactics. There is an old saying that 'they who lie down with dogs get up with fleas'. The buyer who boasts of 'screwing' a supplier is, to stretch the analogy a bit further, sounding a trifle flea-bitten.

Some years ago there was a well-known buyer who used to find out and record what peccadilloes the MDs of his suppliers used to get up to and then threaten to tell the MDs' wives unless the MDs gave him a very special price. Certain suppliers were not above inviting buyers to a sleazy nightclub and threatening the buyer that the supplier would make sure the buyer's wife heard about it, unless the supplier got the order. Which is why Clause 5 exists.

But the buyer who forces a supplier into a position where he or she has to accept a condition that is manifestly unfair makes a dangerous enemy, because there are many ways in which the supplier can 'screw' the buyer; like for example accidentally on purpose failing to make an important delivery!

The law

Section 3 states that the buyer should comply with both the law and the spirit of the law.

The best advice you can be given is to learn all you can. The Chartered Institute of Purchasing and Supply runs seminars from time to time which are excellent updates, and of course the CIPS Diploma course provides an excellent foundation, so here we will just touch on a few that you should be completely familiar with.

1. The Health and Safety at Work Acts which make the company and its servants responsible for safety in the workplace. In certain cases the buyer could be personally liable if acids were brought into the plant unlabelled and an accident occurred due to the contents being anonymous.
2. The Sale of Goods Act which basically states that goods should be fit for the purpose they were sold for.
3. The European Community Laws which states that contracts above certain values must be advertised in the *Official Journal of the European Community*.
4. Product liability law. This now exists throughout the EEC and the USA. Basically this states that manufacturers must accept responsibility for the safe performance of the products they manufacture and supply. The EEC is not so legislation orientated as the USA which rules that, despite safety notices etc., if a machine can be mis-operated then the manufacturer is liable.
5. *Caveat emptor* (buyer beware) a Latin phrase signalling that the onus is on the buyer to ensure that the contract precisely reflects the buyer's wishes.
6. Another aspect of the law which causes apoplexy in most buyers is concerned with at what stage an order is placed. This comes under the heading of Offer and Acceptance. The buyer raises an enquiry accompanied by the buyer's terms and conditions to which the supplier responds with a quote. The buyer then raises an order. Unless the supplier accepts the order formally there is no contract which is why you will note that the example orders in this book have a tear-off slip for the supplier to acknowledge receipt. However, often the supplier responds with his own terms and conditions which are at variance with

the buyer's wishes. Bearing in mind the strictures of *Caveat emptor* the buyer must negotiate. The buyer, however, depending on the market he or she is dealing in is at liberty to assume that silence means consent.

7. It is illegal in the United Kingdom (but not in some countries) to apply penalty clauses. The legal position is that this places the supplier 'in fear' the Latin phrase is '*in terrorem*'. This is not to say that you cannot apply rules of performance that you demand from the supplier for example, 'that failure may result in cancellation of the order'. There is also the promise of applying either liquidated damages or consequential loss clauses if the situation demands.

    Liquidated damages are 'an agreed contractual remedy whereby the buyer deducts fixed percentages from the contract value for each defined period of time that the supplier is late on delivery. Such deductions must be genuine pre-estimates of loss.'

    Consequential loss. This is an amount or amounts of money paid by the seller to the buyer which reflect the actual losses sustained by the buyer in the event of contract default by the seller. An application of consequential loss may be that if a supplier is quality-assured, which means that the buyer does not inspect the item and subsequently the buyer is the subject of an action on the basis of a product liability due to the failure of the uninspected component, then the supplier is responsible to pay all costs and fines in the case.

The foregoing seven laws are all ones that can be used against your company; make sure that you 'flow down' the same strictures on your suppliers!

This leaves only section 6 of the policy, 'to attempt to foster good community relations wherever possible', to be considered. Any company needs to have a good standing in the community and this does not mean going out every night for drinks with the mayor! What it does mean is that you don't run trucks at night through the quiet sleeping streets, or behave unfairly to local workers, and be seen as a firm but fair dealer. In this way the town respects its local industry. It also means that your community which is the supplier population also look on you as a firm but fair customer.

It may not have escaped your notice that throughout this chapter while we have been discussing the ways in which your own attitude can colour the way in which you can achieve the status of world-class the greatest attribute is never to let pressure at the buyer's desk dim your critical faculty!

MEMORY JOGGERS

23 **Before you place the order I**
- Make sure you know the price
- Check material cost
- Check labour cost
- Check overhead amounts
- Establish the profit
- Find out if tooling costs apply

REMEMBER – you should be controlling price, not only now but in the future.

24 **Before you place the order II**
- Know the contractual detail from your customers
- Talk to your commercial department
- If your company is paying damages – so should the supplier
- Establish performance criteria on quality
- Check your rights to cancel

REMEMBER – you must not expose your company to unacceptable contractual risk.

25 **When you get a price increase notification**
- Check what the contract says
- Check cost movements
- Check the original quotation
- Obtain competitive quotations
- Check impact on your business
- If the impact is adverse reject it

REMEMBER – supplier's price increases add to your company's costs and make them more uncompetitive.

26 **Knowing intellectual property rights**
- If you are buying a new item make the supplier sign a confidentiality agreement
- Brief the design team not to divulge secrets
- Check patent rights when they are claimed
- Check if a supplier's patent can be 'got around' without breaking the law
- Ask if you can use their IPRs and what it will cost

REMEMBER – IPRs are either yours, the supplier's or someone else's – check them out!

6 MANAGEMENT BY OBJECTIVES IN OPERATION

This chapter identifies the seven essential characteristics of the 'world-class buyer'. It discusses the importance of management by objectives, the buyer's job description and identifying training needs. The skills and knowledge covered in the book so far are put to the test by analysing two legal, but unfair, contracts and showing how they can be renegotiated. We also look at a situation where the buyer has to decide whether it's more effective to make or buy a product.

If your career plan is to progress to senior management, then you've chosen the job which gives you from your earliest days an insight into management which members of most other disciplines would give their eye-teeth to experience.

Seven characteristics

There are probably only some seven dominant characteristics which equip managers to manage, and these are:

1. the ability to motivate others;
2. the imagination to devise schemes to maximize the use of limited financial resources, and the energy to carry these schemes through;
3. the technical and professional knowledge to control their environment, and to evaluate risk;
4. the courage and nerve to carry plans through against opposition;
5. to understand the mechanisms of business politics and use this understanding to assist in the achievement of worthy objectives;
6. the wisdom to negotiate effectively;
7. the understanding of others, their drives and ambitions; and while being sympathetic to them, not allowing this understanding to influence decisions adversely, which must be taken in the company's interest.

You will see that the same qualities are required from the world-class buyer, which is why so many ex-buyers become MDs of major companies.

Most companies provide buyers with not only the opportunity to exercise these seven characteristics and develop them, but with applied training to help them enlarge their skills and further their careers.

The chief buyer sends for you, and after you've decided that your conscience is reasonably clear, and that the buyer's desk is in good shape, you sit down at his desk alive with curiosity.

In his normal grimly cheerful way he pushes a couple of forms across the desk and asks, 'Do you know what this is?'

'Well, yes,' you reply, 'it's the buyer's job description!' (See Figure 6.1.)

'Right then,' says the chief buyer, 'how well do you think you've done so far on these various sections?'

Now this is an unexpected question for a normal working afternoon, but doing your best you say modestly, 'I think I'm doing quite well on items 3, 4 and part of 5, but of course I'm single-handed on consumables, so I haven't got an assistant, I'm not doing much about some parts of section 6 or 7; and regards 9 I'm studying for my CIPS Diploma.'

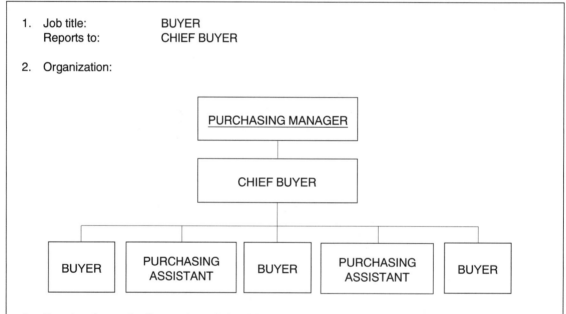

1. Job title: BUYER
   Reports to: CHIEF BUYER

2. Organization:

3. Functional reporting lines, other relationships

Each buyer controls an annual turnover approximately £1m minimum (turnovers vary according to complexity and other factors).

These expenditure responsibilities will cover a range of materials, services and requirements on which the buyer has, or can rapidly develop, speciality market knowledge, both UK and worldwide.

The objective is to acquire these requirements at the lowest ultimate cost, by identification and establishment of the most effective and cost-efficient suppliers available.

Figure 6.1 Buyer's job description

The work comes from various departments in the shape of requisitions, production releases etc. and the responsibilities include:

(a) establishing lowest ultimate cost for new projects at the quotation stage;
(b) acquire materials, goods and services required for current needs at the quotation stage;
(c) non-production materials required by end-users;
(d) capital equipment;
(e) prototype materials required by design engineering, etc.

In addition to the foregoing close contact should be maintained with:

quality control
production engineering
accounting/finance
design engineering
safety department, etc.

So the buyer has to be 'au fait' with their requirements in order to achieve lowest ultimate cost objectives.

Close links are maintained with suppliers at all levels within their organizations to ensure that the company is obtaining the requirements from the supplier at lowest ultimate cost.

4. Responsibility for bringing work into the firm

In addition to the prime objective, which is source selection to provide the company with suppliers who meet the company's needs at the lowest ultimate cost, there is a secondary role.

This is to consider where appropriate value analysis, cost analysis, make v. buy can work towards achieving lowest ultimate cost, either with suppliers or **within the company**.

5. Managerial responsibilities

In certain areas, the buyer will have a small team consisting of an assistant in the form of a junior buyer or a purchasing assistant but apart from this, does not normally have managerial responsibility **within** the company.

Nevertheless, by use of strategic and tactical planning, the buyer manages the efforts of suppliers to meet the prime objective.

Liaison is maintained with internal 'customers' in order to help them manage their own functions by suggesting more cost-effective methods in acquiring, and use of, their material and service requirements.

6. Undertaking work

By various requisitioning procedures as outlined in (3), work of varying complexity and urgency is undertaken. Considerable discretion must be showed in order that work is dealt with in such a manner as to ensure that materials required by the 'customers' are delivered on time.

In order to obtain these at the lowest ultimate cost, a range of initiatives are created which include:

(a) study of potential/actual economic movements;
(b) study of worldwide markets and commodities;
(c) study of potential suppliers and source selection;

Figure 6.1 *continued*

(d)   manipulation of markets in order to create leverage with suppliers giving the company competitive advantage;

(e)   historic data used to forecast likely future demand.

From these processes which go to create market knowledge, enquiries are made in the appropriate market, negotiating price agreements which meet lowest ultimate cost objectives with the most appropriate and efficient suppliers.

In pursuance of these objectives, regular meetings are held with suppliers, sometimes at the buyer's premises, sometimes at the supplier's works in order to further the buyer's projects. In addition, regular meetings must be held internally with production control, manufacturing, sales/marketing, quality control, design engineering, accounting, factory management, as well as meetings within purchasing with the staff and management.

7.   Innovating

It is axiomatic that there are always further cost benefits which are available. Methods include:

- material substitution;
- component rationalization;
- improved supply/inventory methods such as bond stock, consignment stock etc.;
- inventory reduction;
- improved supplier performance;
- supplier concentration;
- importation skills;
- currency control;
- use of competition;
- make v. buy;
- supplier liaison;
- contract writing;
- joint developments;
- supplier manufacturing methods;
- value analysis.

The buyer will always be reviewing the foregoing against the range of commodities for which responsibility is taken in order to uncover new opportunities.

In this regard, the buyer needs to be at a high level of skill and knowledge which is constantly improved on in the fields of:

- commercial law;
- UK/foreign contracting;
- methods of manufacture;
- labour and overhead rates;
- stores/inventory;
- budgeting/planning/finance;
- procedures/systems;
- market knowledge;
- negotiation psychology;
- best course analysis.

Figure 6.1 *continued*

8. Workflow

As has already been alluded to in (6), the buyer must always be able to align the expeditious conversion of requisitions into enquiries and then to completed orders, while creating and sustaining an environment of efficient cost-effective suppliers.

This requires good levels of skill in time management and job prioritization in order that the two separate aspects of the buyer's role are harmonized.

The buyer is often required to work to extremely tight deadlines and thus often works under pressure.

9. Skills

The skills listed in (7) are acquired in the Chartered Institute of Purchasing Diploma, or Higher National (Business Studies), plus the Purchase Specialities or in BA Business Studies, followed (or in parallel) with experience gained in a purchasing working environment.

After training, buyers should be proficient in the first commodity ranges, in 9 to 18 months, then should be rotated on to other commodity ranges, in one year to two year cycles, since the wider the commodity range experience, the more effective they become and the more promotable they become.

Figure 6.1 *continued*

Identifying training needs

'Where do you think you could benefit from further training?'

'In two areas, I think, firstly with the EC being our major trading partner, I'd like to learn at least one mainland European language, and preferably French, and at the same time I'd like to learn much more about negotiation – I'm doing quite well on quote and select purchasing, but I'm finding difficulty in really cracking open some situations that arise, and I think some good negotiation training would really help.'

'That's a good assessment,' he smiles, 'because the next thing I want to talk about is management by objectives,' and with that he produces another form (see Appendix F).

'Now you'll see at the bottom of the page there's a section for Training Needs, and I agree with you that you should be given training on both subjects. This agreement becomes part of my MBOs because I now have the objective of persuading the purchase manager to allocate funds from his budget. Assuming that he agrees, then you have to commit to reach say Intermediate Standard in say 12 months.'

Structuring the MBOs

'That's good, because that's what MBOs are about. We agree a target, and a date by which it will be achieved, and then you set your stall out to get to the agreed point at the agreed time. The job description and the MBO system are tools for me to manage you and you to manage yourself, and if you can manage yourself you can manage others. I've seen your savings reports, and I think you're doing well, but I don't know what your "long range" plans are, i.e. the next 12 months and I suspect you don't either. So part of this exercise is to help us plan your work, which in turn helps me plan my work. Now let's look at the major categories of spend in the consumables buy.'

As a good buyer always does, you are able to list your commodity ranges, the annual turnover on each range and the suppliers which you list as below:

Laundry	£10 600 p.a.	Fixed price 2 years
Standard parts	£200 000 p.a.	Fixed price 1 year
Paint oil and grease	£70 000 p.a.	Under negotiation
Stationery	£40 000 p.a.	Fixed price 1 year
Electrical requirements	£60 000 p.a.	
Window cleaning	£15 000 p.a.	Fixed price 1 year
Cutting tools	£100 000 p.a.	
Stillages and pallets	£40 000 p.a.	
Office furniture	£60 000 p.a.	
Janitorial services	£50 000 p.a.	

Rental contracts:

Cars	£200 000 p.a.
Copying machines	£50 000 p.a.
Fork-lifts	£60 000 p.a.
Portakabins	£40 000 p.a.
Toiletries	£8000 p.a.
Waste disposal	£100 000 p.a.

The range of tasks

'The total annual turnover comes to £1 075 600. Of course there are all sorts of odd requirements that I get from other departments but that is more than 90% of my spend.'

'So,' says the chief buyer, 'apart from those areas where you have negotiated a year or more's stability, all the others could be requesting price increases this financial year. Also I get complaints about the efficiency of some of the suppliers of these commodities, so without being too specific at the moment there are two objectives emerging; the first being to ensure that at absolute minimum any price increases awarded during this financial year are offset by savings in other areas, and second that those suppliers that are unsatisfactory are either shaken up and made to conform to our requirements, or replaced with someone better. Do you agree?'

There was really nothing else to say but, 'Yes.'

Then he continues, 'Let's chart the anniversary dates of the orders to see what time of year these suppliers are likely to want to talk about price increases,' and the chart is drawn up.

Table 6.1 Anniversary dates

	Apr	May	Jun	Jul	Aug	Sep	Oct	Nov	Dec	Jan	Feb	Mar	
Product													
Electrical						X							£60 000
Cutters			X										£100 000
Stillages and pallets							X						£40 000*
Furniture				X									£60 000
Janitorial										X			£50 000
Rentals													
Cars								X					£200 000
Copying machines					X								£63 000*
Fork-lifts										X			£60 000*
Toiletries					X								£8000
Waste disposal							X						£100 000
Total													£741 000

The spends are all last year's figures, but with the exception of furniture, our requirements will be about the same next year.

Notes
1. Asterisked groups are where suppliers are not conforming in all respects to requirement standard (as identified by the chief buyer).
2. Anniversary dates have been derived from previous price increase awards and assumption made that suppliers will re-apply 12 months after last award.
3. If the national inflation figure was awarded to each supplier the company would be paying, say, 3% of £741 000 more, eg £22 230 **for no extra goods or services**.

Objective setting

'Well then,' says the chief buyer, 'there are your objectives.'

'Eliminate the quality and service complaints we get from the stillage and pallet supply, and the complaints that we are paying too much for our copying machine, and fork-lift rental schemes, and contain next year's price increases to zero, or less than zero!'

'I can accept that, with no problem, except for two things. One is how will we be able to agree on the levels of success I've achieved; and the other is if I do achieve a measure of success does my salary increase?'

The chief buyer laughs. 'The answer to the salary question is, "no", but clearly you're more likely to get an increase if you've done a good job. As to the first part that's fairly easy. You report each month those savings you have negotiated, bringing prices down below the price last paid, and those where price has gone above last price paid. So if netted out you have not exceeded the equivalent spend for last year you have achieved the objective; and the more you reduce prices, the better. Now as far as the stillages, copying machines and fork-lifts are concerned, I get at least one memo of complaint a month from either accounts or production about them. When those memos stop coming – that will be your success criterion!'

The chief buyer writes up the MBO form; you sign as accepting the objectives, not forgetting the recommendations to learn French and to go on a negotiation course and then return to the buyer's desk.

Initial plans

Once again there is a 'ducks in a row' problem to sort out. There are two months to go before the start of the financial year, but clearly there are two separate lines of approach as regards the products listed on the anniversary sheet. In a lot of cases there are several suppliers supplying parts of each commodity range and the anniversary date only represents a 'mean date'. In some there is only a single current supplier involved. In some cases the rationalization route would be the one to choose, in which case there is nothing to stop you starting the exercise now, because it would be some time into the financial year before you could come to a decision; but even before that there is the need to familiarize yourself with the items, and your 'customers'.

An investigation commences

But the second group of items could be investigated right away. What is wrong with the stillage and pallet buy, why are production constantly complaining, and what is upsetting accounts about the copying machines, and the fork-lift truck contracts?

For the world-class buyer the phrase, 'There's no time like the present', is a very useful motivator so it's time to call on the accounts department to ask some questions.

The accounts manager's opening comment when you explain why you have to come to see him is, 'Well, it's about time purchasing decided to respond to my complaints. Have you read either of the contracts yourself?'

Having admitted that you haven't he takes out the relevant contracts which have both been written (by the suppliers!) some three years ago and signed by a manager who had left the company some year or more ago, and you sit down to read them (see Figures 6.2 and 6.3).

'Well,' says the accounts manager, 'what do you think?'

It is agreed that Snibbo will place the following machines in the locations noted below. This allocation of resources has been agreed between Miss Kelly, Sales Manager, Snibbo and Mr P Stick Administration Manager of The Company.

2 × Snibbo 2000	Design Engineering
1 × Snibbo 1500	Production Control
2 × Snibbo 2000	Marketing
1 × Snibbo 1500	Accounting
1 × Snibbo 4000	Production
1 × Snibbo 500	No 11 Store
1 × Snibbo 500	No 12 Store
"	No 14 Store
"	No 15 Store
2 × Snibbo 300	Annexe B

Purchase prices (new)
Snibbo 2000 £12 000
Snibbo 1500 £10 000
Snibbo 4000 £15 000
Snibbo 500 £6000
Snibbo 300 £4500

Rental agreement.

This sum includes regular maintainence according to our schedules and is to be paid monthly. For the first year of the contract the rental will be £4366 per month, on each subsequent anniversary, the rental payment per month will rise by 10% thus:

Year 1 £4366 monthly
Year 2 £4802.5 monthly
Year 3 £5282.5 monthly
Year 4 and subsequent years £5282.5 monthly

Only Snibbo brand copying paper can be used which is available from Snibbo direct at £6.00 per quire.

Cancellation clause

In the event that the customer desires to cancel the contract, or any part thereof during the first three years of the contract the full new purchasing price of the machines must be remitted to Snibbo.

Figure 6.2 Contract between Snibbo Reproductions and The Company

It is agreed that the Do-Do Fork-Lift Co. will permit the company to hire electric fork-lift trucks for service in Stores nos 11, 12, 14 and 15 at the premises at Binns Road, Everytown on an annual hire basis.

Machine specification:

Do-Do 24 LX Model 1994
Quantity 4

Servicing: machines will be collected by Do-Do quarterly for overhaul. Routine servicing will be carried out free of charge.

Damage which has occurred while in operation at the company will be charged to the company.

Monthly rental per vehicle £1250 per month per vehicle per annum. In the event of the customer wishing to cancel the rental during a hire year the customer shall be liable for the whole of the rental for that year.

Contract signed by M. Speedy (Sales Director) Do-Do Ltd and P. Stick for The Company.

Figure 6.3   Contract between Do-Do Fork-Lift Co. and The Company

Skeletons in the cupboard

Cautiously you reply that they are two of the most unfair contracts you have ever seen, but what are the specific complaints?

The explanation (with expletives deleted) goes like this:

1. Over a year ago there was a change of routines at Binns Road and now the production machine covers all the photocopying for 11, 12, 14 and 15 stores.
2. Annexe B has been closed.
3. Marketing has lost staff due to redundancies and now need only one machine.
4. The instructions embodied in the contract state that in the event of a machine breaking down a Snibbo mechanic would be on site within two hours; in fact two **days** for a mechanic to arrive is much more the practice.
5. Anyone's photocopying paper is as good as another's and less than a third the price of Snibbo paper. It is only specified by Snibbo for obvious reasons.
6. What is really impossible is that we are paying a monthly rental for machines we don't want and paying for them to be serviced when the ones that we do want to use aren't serviced as quickly as Snibbo has contracted to do.

You agree to get things sorted out as quickly as you can; then you ask what is wrong with the fork-lift contract.

His reply is quite startling. 'Well, as perhaps you know the decision was taken about four years ago that in the Binns Road Plant it was felt more ecologically sound to use electric rather than diesel powered trucks. Since we weren't sure if the electric trucks would be as powerful as our old diesels we "mothballed" them while we carried out extensive operational tests with the electrical ones we'd hired. Well, about six months ago I felt production had had long enough to make an evaluation, so I dropped them a memo to see if I could recommend that we sold the diesels. Imagine my surprise when they said that after the first year, two of the electric fork-lifts had disappeared, and they were now using two diesels alongside the two electric trucks! **But we're still paying for four!'**

'What do you think has happened to them?' you ask. 'I don't know, but then it isn't my job to find out – but it is yours!' As you go back to the buyer's desk you suddenly feel that 'going home time' couldn't come fast enough.

Analysing suppliers' contracts

Both these contracts have been constructed by suppliers, and world-class buyers would under no circumstances put their name to a contract like that without carefully analysing each clause, because – you can be certain of this – some of those clauses would be traps which could prove very expensive!

The world-class buyer always writes contracts with legal support from the company's lawyers.

The position you are now in is difficult because here the contracts have been agreed by an officer of the company, and are technically legal – but the contracts no longer serve the purpose. However, provided the other party is prepared to re-negotiate then it is possible to re-open negotiations at any time.

Before anything else you must firstly check that what the accounts manager has told you about the reduced need for Snibbo photocopying machines, and the very poor servicing support that Snibbo are providing, is true. Secondly you must establish the value for money (or right price) aspects of the contract.

Snibbo had provided the prices 'as new' for the machines (these prices should also be verified), but assuming the prices are what they would have been at the time, the total value of the machines can be computed. It is:

Snibbo 2000 × 4 @ £12 000 = £48 000
Snibbo 4000 × 1 @ £15 000 = £15 000
Snibbo 1500 × 2 @ £10 000 = £20 000
Snibbo 500 × 4 @ £6000 = £24 000
Snibbo 300 × 2 @ £4500 =   £9000
Total value of items rented = £116 000

You have paid in Year 1 £4366   × 12 = £52 392
                  Year 2 £4802.5 × 12 = £57 630
                  Year 3 £5282   × 12 = £63 384

So up to the end of year 3 you have paid £173 406 and you are now coming up to Year 4 with the prospect of paying out £5282.5 per month ad infinitum.

Additionally, assuming the use of 1000 quires of paper used per year you've paid out £9000 more than is necessary because Snibbo has made it a condition of contract that their paper is used. It can be seen just how badly the company has been caught!

Snibbo has clearly suspected that their chances of holding the rental for three years is in doubt, so they have (to protect themselves) put in the clause which says that if a machine is no longer required, and the buyer seeks to cancel, the price of the machine as new must be paid by the buyer.

It can also be reasonably assumed that the prices as new are inflated in Snibbo's marketing strategy so that in addition there is something in the order of at least a 10% mark-up in the prices they have quoted as 'new'. So that the machines have been fully paid for by the company by the end of year 2.

If you also consider that the purchase price 'new' of the machines that are now in use would be not more than:

3 Snibbo 2000 @ £12 000 = £36 000
1 Snibbo 4000 @ £15 000 = £15 000
2 Snibbo 1500 @ £10 000 = £20 000

this equipment cost = £71 000 + a service contract at, say, £10 000 per annum.

There are a range of actions you can take having reviewed the situation.

1. You can cancel the contract and tell Snibbo that your dissatisfaction with their service agreement is such that since two-hour service response was a condition of contract which they have reneged on, they can come and take their machines away.
2. You can argue that since some of the machines were not in use, you want a refund on the service content allocated to their servicing from the time that the machines ceased to be used.
3. You can make a small offer to buy the machines that are still in use provided you can find a servicing company to take on the servicing of them, and you want them fully overhauled at Snibbo's cost before you do this.
4. You can argue for a refund on the rental of the machines that were not in use from the time that they became surplus on the basis that according to your calculations they have **already** been paid for.

Clearly for the service you actually require, with hindsight, the company has paid more than £100 000 more than they needed – much of which has gone to Snibbo as pure profit.

There are several learning points here, apart from trying to save as much as you can from the wreck:

1. Snibbo hasn't done anything wrong. Your company has made four mistakes:
    (a) Apparently no comparison has been done on a rent v. buy study. Clearly buying would have been the cheaper option as against a minimum three year rental agreement.
    (b) There is no reversion to the company at any time of the rented property.
    (c) The purchase at full price for cancellation during the first three-year period should never have been accepted.
    (d) The company should have written a contract themselves and not used Snibbo's form of contract.

2. It is probable that the Snibbo negotiation will become fairly heated, so you would be well advised to brief your chief buyer and perhaps involve him or her in the negotiation. You should also arm yourself with quotes from competition photocopier suppliers, and suitable service contracts because Snibbo might become vindictive and take all their machines away in a 'huff'.

Now there is the affair of the fork-lift trucks. When you consider that the rental was taken out on an annual basis to evaluate diesel v. electrically powered trucks the deal was fairly reasonable. What has gone wrong is that it was two and a half years before the accounts manager asked an innocent question. A review date should have been set certainly after a 12-month evaluation period probably between purchasing, production engineering, and production to recommend the purchase, hire or rental of electrically powered machines, or alternatively revert to diesel power.

There are three tasks here:

(a)   What is the production/production engineering preference?
(b)   To obtain quotations for both types of machine, and prepare a cost benefit and lowest ultimate cost presentation to management recommending a course of action.
(c)   Last, but certainly not least, why is the company paying monthly rentals for four machines when it's only got two?

A case for Sherlock Holmes

Discussions with production engineering and production reveal that the diesels are more powerful than the electric ones for some tasks, and, although they consented to the trial because of management's interest in the environment, in the type of work that they had to do, the diesel was more productive and in any cost benefit study if the price of the machines were the same the diesel was the better machine for the job. In fact, the production manager wasn't at all upset when two electric fork-lifts disappeared after Christmas two years ago. It was assumed that management had decided to take two machines out of the trial and so he'd been happy to take two of the diesels out of mothballs and bring them back into service.

It was quite clear that the production manager had no idea what had happened to the two machines. So the next point of enquiry was security. The security manager was quite emphatic that with his security arrangements nobody would be able to get into the plant and steal two fork-lift trucks. So what has happened?

Back at the buyer's desk you look again at the contract and a clause strikes your eye.

'**Machines will be collected by Do-Do quarterly for overhaul.**'

A phone call to security shows that on Boxing Day two years ago a Do-Do truck was booked in and out.

A quick phone call to Do-Do leaves their service manager with a very red face. 'Yes, they had collected two for quarterly overhaul, and due to an error in their computer they had not been returned to the company; but why hadn't the company asked for their return?'

The answer to this, which it is not the time to tell Do-Do, is that the production manager was glad to get rid of them!

Do-Do very promptly refunds the hire fee for the two trucks, and shortly after your cost benefit study shows that the company preferred to stay with their diesels.

The learning point here is that on evaluation studies involving the use of machines under temporary contract it is purchasing's job to ensure that test programmes are adhered to, in order to avoid unnecessary expense.

The stillage problem

There is another matter to talk to the production manager about. It seems from the memos he's been sending to the chief buyer that he basically needs more stillages in the system but doesn't want to pay for more.

'We've got a permanent material handling problem,' he says, 'it boils down to the fact that we don't have enough stillages to fulfil our requirements. My people have done studies very often which show that we need to have a population of:

    1000 Type A 6 × 4 ft
     800 Type B 4 × 4 ft
    2000 Type C 3 × 4 ft

'Stillage life should be three years, so I have a replacement budget of £40 000 per annum to replace one-third of the population each year.

'Every month my stock section have a round-up, and count up what stillages are in circulation, and the number of stillages which have been damaged during the month, waiting to go back to the supplier for re-welding, etc.

'Typically I'm some 300 to 400 below my minimum requirement.'

'So what do you want me to do about it?' you ask. 'Surely it means that you must "up" your budget and bring more stillages in.'

'It's not as simple as that,' he replies, 'accounts run a stillage account and they say that over the last two years we've actually paid in repairs and new stillages enough to have a population of 4500 against an average stock of 3400 so effectively according to them I'm 1100 light and I don't feel disposed to increase my budget allocation until I find out where those have gone.'

'I still don't see what purchasing can do except to check prices and deliveries to crosscheck accounts figures.'

'Well, there is something purchasing could do, I think; it's to do with the way you handle the supply of material to sub-contractors, platers, heat treatment, and rejects. Purchase raise orders to cover these jobs, production control instruct us to pack the material into stillages and send the material out. Often we send out three stillages and only get one or two back and nobody contacts the supplier for the return of the others.'

A make v. buy opportunity

'We could certainly help you there,' you say, 'we could arrange to invoice the goods out with the number of stillages in which the material is contained, and charge out the stillages at say £40.00 or whatever the price per stillage is. If we don't get the same number of stillages back within a month we bill the supplier, and either we get the stillages back, or the money!'

The production manager frowns. 'Well, it would take some extra administration in following up the suppliers, but it would be worth it to get accounts off my back.'

'There is something else,' you offer, 'at present you save your damaged stillages until the end of each month before you send them out for repair, and presumably they come back the following month when the supplier collects the next load of damaged pallets.'

'That's right.'

'Well, I could do a mini make v. buy study on the repair process. Are your welders fully occupied on production?'

'No, they are about 60% employed, on average. Their job goes in cycles, sometimes they are very busy, other times they are waiting for work.'

'Then if damaged pallets could be re-welded as soon as they are damaged you could increase the working population of stillages, get better labour utilization from the welders and save the costs of getting the repairs done at the supplier.'

'That would be a real help,' says the production manager.

You leave his office well pleased. You've achieved three of your MBO targets, you've got closer to the lowest ultimate cost on stillage repair which would give you another saving to claim, and you've made a satisfactory impression on the accounts manager and the production manager.

The learning point in this last example is that purchasing is the bridge between factory costs and the supplier, and the world-class buyer is always on the look out for make v. buy opportunities in the search for the lowest ultimate cost.

MEMORY JOGGERS

27 **You need a grasp of detail**
- Know your spend per commodity
- Know your spend per supplier
- Know your total spend
- Know if the contracts are being performed
- Know the markets
- Know your suppliers, commercially and technically

REMEMBER – you are accountable for your commodity portfolio, have the detail to hand, you never know when you will be asked.

28 **Management of objectives**
- You need achievable objectives
- Discuss them with your boss
- If you think they are not achievable – say so but justify it
- Always set tough targets
- Monitor your progress

REMEMBER – you must provide self-motivation for hitting your objectives, the will to succeed must not be sapped!

29 **Your training requirements**
- Analyse your strengths and weaknesses
- Where can you improve your knowledge?
- Where can you improve your skills?
- What new subjects are developing
- Do I read enough?

REMEMBER – you need continual training and development, never stop learning.

30 **Suppliers' contracts**
- Find out how many there are in your spend area
- Read them carefully
- Identify the contractual risk
- Establish the expiry date and period of notice
- Check the supplier's performance
- If they are not performing you may cancel

REMEMBER – suppliers generally don't write contracts to help you so – **WRITE YOUR OWN!**

31 When a product is for test

- Ensure you have an agreement whereby it can be returned.
- When does the test end?
- What represents acceptable trials?
- What are you liable to pay?
- Who insures the product on your premises?

REMEMBER – you must control this situation otherwise you will find that the product remains even if it is really unsuitable!

32 Alternative approaches to buying

- Do a make v. buy study
- Do a buy v. make study
- Do a hire v. buy study
- Do a lease v. buy study
- Do a rent v. buy study
- Make sure you establish all the relevant costs

REMEMBER – there are valid alternatives to outright purchase, these must be considered but your costs must be very accurate.

7 FROM CONSUMABLES TO CAPITAL BUYING

This chapter takes the reader on from buying consumables to the more complex task of buying capital goods. Some new skills are introduced such as analysing technical requirements, overcoming internal politics, using the capital appropriation request, preparing a negotiation agenda, using neutral specifications to ensure a level playing field and 'backing out' options.

With the three contract problems cleared away, and enquiries being launched on commodity groups in order to obtain competitive quotations before the contract anniversary dates, it really seems as though the buyer's desk is under control – until the day that Alice Green-Browne, the capital buyer, leaves the company.

The day she leaves, the chief buyer sends for you to ask, 'What do you know about buying capital equipment?' His reply when you say 'Not a lot!' was 'Well, you will soon learn. We are moving you to the Capital buying desk from tomorrow.' He then told you young Howard Ellis would be taking over your job and that you would have to help him take over, and then left you to contemplate your new responsibility.

You know that capital goods have two definitions:

1. that unlike consumables, or production parts which are paid for out of revenue, capital goods are paid for out of capital funds, and as such the cost of borrowing, and tax benefits etc. become involved;
2. that capital items are bought for long-term needs such as buildings, machine tools, and plant.

Looking through Alice's desk you find that she has been a meticulous recorder on a range of issues and discussions, that you have not been doing. She has a thick A4 notebook in which she has kept details of meetings she attended, and from these notes she has issued her own minutes. She has also kept notes on the people she met, their likes and dislikes, where they lived, how they negotiated etc. These seem good ideas so you decide to adopt them yourself.

Some invaluable advice

In fact, Alice has left you some absolutely invaluable advice for the future world-class buyer.

1. Keep notes of all meetings, dated, and details of those attending.
2. Issue minutes yourself; they could become important if there are any future disputes with the supplier.
3. It is advisable to keep thumbnail sketches of the people you meet. Most sales-people do it so that when they visit you, having quickly checked their notes they can say, 'Last time we met you were considering going to Italy on holiday. How did it go?' It gives you a feeling of rapport with them, and it's useful that you too can use the same tactic.

An impending battle

It is common knowledge that the purchasing manager interests himself in capital purchases and so it is no real surprise when he sends for you to talk to you about your new job. What is a surprise is what he tells you.

'We have a battle to fight, and you need to understand the elements of our task. Our managing director is a good boss in many ways, but he's absolutely putty in the hands of the plant and production engineers. They decide sometimes, on heaven alone knows what basis, to make a presentation showing how much more profitable a new machine or a new building would be than the current situation. He then instructs them to go out on enquiry, get quotations, and then to raise an appropriation (capital approval) request for his approval.

'When the AR is signed they get to work with the supplier they have chosen to develop the project. They then lose time until it's almost impossible to bring the feature in at the date they promised the managing director, then they drop the problem into purchasing's lap to raise a contract and to bring the feature in on time.

'The managing director seems to believe that if there are contractual problems it's purchasing's fault as it also is if the project runs late! What they really do is to develop a supplier in secrecy, often after they have been persuaded that this is the only supplier possible. Their selection criteria are very much open to suspicion.

'The managing director insists that the chief engineer shows him three quotations; often the two comparative quotations are in fact "no quotes" from suppliers who don't even make a comparable product! They use the "no quotes" as a justification for their choice to demonstrate how difficult it is to obtain this high-tech facility.

'The engineers, to show what influential decision-makers they are, always tell the suppliers that they've got the job and that seeing purchasing to establish the contract is just a paperwork formality. They will often give the supplier a letter of commitment, prior to telling the supplier to "just pop along to purchasing and get the contract business over with."

'They have therefore left purchasing with no negotiation space at all. So what we are left with is the possibility of negotiating a retention sum, and perhaps some form of liquidated damages.'

The right way to buy a capital item

What should happen before raising an AR is the following:

1. Some form of discussion, perhaps a board meeting, or a recommendation from some other area of the organization who has identified a need for change. It could be for a new building, or a new machine, or the replacement of an old piece of equipment.

2. Let's assume that production have produced a report to the board saying that a process machine is breaking down too often, necessitating expensive repairs, causing losses of production because of extended 'down-time', and necessitating operator overtime to be paid, in order to catch up with production quotas. These costs are adding to the unit cost of the items produced across the machine.

3. At this stage, planning and production engineers, together with purchasing, should come together to write a 'neutral specification', which is not modelled on one potential supplier's product so closely that no other supplier would quote for the same job.

   The neutral specification should define the task, stipulate the necessary production requirements, with reference to manual or automatic loading and unloading facilities etc. The actions should be the same as if you had decided to buy a camera to replace the one you have had for the last ten years. Clearly you want to take pictures with it, but do you want automatic focus facilities, colour filters automatically selected, or do you want to be able to make your own selection? How about automatic flash facilities? Do you want the ability to cancel the flash facility in certain circumstances? If you'd seen a Brand X camera, and said to yourself, 'That's the one I want', you have denied yourself the opportunity to look at competitive prices and alternative specifications produced by the competitors to Brand X. So the neutral specification is vital.

4. Purchasing then launch the enquiry to the suppliers who build and supply similar machines to the theoretical machine described in the neutral specification.

5. When the quotations are returned the same team that wrote the neutral specification make a features study from the specifications offered by the suppliers.

6. From this exercise a range of prices emerge.

7. A quotation analysis is prepared taking into account the features offered. It is probable that none of the quotations precisely meets the neutral specification. Returning to the camera example you may have had in your specification two flash attachments that nobody has included in their quote.

8. A provisional cost benefit analysis can be prepared which would include, say,

a 10% allowance for the cost of, as yet, unidentified features that may emerge as required during the processes after the order has been placed. The cost benefit analysis should aim to pay-back over a finite period, say one or two years. It should also include an analysis of the cost of doing nothing.

9. At this stage a presentation in the form of a capital appropriation request should be made. The purpose apart from getting approval to spend a certain sum over a period leading to the introduction of the new machine is to allow the company to prioritize their borrowing requirements. For example, although the machine we're wanting to replace is causing some problems, it does not seem to be a first priority if for example the factory needs a new roof immediately.

10. Given that AR approval is granted, the engineering and purchasing group should start discussions with the best two or three contenders on both commercial and technical aspects, and over a process of some weeks to arrive at the supplier who is the most satisfactory; with it being made clear that no matter how technically satisfactory a supplier is, he or she does not get the order unless he is commercially satisfactory.

11. Commercial satisfaction must provide for staged payments, suitable retention sums, liquidated damages and/or consequential loss provisions, plus supplier support until a technical satisfaction note is signed off by the company.

12. Once the order is placed the buyer holds regular meetings with the supplier and the appropriate engineers to check on stages reached to approve payment at stage payment intervals, and if extra costs arise due to necessary change to ensure that they are necessary and justified.

The purchasing manager says, 'This procedure is used in many companies and I intend to introduce it here!'

A most expensive blunder

'Just to give you one example as to why it's so important,' the purchasing manager continues. 'Last year the engineering manager decided to accept a supplier's contract for a transfer machine costing £1 250 000. The job was then passed to purchasing to try to force the supplier to come in on time when it was discovered that the supplier was going to run late! There was only a 10% retention fee in the contract so we hadn't got a prayer. Anyhow the upshot of the affair was that the machine came in late by six months, and there appears to be no chance that it will ever work. The supplier has accepted the loss of the 10% and just walked away from the problem. The supplier claims that the fault in the machine is due to the fact that our engineering had asked for modifications which have caused the machine not to work. That, of course, is nonsense because they shouldn't have agreed to implement the change if there was a risk of that happening. Believe it or not the chief engineer had the brass neck to say that purchasing should have used its "commercial power" to pull "the fat out of the fire", but I'm afraid I see we have no alternative but to swallow the loss. Still that's what you get when unskilled commercial people deal with suppliers. Mind you, I suspect that there may be some dishonest practices going on, otherwise why should they be so secretive?

'What I've done to help us try to get the process I've described into operation is to arrange with accounting that I see a copy of each AR as it is presented to the board as a means of reviewing just what the engineers are playing at! Now let's look at this AR I've just received to see what they're up to this time!'

It is quite apparent from what the purchasing manager has said that the managing director is too easy with the engineering people and is not using the purchasing function to fulfil its proper role. It is also clear that the purchasing manager is not prepared to let matters rest there. It is necessary to prove purchasing's professional value, and at the same time to win a political battle. Together you study the AR (see Figure 7.1).

Proposal

The current Friction Welding System in No 3 Shop welds 21 4NS valve heads to EN18 stems at the rate of 2000 per hour. The proposal is to replace the current system with one capable of producing at the rate of 4000 per hour.

Justification

The current system is nine years old. The process time is slow by today's standards. Over the last six months there have been three major breakdowns, each of which has caused the loss of a week's production. This has had to be recovered by massive overtime. Additionally, due to the increasing age of the machine, resetting is necessary on a daily basis, instead of the planned routine of once weekly.

Production status

Current schedules require output of 16 000 valves per 8 hour shift. These requirements only merit day-shift production. Marketing forecasts predict a requirement for 20 000 per day in 1997.

Current standard cost

Excluding cost of raw material the standard cost is £1.00. Over the last six months the off-standard performance has resulted in the actual cost remaining at £1.05. The aggregated cost penalty over the last six months is:

.05 (penalty) × 16 000 (daily output) × 5 (shifts per week) × 20 (no. of weeks) = £80 000

Plan

The proposed supplier, Noccini, Milan via the agent, T. Boiler Ltd, has produced a Specification proposal as follows: their friction welding system PMX 7 can be adapted to our requirements and post-modification be capable of an output of 4000 welding operations per hour.

Figure 7.1 Capital appropriation request

The estimated cost of the new machine (including estimated % applied for development costs) = £850 000.

Benefits

The new system is numerically controlled, with automatic loading and unloading facilities reducing current operator manning from 5 to 3.

Savings

1. Eliminate £80 000 per half year = £160 000 per annum.

2. Redeploy 2 operators = £24 000 per annum.

3. Cycle time reduced by 50% (assuring 1997 production target)
    = 0.5 × £16 000 ×5 ×52 = £2 080 000 per annum.

Total annual saving = £2 264 000

Cash release requirements

(a)	Immediate release of	£300 000
(b)	+ 4 months	£300 000
(c)	+ 4 months	£200 000
(d)	On issue of Engineer's Acceptance Certificate	£50 000
	Total	£850 000

Payback = 0.375 years

Notes

1. No competitive source has been found.
2. The supplier is very busy, but is prepared to reserve a 'window' for our project, provided the order is raised in the next three weeks. This will ensure delivery at the required time.
3. The machine offers extra accuracy factor by weighing each valve and stem prior to friction welding process commencing. This will necessitate valve heads and stems being made to tighter tolerance than hereto and an Engineering Change will be instituted in due course.

Signed   ....
A. Payne, Chief Engineer

Signed   ....
B. Gasket, Engineer i/c Project

Approved   ....
B. Spot, Managing Director

Figure 7.1 *continued*

The appropriation request critiqued

'Is it true' you ask, 'that the friction welder is breaking down that often?' 'Yes,' the purchasing manager answers, 'but you'll note they only run it on the day shift, so in fact they've got the whole of the nightshift to fall back on, so it's not so serious, or immediate a problem as the AR makes out. Incidentally, in many companies they run process machines exclusively on the night shift because most overheads are only costed to the day shift, but that's a point for another day. Let's not debate whether we need the machine now or later, but rather look at what is missing from the AR.

1. 'They have not considered buying the valve welding out. Despite the fact that engineering claim payback inside one year, if we could find an acceptable unit cost by buying out we could leave the money in the bank to earn interest or invest it. I'll get one of the production buyers on a make v. buy study straight away.
2. 'They have not gone out for competition, so here's a job for you, go and see Ben Gasket who is the project engineer, and see if in fact they did get any other quotations beside Noccini – if not we'll put out enquiries including Brown and Light who made the present machine.
3. 'We need to analyse Noccini's quote, and plan the strategy we'll use if we decide to stay with them. Also we must decide in that case whether the order is placed with the agent, Noccini or even both.
4. 'Do you see how they're proposing to pay the supplier? Engineering are planning to make the same blunder they did last year. In fact the minimum I'd accept would be, say, 15% with order (and ideally nothing), 20% when all design is completed, 40% when all material has been acquired and 25% retention money. I cannot understand why engineering can't learn by their own mistakes!'

The following morning you are in Ben Gasket's office and you explain that you are the new capital buyer. As the atmosphere thaws you are shown the quotation from Noccini's agent. The enquiry has actually been sent to them and in turn they have forwarded it to Milan. Looking at the quotation it is easy to see that the quotation and the preliminary specification have been written in Italian and returned to the UK agent, who has had it translated into English and then sent it to the company addressed to the chief engineer.

What does the new machine do?

'Before you ask,' says Ben, 'I haven't got any competitive quotes; when the chief engineer went to the last machine tool exhibition he saw the Noccini system and liked it. You know he's been to Italy twice to see Noccini.'

'Is it a unique system then?' you ask.

'It's got some interesting features, but no, it's not unique, Brown and Light made the one we've got now, then there's Smith and Jones, and of course Dartmoor Ltd all produce basically similar types of machine. Although I would imagine they approach the main function in different ways.'

'Then it's a fairly standard type of machine?'

'It's quite an old technology really, you see,' says Ben. 'The basic process is to fuse, or friction weld a valve together. A valve looks like a mushroom, so if you imagine having to weld the stalk of a mushroom to its head you've got the general idea. This has to be done on a fast repetition cycle. This means that the two pieces have got to be presented to each other very precisely, held together at a certain pressure for exactly the right amount of time to allow the welding process to be completed. This requires some sophisticated material handling processes. The heads and stems, which are brought out have to be loaded into a system which "fingers" the two work pieces, like human hands holding the two pieces between finger and thumb, for the requisite heating cycle, then putting the finished valve into a special rack for movement to the machine line. As you can imagine that since we want to weld ten at a time this needs a complicated conveyer system to feed the welders. This can be done, either on a sort of linear conveyer belt, or on a rotary table system. The rotary system requires more transmission mechanics, and of course in either case there is a considerable need for computer control. The advantage of the rotary system is that it takes up less space and we're desperately short of that in No. 3 shop. I should add that tucked in at the end of the cycle is a non-destructive test unit (NDT) which checks the integrity of each weld before the valves go for machining. The NDT is a vital part of the process, because these valves must be 100% OK before they go to machining!'

Before you leave Ben's office you take a copy of the Noccini information and then go back to the buyer's desk to study it in detail (see Figure 7.2).

A 'neutral specification'

Between the detail on the CAR, the Noccini quote, and the explanation that Ben Gasket has given, it is clear that the salient features of the machine are quite simple to synthesize into a 'neutral spec.'.

In Chapter 4 we discussed the checklist for developing a specification:

1. Define the task

To weld at a rate of 4000 per hour valve stems to heads. To provide a rotary system with mechanical, electronic systems including NDT in process. (Include engineering drawings of valves.)

2. When to be carried out

System to be installed and working by Jan/Feb 1996.

3. How to be carried out

The potential supplier should submit proposals, specifications etc., together with prices, within three weeks of receipt of this enquiry.

NOCCINI S.P.A.

224–230 Via S. Loren
MILANO
ITALIA

Gentlemen,

In response to your kind enquiry addressed to our UK Agent dated 30/3/1995 we offer the following:

Design and development of a rotary friction-welding system based on our standard machine the PMX 7.

10 welding stations on a rotary table.

Selection/pressure, heat application/duration controlled by NC.

Post-weld NDT in-cycle testing with automatic rejection facility.

Cycle time 4000 per hour.

Three operator station   –   input control
welding
off-loading

Please refer to specifications and drawings attached to this quotation for electrical, electronic, and mechanical data of PMX 7.

Because some of the features requested by your Mr A. Payne are not in our standard range, the prices below are indicative only, and the detailed price can only be fully established after further detailed discussions have taken place which our UK Agent, Mr T. Boiler, is well qualified to undertake on our behalf.

Delivery 9–10 months from receipt of order

Price:– £850 000 sterling

Payment terms:

The quotation price is fixed for 90 days. However, in the event of Italian inflation rising above our forecast beyond this date, prices may be adjusted upwards accordingly. This increase may be applied at any time.

Figure 7.2   The Noccini quotation

£300 000 with order
£150 000 on submission of finished drawings
£150 000 on acquisition of computer, motors and robotics
£200 000 on inspection of our finished machine at our works in Milan

We offer a sum of £50 000 for your retention until you provide us with your Certificate of Satisfaction.

Price does not include delivery.

Figure 7.2 *continued*

4. Time to be carried out

Potential supplier should provide major time milestones toward the completion of the system proposed.

5. Equipment required

Potential supplier should have full design and manufacturing facility.

6. Satisfaction criteria

Competitive pricing of system, and unit cost production. Full engineering support provided during introduction cycle. All stages when established to be strictly maintained by supplier. Full professional and technical support during the development process.

A further discussion with Ben Gasket to flesh out further 'neutral spec.' data and the enquiry can be launched.

Rather than go through this process, a common fault among some engineering and purchasing functions is simply to send out a copy of the equivalent of the Noccini quote and specification. This has the effect of putting other competitors at a disadvantage immediately since they would solve the problem in a different way and cannot/will not quote for someone else's system. In this way the buyer loses the ability to attract alternative quotes with potentially more attractive solutions.

The purchasing manager reports back to **you** the day after you've put out the enquiries to the machine tool suppliers!

'I'd like you to have a look at this list of points I'm going to put to T. Boiler the UK Agent of Noccini, who is coming up to see me this afternoon and I'd appreciate your comments. Also I'd like you to stand by because I'll want you with me at the meeting this afternoon.'

It is in the form of a typed agenda.

'I usually produce an agenda when I've got a supplier meeting,' the purchasing manager explains. 'It allows me to keep control of the meeting and, to form the basis of any minutes I want to produce after the meeting. In fact it's a useful tip for any negotiator to use.' (See Figure 7.3.)

Subject: Matters arising from the quotation from Noccini S.P.A. Milan via Mr T. Boiler.

1.   Mr T. Boiler to explain relationship with Noccini.
2.   How is the price of £850 000 broken down? What is estimated labour hours, design hours, etc.
3.   What are the differences between the Standard PMX 7 and subject quote?
4.   What is the price of a Standard PMX 7?
5.   How does Mr Boiler propose to liaise between Noccini and the Company?
6.   How will engineering support be provided during the installation process?
7.   Staged payments and retention fee not satisfactory. The Company considers staged payments are requested too soon, and at sums too high to be acceptable and will not be considered as quoted.
8.   Retention sum should be a minimum of 25% of final price.
9.   Price on order will be fixed, and no change to final price quoted will be allowed except where changes requested by the Company are introduced. These are to be costed and not introduced until a Purchase Order amendment is issued.
10. Noccini are to be informed that the Company has not made any commitment to the purchase of the Noccini system.

Figure 7.3   Agenda

A preliminary skirmish

There is nothing extra that you can add to the agenda and when T. Boiler comes into the purchasing manager's office you feel prepared to learn.

T. Boiler explains that he is a commission agent and that he is the agent for several Italian companies and that as a qualified production and planning engineer he is well qualified to represent Noccini to the extent that he's done a three months' training course with Noccini recently and that he visits Noccini's Milan works practically every month.

He is vague about the hours involved in the breakdown of costs for the £850 000 but he agrees to telex the question to Noccini for an urgent response.

He produces some photographs of the PMX 7. It is a four-station welder, manually fed, manually loaded and the NDT testing is not integral with the machine. The price is £50 000. This prompts the question from the purchasing manager as to how many integrated systems similar to the system under discussion they've actually supplied to other customers. His reply is that the prototype has been on display at various machine-tool exhibitions and they are currently handling six enquiries but as yet none has been sold.

With regard to engineering support he says that engineering support will be provided by Italian engineers who will reside in the UK for the necessary time.

However the company will be required to pay hotels and subsistence allowances during their visit.

The purchasing manager is getting a little short with T. Boiler, and he says a trifle tartly, 'You're a bit optimistic expecting 35% of the order price with order aren't you?'

Boiler smiles. 'Those payments are negotiable of course.'

'That's good,' says the purchasing manager, 'we'll discuss that subject again when I know more about your price breakdown. Now I suppose you realize that if you get the order we will give you a fixed price with no escalation allowances, with the exception of any engineering changes which are mutually agreed on necessity and cost. Also we view engineering support as part of the Contract so certainly we would not pay their costs whilst in the UK. Also of course once a date has been agreed we will require a Liquidated Damages Clause which will reduce the value of the Contract by 2 ½% for each week or part of a week that you are late on delivery to a maximum of 20%.'

'I don't think Noccini will go along with all that,' says Boiler, 'particularly since your chief engineer has visited Milan twice recently and has given them the idea the order is pretty well, "in the bag" but I'll pass all the questions you've asked back to them and I'll come and see you again as soon as I've got the answers.'

After Boiler has left the office the purchasing manager says, 'I was given a quote for getting the welding done outside. Incidentally the sub-contractor uses a Brown and Light 1700 which is quite similar to our present set-up. Their quote is 0.98p each which is actually **cheaper** than our current price at standard cost. So we could on a make v. buy basis recommend that we source out the valve welding. We'd save against standard cost $.02 \times 16\,000$ (daily output) $\times 5$ (days per week) $\times 52$ (weeks per year) $= £83\,200$ p.a., but of course for an outlay of £850 000 we could enjoy after pay-back a unit saving of $0.50p \times 16\,000 \times 5 \times 52 = £2\,080\,000$ p.a. So the right solution is to make-in.'

'What did you think of Boiler's attitude?' you ask.

'Obviously he wasn't expecting the reception he got, because he certainly wasn't as prepared as he should have been and I think probably the chief engineer has given them the idea that the business is almost theirs. What really worries me is that they're only at the prototype stage. I'm hoping one of the alternative sources is already in production with something closer than the PMX 7 is to what we want.'

As you go back to the office he says, 'I'm sending a copy of the minutes to the chief engineer, the accounting manager, and Ben Gasket and of course a copy to you as well.'

It is later that afternoon when Ben Gasket phones you. 'I've just received the minutes of your meeting with Noccini's representative. Your boss gave him quite a going over, didn't he? Personally I think it was a good effort. Indeed, I think we always ought to do a lot more research before we select a supplier, but what my boss is going to say when he reads his copy, I dread to think. Still, more power to your elbow, and if I can help in this assessment, provided it doesn't bring me into head-on conflict with him, you can count on me.'

It is a comfort to know that you have at least one ally, and it is with a slightly more comfortable feeling that you hang up.

The Noccini people are obviously very much on the ball because the following afternoon T. Boiler is back in the purchasing manager's office with the information shown in Table 7.1.

Table 7.1   A cost breakdown by major feature

Stem hopper	£5000
Head hopper	£5000
Agitator/drive/chute	£7000
Electronic weigher	£10 000
Accept/reject mechanism	£50 000
Loading to rotary table	£15 000
Temp./time cycle controller	£30 000
10 welding stns + 'fingers'	£140 000
Drop-to-table mechanism	£40 000
Non-destructive test	£48 000
Accept/reject classification mechanism	£40 000
Load to racks	£20 000
Linkages/gears/drives/motors	£200 000
Miscellaneous electronics	£90 000
Turntable	£150 000

Grand total £850 000

Bought-out-items	£453 000
Raw materials	£57 000
Design	£70 000
Labour	£100 000
Overhead	£170 000

'I've also discussed with my principals the 25% retention price you suggested, the provision of engineering support post-launch and they are prepared to agree in both cases. Presumably now you are prepared to give me the order.'

'No, I'm not,' says the purchasing manager, 'I want to remind you that this is a competitive enquiry, and as I said yesterday, I want a considerable improvement in your staged costs. You're asking far too much up front, and I also want you to accept liquidated damages of 2 ½% for every week or part of a week that you are late to the established installation date. Oh, and one more thing, the price we agree will be fixed except for mutually agreed changes.'

'You don't want much,' says T. Boiler ironically.

'No,' says the purchasing manager, 'all I'm looking for is a good machine for a fair price.'

'I'll be back to you by this time next week, with our final offer,' says Boiler as he leaves the office. During the next few days quotations are received from Brown and Light, Smith and Jones, and Dartmoor.

The quotation analysis shows that there are some different approaches being considered.

In order to create a 'level' playing field it is decided to break down the quotes in line with the fifteen features that Noccini has identified in order to construct a feature analysis (see Figure 7.4).

1. Stem hopper
2. Head hopper
3. Agitator/drive/chute
4. Electronic weigher
5. Accept/reject mechanism
6. Loading to rotary table
7. Temp/time cycle controller
8. 10 welding stns + 'fingers'
9. Drop-to-table mechanism
10. NDT
11. Reject classification mechanism
12. Load to racks
13. Linkages/gears/drives/motors
14. Misc electronics
15. Turntable

Feature	Noccini	B & L	S & J	Dartmoor
1	£5000	£4000	£6000	£3000
2	£5000	£4000	£6000	£3000
3	£7000	£8000	£5000	£6000
4	£10 000	N/A	£10 500	N/A
5	£50 000	N/A	£52 000	N/A
6	£15 000	£12 000	£16 000	£14 000
7	£30 000	£30 000	£29 500	£30 500
8	£140 000	£160 000	£120 000	£165 000
9	£40 000	£37 000	£39 000	£42 000
10	£48 000	£50 000	£44 000	£60 000
11	£40 000	N/A	£41 000	N/A
12	£20 000	£18 000	£22 000	£16 000
13	£200 000	£180 000	£180 000	£195 000
14	£90 000	£80 000	£85 000	£79 000
15	£150 000	£140 000	£138 000	£152 000
Totals	**£850 000**	**£723 000**	**£794 000**	**£765 500**

Figure 7.4　Quotation analysis by major feature

Technical information

The purchasing manager and the design manager have been discussing the chief engineer's idea of controlling the weight of the raw stems and heads. The design engineer finishes the discussion by saying, 'Look, it's asking for trouble, the valves have to be very precise as to weight and dimension before we fit them, that's why we machine them to such refined limits, but we need a machining allowance, so within the current limits the raw material we get is fine. The range between top and bottom tolerance is such that with the same temperature and time, the weld is as good on top tolerance as it is on bottom limits. It will add a lot of unnecessary cost to the raw material to buy it in more closely toleranced, and if we follow that route, I would be concerned about our machining. Anyhow why does the chief engineer want the raw heads and stems weighed before welding?'

'Apparently the supplier has told him that the welding stations are very sensitive to the weight of the raw valves and they won't give a proper weld unless the weights are extremely tightly controlled,' says the purchasing manager.

'If the welding stations are that critical' the design engineer replies, 'the machine will be stopped half the time because it will only accept material within such fine limits it'll reject half the work presented to it. I'm not going to waste my design team's time on stunts like that when we're so busy.'

It is interesting too that of the four quotes two do not envisage weighing before welding, one of which is Brown and Light who supplied the current machine. It will be necessary to invite all suppliers in to discuss the quote and you decide to invite A. Fawkes of Brown and Light in first.

Taking the purchasing manager's advice you prepare an agenda before the meeting. It will be more extensive than the purchasing manager's discussion with Noccini's representative. Aside from payment terms, liquidated damages, engineering support, spares, delivery dates, it is necessary to find out why they have not considered it necessary to weigh before welding.

At the last minute the purchasing manager says that the meeting can take place in his office, and you can lead the discussion.

Uncovering supplier uncertainty

Agenda

1. Staged payments. We propose:
   Staged payments based on agreed milestones, and a retention sum equivalent to 25% of order value subject to the granting of an approval certificate from the company.
2. Engineering support is provided by the supplier until the system is working properly during the installation of the machine.
3. Since once the introduction date is agreed the company will be putting into effect other down-stream changes dependent on your machine's being delivered at your promised delivery date, we propose to apply liquidated damages at the rate of 2 ½% of the order price for each week or part of a week that delivery is late up to a maximum of 20%.
4. We will require a year's warranty on all parts (which are not consumable) and a list of necessary spares which may be required thereafter to be held on consignment stock.

5. This machine is much more powerful than the current machine. Can you show evidence of machines which are carrying out ten station welding at a production rate of 4000 per hour currently in service?

6. There is some suggestion that within the faster production welding cycle the tolerance of the work pieces must be more uniform, and consequently must have a weighing machine ahead of the welding process in order to act as a filter. You have not referred to this possibility in your quotation.

7. Should we decide to select your machine to replace our current machine the order will be placed at the mutually agreed price. No escalation will be permitted except for any mutually agreed changes which may present themselves as necessary during the development of the system.

The meeting with A. Fawkes is very much to the point. He reads the agenda through, then says, '1 and 2 yes, 3 I'll talk to the Board, 7 I'll talk to the Board. As regards 5 and 6, we've got ample examples at our customers where they are welding at the rate of five per minute per station, in the lab we can with very high heat weld considerably faster, so your rate of nearly seven per minute seems perfectly feasible. Our designers are working now on preliminary studies. We do not believe you need to change your work pieces; it's a question of getting enough heat generated fast enough. If we don't think it's practical with ten stations we may suggest you go to twelve stations.'

The purchasing manager interrupts A. Fawkes with a question. 'If you're not sure that ten stations can produce 4000 welds per hour why did you quote for it?'

'We've assumed that your objective is 4000 per hr and the number of welding stations is secondary. Since an individual welding station would cost you about £16 000, then if we decided that you needed more than ten, then you can work out how much above the current quote you'd have to pay. But this would eventually come out during development and we'd have to design with that possibility in mind.'

A lesson for the world-class buyer

After A. Fawkes has left the office the purchasing manager sits back. 'I'm glad you have had this example so soon in your career. Often when engineers raise specifications they will try to set up a development programme aiming for the nearly impossible. So always check the supplier's capability, despite what the engineers tell you!'

By the end of the week the suppliers S & J and Dartmoor have both been to the purchasing manager's office and on the technical side their view is close to A. Fawkes's views:

1. To stand a chance of producing the 4000/hr rate with ten stations only, tight control on the dimensions of the raw stems and heads is vital. This means inserting a weighing machine and an accept/reject process imposed in front of the welders.

2. Without weighing, which design do not consider desirable, more welding

Table 7.2 The level playing field

	Noccini	B & L	S & J	Dartmoor
Quotations as received	£850 000	£723 000	£794 000	£765 500
Deduct features 4/5/11	£100 000		£103 500	
Total	£750 000	£723 000	£690 500	£765 500
Unit cost of extra head	£14 000	£16 000	£12 000	£16 500
Commercial				
Payment with order	*10%	15%	12%	20%
Payment on design completion	*30%	25%	25%	30%
Payment on material receipt	*35%	30%	40%	45%
Rentention %	*25%	30%	23%	5%
Engineers' support	*Free	Free	Free	Free
Liquidated damages	*No	Yes	Yes	No
Design	Against	For	Against	For

If S & J are willing to work to multiple heads solution recommended; if not B & L recommended. *Final quote.

stations will probably have to be introduced and this feature could be designed in with the extra costs of the extra stations having to be paid for.

This requires a further meeting with Ben Gasket the project engineer. It is now possible to cost the alternatives of controlling the weights of the raw material (which the design manager is against) as opposed to perhaps going for more welding stations.

Creating a level playing field

The table that purchasing and Ben Gasket produce will serve as part of the evaluation that the chief engineer is going to have to see, and will form the battleground the purchasing manager will use to prove his point (see Table 7.2).

'It's interesting to see how the choice of suppliers changes as you go for backing out the options,' says Gasket. 'How is your boss going to persuade the chief engineer to drop Noccini?'

'I think I'd better leave it to him,' you say, 'but just look at how much purchasing have saved. We've proved that the option costing over £100 000 is replaceable by increasing the number of heads, possibly two at between £20 000 and £30 000, we've got much better retention terms, liquidated damages, and free engineering support and we've saved the cost of an engineering change to the stems and heads. Plus the problem the design engineer foresaw with the machining.'

What goes on between the chief engineer and the purchasing manager the world-class buyer can guess at but from then on no CARs are raised without purchasing carrying out the actions detailed in this chapter. The final choice is S & J who agree to develop the system on the 'extra-heads' basis, and the next chapter details the construction of the contract.

MEMORY JOGGERS

33 **Minutes of meetings**
- Keep your own notes of the meeting
- Use them to summarize main points at the end
- Make notes of the personalities you meet
- Issue the minutes to the other party

REMEMBER – records of meetings may be required many months after the original discussions and by then your memory has faded; notes are essential.

34 **Contractual basics**
- Develop your own contractual terms and conditions
- Aim for a retention amount – say 20%
- Develop your logic for damages, liquidated or unliquidated
- Make stage payments (if you must) against milestones

REMEMBER – It is the buyer's job to ensure that the contractual detail has been agreed with the seller and that the risk is minimized.

35 **Buying capital equipment**
- Always start from a neutral specification
- Never issue one supplier's specification to another supplier
- Ensure buying is involved at a very early stage
- Involve all interested parties

REMEMBER – capital equipment buying involves large sums of money and the buyer must create as much competition as possible.

36 **Pricing considerations**
- Get the price broken down to at least sub-assembly level
- Price the spares separately
- Get the costs of product support
- Identify 'one-off' costs, such as design

REMEMBER – the price will be a large amount and it is therefore essential that the buyer understands all the constituent elements of the proposed price from the seller.

8 WRITING AN IMPORTANT CONTRACT

This chapter builds on the position reached in the previous chapter to show the detailed commercial, legal and technical requirements necessary to draft a full contract.

Another opportunity presents itself

You are beginning to think that all the hard work with S&J is complete, particularly after all the negotiation effort and influencing of internal people. It has certainly dawned on you that buying capital equipment is not an activity for an amateur. The sums of money are usually large and they are a 'one-off', the supplier seems to have the upper hand and isn't life a fag. It would be easy, you reflect, to become pessimistic about ever completing a major project on time and within cost. And there you are on the crest of a slump as a cynic once explained the feeling. The ringing of the telephone jolts you back into the real world. It is the purchasing manager asking for a meeting, right now! It is with some feeling of trepidation that you enter his office and ask him what you can help him with. This is always a good line with the boss, it has the suggestion that you are keen (and that's how world-class buyers make progress!).

'Have you ever written a contract from scratch?' Be truthful at all times; that is the motto. 'No,' you reply. 'Well now's your chance. We need an effective contract with S&J that protects our interests. Have a go and bring me the draft of the contract. Use whatever references you want and see me if you start to struggle.' You seem to remember saying, without total enthusiasm, 'thanks.'

As you sit down at the desk again the enormity of the task begins to sink in. How should you tackle this latest assignment and show that you are developing your thoughts like a professional buyer? By now you have learned to prepare a mental plan of your intentions, think it through before taking any other action. That way you avoid hasty irrational actions. While it takes more time initially, it certainly saves time later in the process. With a little smugness you reflect on how you are a philosopher nowadays.

Working out a plan

To help you to formulate your ideas you get out a clean sheet of paper.

Action	*Purpose*
1. Get some reference material.	Familiarize yourself with key aspects of a contract.
2. Prepare main contract clause headings.	To deal with key aspects of risk.
3. Draft the main clauses.	Practise writing the detail.
4. See legal department.	Take specialist advice.
5. Review the final draft.	Ensure that there are no gaps in the document.
6. See the purchasing manager.	Present your final draft contract and 'sell it'. Also convince the PM that you have made a credible effort at what is a major task for you.

This seems pretty good to you and now is the time to put it into action.

Getting the reference material

You first look around the office but there is no library as such. This is one aspect of the buying department that you recognize as a weakness. There are copies of trade directories, such as *Sells*, *Kelly's*, *Yellow Pages*; a few dated textbooks such as Lee & Dobler, Baily and Farmer and Aljian. There are no books to be found that deal with writing contracts. Deadend. Your face must tell its own story because Hazel Armander, another of your colleagues asks you if you have considered attending any contract courses. Luckily she has and, since then, has purchased some books of her own (and that is dedication). 'Borrow them if you want, but make sure I get them back. There are some copies of contracts I got from a friend who works for a major engineering company. You may find them helpful!' That is an understatement. They are like gold dust. Not that they make easy bedtime reading, all these phrases – notwithstanding, heretofore, aforementioned. The lawyer's jargon is unbelievable and this sets you thinking that perhaps you could write them more simply and see what your legal department have to say. Your view is confirmed as you read *Drafting Commercial Agreements* by A.G.J. Berg (Butterworths) which advises, 'A contract should be as easy for the lay client to read and understand as is consistent with precision and certainty. Brevity is valuable. In general, legal usages should only be introduced where necessary to avoid uncertainty.' That clinches it so far as you are concerned. The more you read the more you are convinced this task of writing a contract is no straightforward matter. If only you could see the purchasing manager who, right now, is telling one of the directors of the task that you have been given saying, 'If I want to slow one of my buyers down I get them to write a contract.' He then gives a knowing smile and moves on to the next subject. (What you have yet to learn is that with practice it becomes second nature.)

Preparing the main contract clause headings

At this stage you decide to go back to the meeting and discussions with S&J. What issues cropped up? Once again you decide to list them but not in any particular sequence.

1. Payment
2. Fixed price
3. Engineering changes
4. Liquidated damages
5. Retention monies
6. Spares
7. Engineering support
8. Warranty
9. Performance of the machine
10. Development or experimental work

These are major issues which have arisen in the discussions with S&J but when you compare this list with other contracts in Hazel's file you make a note that some things are missing. This produces another list:

1. Cancellation
2. Bank guarantee
3. Passing of title
4. Jurisdiction
5. Arbitration
6. Force majeure
7. Design rights
8. Escrow
9. Sub-contracting
10. Insurance
11. Inspection and tests
12. Supplier's bankruptcy

News of your task travels fast! One of your colleagues walks past the desk and says, 'Good morning your honour!', and another asks do you have directions to the Old Bailey and Wandsworth Prison – just in case anything goes wrong. Sarcasm is the lowest form of wit and so you ignore them all, gritting your teeth, determined not to be diverted from your task. You now have 22 clauses which require something in writing and you keep looking at the blank sheet of paper on your desk. You have the feeling that aspirins and Syndol tablets will come in handy, a headache is coming on. Your thoughts need organizing and so you decide to tackle the first ten clauses, review progress, contemplate the world and decide how you will face the other 12 clauses. The plan hardens in your own mind.

Drafting the main clauses

1. Payment

You decide this is an important matter for the supplier who obviously needs paying for the work that will be undertaken. What did your purchasing manager tell S&J? He said, 'Staged payments would be based on milestones, and a retention sum equivalent to 25% of the contract value, subject to the granting of an approval certificate from the company.' You have since checked the meaning of 'milestones' and are satisfied that they refer to a specific achievement by the supplier where something tangible exists and to which you can expect ownership. Your purchasing manager says staged payments but didn't quantify them. You remember that Noccini stated design was £70 000, less than 10% of the total contract price. They should be able to fund that if they are a reputable supplier who isn't short of cash. You decide that S&J will not have any money with placement of the contract but you reasonably conclude that when they satisfactorily complete design they can have a payment. 5% seems appropriate. What happens then? Well, another key stage will be reached when the supplier has all the materials to make the machine. Another payment could be made here, say 20%, because we don't know the exact amount (but you wish you did). That accounts for 25%. What next? You reason that when the machine is assembled and tested satisfactorily at S&J premises another payment would seem reasonable and you decide a further 25%. That is a total of 50%. It then seems to you that when the machine is installed in your factory and is given an acceptance certificate by your engineer a further payment is due. You decide another 25%. That is a total of 75%. You decide that the balance of 25% will become due six months after acceptance (in other words this is the retention mentioned by your purchasing manager). So there you are: those are the principles of what you want but it now needs writing into a legal clause. You pluck up the courage to write your first clause and wonder what you should do when it is actually written. Champagne? No, can't afford that, but a Woodpecker Cider seems in order. You smile and remember to tell the purchasing manager to keep his hat on when there are woodpeckers about!

Draft clause: 'Terms of payment'

'The Buyer shall pay to the Supplier the following amounts of respective parts of the Contract Price. Payment will be made not later than 60 days after approval of the Supplier's invoice by the Buyer's nominated Engineer.

'5% when design is completed to the complete satisfaction of the Buyer's nominated Engineer;

'20% when all materials have been purchased, delivered and accepted by the Supplier and are allocated to the Contract;

'25% when the machine is built and tested to the satisfaction of the Buyer's nominated Engineer;

'25% when the machine has been installed, tested and accepted at the Buyer's factory to the satisfaction of the Buyer's nominated Engineer;

'25% six months after the signing of a Taking-over Certificate.'

2. Fixed price

Your purchasing manager is adamant that the price will be fixed for the whole of the contract period. You decide that should be easy to write.

Draft clause

'The Contract Price shall be £794 000. This price shall be fixed and unchangeable throughout the Contract period. Should the Buyer formally request engineering changes the Supplier shall immediately inform the Buyer of any effect on the agreed Contract Price change unless previously agreed and notified to the Supplier through the agreed Contract Change Procedure.'

3. Engineering changes

You decide there are some major implications associated with this issue. It seems to you that the supplier S&J should not be allowed to change an agreed design without the authority of your engineer and that even if they do it should not affect the intended performance. It also occurs to you that if your engineer agrees to a change the overall responsibility for the performance of the machine should be left with S&J. The final point that occurs to you is the cost of any proposed changes and who should pay for them. That seems a much trickier situation to resolve and something you should take further guidance on. As you contemplate these issues you keep thinking what your purchasing manager has repeatedly said about engineers changing their mind on a regular basis.

Draft clause

'No Variation or Change shall be made to any feature of the Machine by the Supplier without the express written authority of the Engineer. No such authority shall relieve the Supplier of his duties to ensure performance of the Machine. Should the Supplier believe there are changes in price required he shall immediately advise the Buyer who will decide to accept them or not. Any agreed Price Change shall be confirmed in writing.'

4. Liquidated damages

This legal subject is very new to you and your head is now reeling from the information found in one of the contract law books, by Smith & Keenan and published by Pitman. The first thing you notice is that you can't write a penalty clause in a contract which is to be under English law. Well, you can but it would be illegal. You find this odd because other buyers in the department keep calling them penalties and now you can put them right. The second thing you read is that they should be a 'genuine pre-estimate' of loss, in other words not a guess. That, you decide, rules out the estimators (another of your whimsical jokes!). With all this in mind you have a go at the clause.

Draft clause

'The Buyer shall deduct from the total contract value an amount of 2½% for each week or part of week the Supplier is late to the agreed delivery date up to a maximum of 20%. The Supplier will not be allowed to claim force majeure as a justifiable reason for late delivery.'

(This last sentence suddenly occurs to you because you have just read some conditions of sale which permit the supplier concerned to be late due to strikes, lock-outs, floods, riots, earthquakes and a thousand and one other reasons. This is too one-sided in favour of the supplier and so you intend to pre-empt any move by S&J to have it included in your contract.)

5. Retention monies

You have, of course, already included this in the payment schedule detailed earlier but you now think that it was insufficient to deal fully with the issue. The principle of a retention amount was accepted by S&J and so you must now make sure that all angles are covered. What are these? You ask this and decide another worrying trend has started. You keep talking to yourself! But, that way you have no disagreements and the company is very pleasant. The amount is agreed and so is the length of time. You must now deal with the release of the money when that period ends. And so, you start to write again – writer's cramp is a great danger but your blank sheet of paper is gradually getting completed. This gives you heart and, mentally, you are feeling pretty good about meeting your Legal Department.

Draft clause

'The Buyer shall retain 25% of the Contract Value for a period of six months after the Buyer's Representative signs the Handing Over Certificate. This amount shall become payable to the Supplier when six months has expired and the Supplier has shown that their contractual obligations, during this period, have been fulfilled.'

6. Spares

You are feeling very good about this because you have had a talk to the storekeeper in charge of maintenance and consumables. This has two effects. First of all you have been made very welcome because you have gone where other buyers never reach (a TV advertisement comes to mind). You also find that the storekeeper has a lot of knowledge on the issues. You are shown spare parts bought years ago which have gathered dust ever since then. Some are there and the equipment no longer exists! You have also learned that the lead time varies a great deal and that machines are stopped for weeks waiting for spares. One of your best mates who works for an airline has told you that the price of spares is difficult to control and that there is a huge mark-up (profit), which can be as high as 300–400%. **You are determined to embrace all of this as a life cycle cost issue here**. Any world-class buyer would wish to deal with this matter.

Draft clause

'The Supplier shall supply with the Machine agreed "Essential" Spares on a consignment stock basis. Ownership of the spares shall remain that of the Supplier with Insurance being provided by the Buyer. Payment for any Spares used outside the defects liability period shall become due 30 days after issue of Spares from stock. **The price of such spares shall be held fixed for an initial period of 2 years,** thereafter any price change shall be notified and agreed with the Buyer at least six months prior to its implementation. The Supplier shall not remove any consignment stock from the Buyer's premises without his consent.'

When you finish writing this clause it is 8pm. Time goes quickly when you are having fun. You pull three capital purchase files off the shelf and guess what? **This clause has never been included before!** This you think is a past failing where you can give the company a benefit in future. You certainly intend to make sure that all your efforts are not applied only once. Never again, you decide, will anyone else have to invent the wheel.

7. Engineering support

Your purchasing manager is very keen to emphasize this requirement. 'I've been bitten before. The Supplier's representative hogs your offices, gets the order and then you can't get anyone to respond when there is a problem. I am definitely not having that situation and certainly not when installation is going on.' So there you are: it is a contractual requirement and you have to write the clause. It doesn't seem too complicated **but you must take into account what happens if adequate engineering support is not there when you want it**.

Draft clause

'The Supplier will provide on-site engineering support at the Buyer's premises throughout the delivery, installation, testing and commissioning stages of the contract. The level of such support shall be agreed at least eight weeks prior to delivery. **If, in the view, of the Buyer's nominated Engineering representative, the level of support is inadequate the Supplier shall correct the situation within 48 hours of being notified.**'

8. Warranty

The purchasing manager mentioned one year in the discussion with S&J, but didn't say when the year would start (one of the textbooks mentions this as the 'trigger' date). You have also read that when the warranty expires a service contract will be required and that is another issue to discuss with the purchasing manager but not today! Two other things cross your mind. You have noticed in some of the textbooks that they refer to the 'defects liability period' and this seems a good way to put it. **Another point is how the S&J Warranty is affected by the parts that are supplied by their suppliers and sub-contractors**. It seems to you that you must write a clause which reflects this concern.

Draft clause

'The Defects Liability Period means a period of 12 months calculated from the date the Buyer's representative signs the Handing Over Certificate. Throughout this period the Supplier warrants the workmanship and materials and agrees to replace, with new parts, free of charge within 48 hours from the time and date notified by the Buyer. **There shall be no exclusions to this warranty agreement in regard to any part, parts, assemblies supplied for incorporation in the Supplier's finished product.**'

9. Performance of the machine

The purchasing manager has based many of his calculations and his purchasing strategy on the production rate of 4000 welds per hour and you remember the supplier seeking to qualify what they had said. If the production rate is not achieved the whole basis of the financial evaluation becomes questionable and therefore you set out to make sure the contract reflects this point. Your inexperience of writing contracts is a worry at this stage so you decide to have a go at this clause and tell the legal department that you feel particularly vulnerable with this one. This feeling is compounded by a recent article in a purchasing magazine which said that engineers don't like writing performance specifications.

Draft clause

'The Supplier agrees that they will supply a machine that is capable of achieving a minimum production rate of 4000 welds per hour. Should the machine fail to achieve the performance criteria so defined **the Supplier will pay the Buyer for all costs and cost profits for each weld per hour not achieved**.'

You read this again and again and are quite proud of this last sentence. Basically it means that the supplier pays your company if there is a shortfall in the production rate. That seems reasonable because (a) it is measurable; (b) the costs can be identified; (c) the supplier said they could do it; and (d) you don't have to accept the machine if it fails to achieve the output.

10. Development and experimental work

The negotiations managed by the purchasing manager included a discussion on the aspect of development and experimental work that would have to be done by S&J before they had a final design of the machine which is capable of meeting your performance figures. This work is obviously critical to the success of the project and seems to call for a rather special contract clause. You need to consider the aspects that must be covered. First of all you need a contact in their design and development department. You need access to their works (and you don't have that unless the supplier agrees) and you need access to all their confidential information (and they may not want you to have this). Your engineers should be able to express their views on design data but without removing any responsibility away from the supplier. All of a sudden this contract is getting complicated and yet all your ideas seem valid. The water is getting deeper and deeper. If every capital project needs this level of thought and time to prepare, it adds up to a massive job. Perhaps, you reflect, this is why so many projects go wrong and why there is a strain on relationships. Once again you decide to get this clause right.

Draft clause

'Throughout the design and development phase of the contract S&J shall appoint a Project Engineer who will be the responsible person for this contract. The Buyer shall be given access to S&J's premises at all reasonable times. The Buyer shall be given unlimited access to all confidential design data and drawings which the Buyer undertakes not to divulge to a third party under any circumstances. If the Buyer's Engineering staff make any comment on design data or suggest changes these, if accepted by the Supplier, shall not in any way relieve the Supplier from their contractual obligations.'

At this stage you don't know whether to laugh or cry. This exercise has mentally drained you. Your overwhelming reaction is the shock of the detail you have had to tackle (and the job is far from done). You are quite confident that no similar capital buying task has ever been done in this way. As you reflect on the way in which purchasing was done on consumables and service, you come to the conclusion that things could be considerably improved in that area as well.

You now have to plan the next stage of this task and that is to make an appointment with the legal department to discuss the clauses you have drafted so far. You see this as a great opportunity to learn something from legal specialists and you intend to be quite frank in regard to your very limited knowledge in this area. And so, you pick up the phone which is answered by Suzanne Farrington-Small.

You explain who you are. 'I am employed in the buying department and I have been asked by my purchasing manager to write a contract for the purchase of a new machine. I have drafted ten clauses and need your help' (nice touch this one, it usually gets a positive response) 'before I go any further. I want to make an appointment reasonably soon and wonder if you are free at 10.00 am tomorrow?'

'Just a minute, I'll check my diary. Yes, that looks fine. How long will you need?'

'Well, er, um, let me see, about 1 hour, I think.'

What a shambles, in your haste to make an appointment, you clean forgot to estimate how long the discussion would need. The simple expedient of 10 minutes per clause × 10 would have indicated 100 minutes which would have meant 1 hour 40 minutes. Guess what? The world-class buyer just learned another important lesson. Plan your time in an effective manner because it will create a favourable impression with whoever you are meeting, whether it be your manager, internal colleague or visiting representative. The impression you created with Suzanne can only be imagined – six qualifying phrases in one sentence. That is something of a record. Think of the good news. You can do a better job tomorrow providing you get your act together and know what you want from the meeting. An agenda and some objectives are required and now you must develop these.

The legal department meeting

The agenda and objectives

You develop in mind the things you need to discuss and your objectives. Your purchasing manager has told you to make sure the agenda has some structure and that your objectives are quite clear. You plan the following.

Agenda topic	*Objectives*
1. Introduction	Explain to Suzanne Farrington-Small the background of the project
2. Details of the purchase	Explain the importance of the machine and its technical/commercial nature
3. Why you are writing a draft contract	Explain there is no standard contract for the purchase of capital equipment
4. Draft clause (1)	Ensure payment is at the right time and secured in some way
5. Draft clause (2)	Ensure the price is fixed for the period of the contract
6. Draft clause (3)	Ensure engineering changes are controlled and cost control is achieved
7. Draft clause (4)	Ensure the supplier is accountable for delivery on time and that remedies are available
8. Draft clause (5)	Ensure that retention monies are obtained
9. Draft clause (6)	Ensure that spares provision is properly contracted for and price is controlled
10. Draft clause (7)	Ensure that engineering support is available and is at the right level
11. Draft clause (8)	Ensure that adequate warranty provision is provided in the contract
12. Draft clause (9)	Ensure there is contractual

		provision if the machine performance is not obtained
13.	Draft clause (10)	Ensure that the contract is sufficient to deal with key features of development or experimental work
14.	Summary	To agree the next actions and to acknowledge the help obtained in this meeting

That is a very full agenda and all that remains is to get it typed up and photocopied for Suzanne. That is your planning complete, apart from reading the draft clauses again to make sure you have the detail in your mind. These also need typing up and tabling at tomorrow's meeting.

An encounter with the legal department

You make your way to the legal department and ask where you can find Suzanne. You are directed to an office in a far corner of the room. A number of things strike you immediately. The office is a sea of tranquillity and not the madhouse that is the buying department! There are very few papers on the desks, unlike the desks that you know, which all have a tree from Sweden on them. The phones are not ringing and lifting off their bases. The people you see are calm, unhurried and unstressed. There must be something different about a buying department, perhaps events drive them whereas in the legal department they control events. On the other hand perhaps they are not busy and have no problems. Anyway, you fancy being a lawyer next time around. The door to Suzanne's office is open and in you go to be greeted warmly. So far, so good.

The meeting continues

You present the agenda and Suzanne's response is, 'This is very helpful. Thank you. Perhaps you could give me the introduction and background to the project.' You have rehearsed this so many times that it just seems to flow. She listens very attentively, making occasional notes as you speak. When you have finished, she responds, 'It is very helpful and refreshing to get involved in a project contract at such an early stage. Usually we are told when something has gone wrong and then we haven't got much of a chance to save the situation.' So, there you are. Another lesson for the world-class buyer. You want to be involved early, the legal department want to be involved early. If all key influencers in the total buying process play their part at the right time there is much less risk of something being missed. Suzanne moves events on by suggesting that you explain the clause you have written on payment. You do so and her response is very interesting. It goes along the following lines:

'You have explained that your clauses are not presented in any particular order but before the contract is issued it must have shape and form. It will be necessary to present the clauses in a certain logic and that is a task that will be undertaken by our department. It is also important to recognize that linkage exists between certain clauses. Let us take payment as a case in point. You have identified some crucial issues and we could plan the contractual detail in the form of inter-linked elements, i.e.

contract definitions
plan of work
milestones
payment
title and certificate
retention
final payment.

'It will be necessary to write some contract definitions. For example you have a few references to the buyer's representative. One definition could therefore be
' "The Buyer's Representative means the person defined as such in the Special Conditions of Contract and appointed on behalf of the Company as Engineer for the purpose of the Contract."
'On a similar basis we will need to define technical information and the definition could be "Technical Information means all information supplied in the Specification, together with all drawings, diagrams, calculations, designs, specifications and other pertinent documents as may from time to time be furnished in writing by the Seller to the Engineer in connection with the Contract." '

She then tells you that there will be other definitions required and these can be written by her when you give her more information. The next thing that follows is that you need a plan of work which shows how S&J intend to meet your important delivery date. This can be written as follows:

'The Seller is required to provide a detailed programme for the completion of the Contract using a bar chart or critical path diagram. The proposed programme is to be drafted in such a way as to show the various activities separately, e.g. design, procurement, manufacture, installation, commissioning, etc.'

Suzanne asks you if this is helpful and you tell her that the level of detail is beyond your capability and you welcome her help. You follow this with an apology about the length of time the task will take. With a disarming smile she tells you that you needn't worry because she has a piece of computer software with a 'menu' and can change them to suit your circumstances! You learn another important lesson in life: ask around before you begin a specialized task. If you take a philosophical attitude you realize you have probably learned more by having a go yourself. Your thoughts are interrupted as Suzanne tells you that she will now focus on milestones. Good news, she is happy that you have identified some important milestones in your draft clause and she believes you have put in some necessary safeguards.

'Have you heard about Passing of Title?'
'No.'
'OK, let me explain that you really must ensure that you protect our interests by making sure that at each key stage we have legal ownership of that for which we are making a payment. For example, when the design is complete and we pay 5% we should have the design data and drawings so that if the Supplier "goes bust" we can use the information with another supplier.'

There's something that has never occurred to you! You figure out the same logic must apply to other milestones. In other words you pay for nothing unless you obtain legal ownership. What a fascination.

She moves on to payment and advises you that your draft clause is very good and then asks you if you are paying in Polish Zloty. You are aghast. If you knew her well you would tell her not to be silly, it's pounds sterling, instead you say just that it is pounds sterling.

'Well, it doesn't say that and so we must add it!'

And that is another lesson learned, never assume anything in a contract! Write it down.

Suzanne now takes you back to the issue of passing of title and says that you should include in the contract a demand that you get a formal passing of title certificate signed by the supplier at each milestone payment. Also you should insist that the supplier marks the item that it is the property of your company. This is followed by a comment that your draft clauses on retention and final payment will need some work done on them before they are in an acceptable form.

Unfortunately, at this stage, Suzanne explains that she must attend another meeting and will need to arrange another meeting with you to finalize the other contractual clauses. She tells you that it can be done tomorrow which is very helpful to you. You readily agree and decide to brief the purchasing manager.

'Let me explain one other point before you leave me. Make sure you understand the legal process when you are negotiating a contract.' With that she draws the following chart and you promise to study it very carefully indeed.

Buyer	Seller
Sends purchase enquiry with contractual terms and conditions. ⟶	This represents an invitation to treat. It is not a contract.
This represents an offer to sell. There is no contract. ⟵	Sends a quotation with their conditions of sale.
The buyer sends a purchase order with contractual terms and conditions. ⟶	This is a counter offer and does **not** create a contract.
This is a counter-counter offer and as such does not create a contract unless the buyer accepts it without challenge. It must be challenged. ⟵	Sends an acknowledgement with their conditions of sale.

With that, you bring the meeting to an end and return to your office. It's now time for reflection. This has been quite an experience. It has convinced you that a capital purchase needs some detailed attention to contractual terms and conditions which you need to ensure that the supplier meets their obligations. It is also important to make sure that there is some protection in the contract to cover the situation when the supplier fails to meet their obligations. You have made a good contact with the legal department and the contract should be in final draft from tomorrow. Now it is time to plan to meet the purchasing manager and provide an update.

You brief the purchasing manager

Following the practice you have now adopted you make an agenda for the meeting. It goes as follows:

1. Present the list of 22 clauses.
2. Explain the detail of the first 10 which are in draft form.
3. Explain how you will tackle the other 12.
4. Explain the meeting with the legal department.
5. Detail the next actions.
6. Detail what should happen next with S&J.

Where you ask for the meeting, it is arranged for 2pm that day, and away you go. 'So, how have you got on?' said your boss. The next hour is pure joy for you. Complete mastery of the brief as you go through the agenda with barely an interruption from him. 'What should we learn from this exercise?' you are asked, 'and make it brief.' Your reply is straightforward and logical.

1. We need standard terms and conditions of contract for capital equipment.
2. These may be in need of amendment for each major capital purchase.
3. The terms and conditions must be issued with the purchase enquiry, and that should only be issued after we have a proper specification from the engineers.
4. We must negotiate the detail with the supplier, prior to issuing the contract. In this case we will need another meeting to finalize some of the contractual detail.
5. We probably need to examine all our major purchases and do a contractual risk assessment.
6. We should ask the legal department to run a one or two day course on contracts for all the buyers.

The purchasing manager said 'That is an excellent job so far. Well done! Go and finish the contractual detail with Ms Farrington-Small and bring the finished contract to me. I will then bring in S&J and both of us can explain the contract. I don't see much of a problem because the major points have been raised in the earlier meeting. I will arrange to talk to the engineers and explain all this to them, otherwise they may drop us in the proverbial mire by saying something we will later regret. See you later.'

As you leave the purchasing manager's office he smiles and says to himself, 'That one is coming on fine. One day I'll make a buyer of that character – but the training must continue. I now need another nasty to further the education!

MEMORY JOGGERS

37 **Writing a contract**
- Work out a plan before you start
- Prepare the main contract headings
- Draft the main clauses
- Discuss them with legal/commercial experts

REMEMBER – writing contracts is a very serious matter and the detail cannot be left to chance, therefore the planning is critical.

38 **Reducing contractual risk**
- Don't accept the seller's conditions of sale
- Don't compromise your contractual requirements
- Make the supplier accountable for breaches of contract
- Realize that contractual terms and conditions can cost money if you get it wrong

REMEMBER – the battle of the forms must end with the buyer making sure that the buyer's contractual terms and conditions prevail.

39 **Anticipate the seller's objections**
- The seller will not want consequential loss in the contract
- The seller will want force majeure
- The seller will want the contract jurisdiction in the country where they are domiciled
- The seller will wish to limit the guarantee period

REMEMBER – the seller will seek to minimize contractual risk – for them! You are paid to protect your business and that you must achieve.

40 **Negotiation of terms and conditions of contract**
- Make the seller detail any objections they have to your conditions of contract
- Work out the possible cost and risk to you if you deviate from your requirements
- Make the seller responsible for key aspects such as delivery and quality
- Emphasize how important your contract is and why performance is vital

REMEMBER – the negotiation of terms and conditions of contract is very difficult and you must understand the absolute detail in order to be successful.

9 A NEGOTIATING COURSE

All negotiations can be reduced to one of six classic situations. This chapter looks at each situation in turn by analysing six separate case studies, defining the problems and suggesting solutions.

'You are going on a negotiating course.'

(These were the words with which the purchasing manager acknowledged that you had requested attendance on such a course, the chief buyer had recommended via the MBO system that you should go, and the purchasing manager agreed. The system worked!)

'You are at a stage in your development where you are beginning to have to deal with complicated procurement issues where the sales people you are meeting are well trained in their product knowledge and skilful negotiations.

'Unless you can match them skill for skill you'll always come off second best and I refuse to allow us to be put in that position.

'The course we have put you on is a three-day negotiation skills course at a training centre near Shrewsbury. It's run by Farrington Ltd who are long established consultants and trainers. What I like about them is that there is no academic nonsense about them – they are practical people who expose you to real life examples.

'The attendees are all buyers and come from every area: industrial, commercial, government, pharmaceutical, etc. and it's a priceless opportunity for a buyer from whatever area to learn how others work.

'The course is not a rest cure because you will be exposed to new ideas and concepts and you will quite likely find yourself put into situations which to say the least you will find challenging – and stimulating!

'But that's what proper training is about.

'When you come back I want to see four things from you – after all I'm paying good money to ensure that you have acquired the elements of this most important skill:

'1. a clear mind as to how to improve our success rate in the forthcoming negotiations we've got coming up both on capital and production projects;
'2. I want you to be able to go into a negotiation with your objectives set out and equipped with the skills and methods sufficient to influence others to accept your objectives over theirs.
'3. more effective:
    (a)   cost reduction performance,

    (b)   contract construction,

    (c)   relationships with suppliers – because the Farrington Organization will teach you to be able to think the way suppliers do,

    (d)   internal relationships – particularly with that finance lot!

'In fact, thinking about it I'm going to put myself down for one of their senior courses.

'Good luck and off you go.'

The negotiating course begins

The journey to the hotel is uneventful. Just a few million traffic cones along the motorway; an uneventful meal at the Little Chef; a few circuits of the town before you find the hotel car park and then check in. Your tutor is there to meet you and to stress that the course will begin promptly at 9.00 am. A quick visit to the 'refreshment area' and in you go to the 'Excaliber Suite'. You take in the atmosphere. Panic, terror and apprehension come to mind. There are twelve of you on the course and the others come from retailers, banks, an airline, the Civil Service, two engineering companies, a shipyard and a merchant bank. What a mixture and you wonder what do they call a collection of buyers? A sod? And what would they call a purchase – a lottery? In this situation you think 'a confusion' may adequately summarize what you see in front of you.

The course introductions are a blur. You stumble through your introduction, get a few words in the wrong place, and feel very nervous. There is one who stands out who you think is a Blott by name and nature. His opening goes along the lines, 'I spend most of my department's money. My title is purchasing executive and I know I get the best deal from my suppliers. Many of them have told me how tough I am and have said that no-one else gets the prices that I squeeze out of them.' So there you are! You have the feeling that the tutors have a gleam in their eye as they weigh up the Blott. Mind you, your purchasing manager said that there is always one on every course. 'Make sure it's not you,' was the advice.

'Thank you for the introductions. You are very welcome on this Negotiation Skills course. We will make sure that you have lots of opportunity to join us as well as listening to the tutors explain some key aspects of negotiation. We believe that good negotiation skills, properly used, will obtain major benefits for your organizations. It is therefore necessary that first of all we actually understand what negotiation is. Does anyone have any ideas?' At this time most people take a big interest in their shoes and the desk top. Terror, in case the tutor picks on them. Is that a voice?

'It's getting the best deal for your company.'

'Thank you,' the tutor responds, 'But how do you know what the best deal is?' The emphasis here is on the word best. 'It implies you have some comparison to make with everyone else in the market and know all the costs. I suggest that most buyers are not in that position. Sorry, but I can't accept that. Does anyone else have any ideas?'

'It's trying to persuade someone else to do what you want.'

'Thanks,' says the tutor, 'that is getting closer and we need to understand how we may persuade someone to do what we want. Babies do it all the time, don't they? They scream, yell, cry, stamp their feet and blackmail their parents in all sorts of ways. That is also how some buyers try to do it.'

'Let me explain what we think negotiation is. There are many definitions which can help us.

'Aljian, one of the best writers on purchasing said it provided a legitimate and ethical means for the buyer and seller, through give and take, to eliminate unjustified or unnecessary ingredients of cost. This implies that there will be concessions given by both parties and that it has something to do with cost. A simpler explanation is that negotiation is a process by which two or more parties attempt to resolve a disagreement or difference of opinion. This gets us to the point of recognizing that it is a process and that is something we have to accept. You will find that the process needs very careful handling at all the key phases. Does anyone have any questions at this stage?'

'Yes,' says the civil servant, 'I think negotiation is unsavoury and unethical. After all the potential supplier has made their best offer when they submitted the bid. Why must we then take away their profit?'

'That's an interesting comment. It is important that we all recognize that the government in the United Kingdom have recognized how important post tender negotiation is, and they now actively encourage it, providing the circumstances are right. Just because you challenge a price doesn't mean that you are lowering the profit. Perhaps they should buy the materials at a lower price, perhaps the item could be made more efficiently and perhaps too much overhead recovery is being sought. It is therefore important that none of us thinks that this thing called negotiation is unethical. I will use this question to explain when we should negotiate. Let me outline it on the whiteboard.' The tutor then takes you through the following points.

When we should negotiate

1. Where it is believed that the bid cost elements are uncompetitive.
2. Where the bid is unclear on major features, e.g. the delivery date does not have any accompanying production plan showing milestones.
3. Where contractual safeguards are required (you immediately think of your discussions with S&J on the machine).
4. Where long-term product support is needed and the way in which it may be achieved is very unclear.
5. Where you believe the bidders are not pricing competitively and/or where collusion is a possibility.
6. When there are few suppliers in the market.
7. When the bidders are reluctant to explain how they arrived at the selling price.
8. Where the purchase has a unique element, such as a one-off purchase where the buyer has little expertise.

'And so, you will all see that there are perfectly valid reasons why we must negotiate. Indeed, I will go further. If we do not negotiate we are acting in an unprofessional manner. We will certainly fail to obtain the optimum deal that is available in the market. There will also be many suppliers who will feel aggrieved that they put a lot of effort into preparing a quotation and then they were not given the chance to explain their approach to pricing and contractual matters. Now, we will deal with this business of trying to change someone else's mind. Can anyone help me with different ways?'

'Screw them!' That is the first suggestion. 'Explain where they have got it wrong.' That is the second. 'Tell them they will lose the order unless they change their mind.' That is the third. 'Threaten to go to a competitor.' That is the fourth. 'Tell them you have a lower price, even if you don't.' That is the fifth.

'Stop,' says the tutor. 'I have written these down. Have a look at them. Is there a common element? The use of threats is a theme. Only one of you used the word "explain". One of you suggests telling a lie and bluffing. This is a dangerous approach because if you get tarnished with this image you are doomed as a world-class buyer which is what I presume you are all aspiring towards. There are only six ways to change someone else's mind, but before we go into that level of detail, I am going to give you a little exercise to have a go at. You will be placed into teams and asked to develop a negotiation plan. When you have finished we will get one of the teams to role play the problem with one of our tutors and we will use the video equipment to tape the meeting, which shouldn't last any longer than 15 minutes.' You are placed in the 'A' team and you disappear into the padded cell called a syndicate room.

Negotiation exercise 1

The tutor hands you a piece of paper which is headed 'Negotiation exercise 1'. It reads as follows:

You are a buyer employed by the Mega Company. They sell products around the world and have an annual turnover in excess of £500 million. Your personal expenditure exceeds £30 million and you buy a specialized range of engineering equipment. Your company has just been awarded a contract to sell a major installation to Canada. Included in the specification is a specialized electronic control box manufactured by Ellis-Guy Ltd who are located in Glasgow. They are a small firm with only 12 employees and a turnover of less than £750 000 per annum. They have quoted a price of £69 500 and a delivery of 18 weeks. The delivery is OK and the price has no comparison because no one else can quote for the item. You have a brief as the buyer to seek a 5% reduction in purchase prices because your sales people in their last meeting with the Canadians had to reduce their price by 5% to get the order. You are to meet the Sales Director of Ellis-Guy Ltd for the purpose of negotiating the price.

You are in the same team as Mr Blott who immediately takes over your team. 'Leave this one to me! It's simple, we are a large company and they are small. They will badly need our work and 5% will easily be possible. It's just a question of using our power. I would reckon five minutes would see us finished. The plan is complete.'

'But,' you interject, 'my purchasing manager spends a lot of time working out how he is going to do it and preparing an agenda. Don't you think we should do that?'

'No,' says Mr Blott, 'it's unnecessary in this case and anyway the tutor is looking for a quick kill on this one. That's why the brief is so simple. Go and tell him we are ready and don't forget, let me do the talking.'

You think to yourself that he has done it all so far, so why change the habits of a lifetime! Blott by name and Blott by nature. One of your team goes to tell the tutor your team is ready and you are told the role-playing will begin in about ten minutes' time.

When your team enters the room, everyone else is in there and there is a table in the centre of the room. There are three chairs on one side and one on the other. The tutor speaks. 'Make yourselves comfortable. Who is leading this negotiation?'

'I am,' responds Mr Blott.

'Right, you sit in the centre chair and I will send in Mr Ellis who is representing the seller. Are you ready?'

'Yes,' says Mr Blott, exuding confidence, arrogance and self-assurance.

The meeting begins as Mr Ellis enters the room.

'Sit down and listen to me,' says Blott.

'We have your quotation and it is nonsense. The price is too high by 30% and unless you do something to meet our needs you will not get the order. I must also tell you that no more orders will come your way unless you can convince me personally that I should deal with you. Your prices are really ridiculous and it's no wonder you are a small company.'

You sit there and can't believe what you have just heard. You feel like throwing up at the crass stupidity of Mr Blott. So far Ellis has not spoken but he does now!

'Thank you for calling me in. We welcome the chance to meet you and to discuss the bid we submitted. There are two things I have to say. First of all the price is wrong and I apologize for an error. We genuinely got the costings wrong and missed out some special electronics. They will add £2500 to the quoted price. If that causes you a real problem it wouldn't be an embarrassment if you decided not to purchase the item. We have a full order book and we have another customer who wants this control equipment. What do you want to do?'

Nice one, you think. Blott's veins in his neck stand out like snakes! His eyes are bulging and he launches into a tirade. 'That is preposterous. I have never heard such nonsense. Error, my foot! Dishonest, I call it. You didn't seem to hear me when I said the price must fall by 30%. That's it. Take it or leave it!'

Ellis fixes Blott with a knowing look and says, 'I will leave it then. Thank you, offer withdrawn.' With that he leaves the room.

Your tutor then gets the room back into applepie order and asks for views on what people have just heard and seen.

'No one would do that in real life,' says Blott who is still smarting from the experience.

'Wrong,' says the tutor. 'You used power and coercion but forgot that it is never one-sided. While the other company is very small they also have some power. You used bluff and you set an unrealistic target. You left no room for manoeuvre and they called your bluff. You made no attempt to introduce the topic or yourself and gave the visitor no chance to join in the meeting. You didn't have an agenda and the planning considered no alternatives or the seller's likely response. I am very grateful for Mr Blott's efforts. It's not easy doing the role-playing and all that really matters is that we now learn from these situations. We learn from that exercise that power and coercion is a very dangerous approach. It is rarely one-sided and must only be used as a last resort. It is a very destructive form of negotiation and will heighten tensions. Most likely, it will also damage relationships. It has to be said, however, that there are some suppliers who will only respond to power and coercion. Happily, these days, they seem to be in a minority but if all else fails, then they will have to be dealt with in that manner. I hope you enjoyed the meeting. We have certainly learned a lot from it and now we will have a go at the second negotiation exercise.'

Negotiation exercise 2

Your team goes back to the syndicate room and are handed the second exercise which reads as follows:

In this situation you are the buyer for Grovex Pharmaceuticals. You purchase packaging material for OTC (over the counter) products. In a few months' time there will be a new product launch and you must buy the packaging. This consists of a printed pack. You have a packaging development department who have a great deal of experience in this area. They have sent you a specification and an internal costing. The latter uses their expert knowledge and gives you the following detail.

	£
Material-board	0.75
Inks	0.08
Folding	0.03
Labour	1.05
Overheads	1.05
Profit	0.30
Total	3.26

Your enquiries have been made and you have three quotations on your desk. The quoted prices are Abex £5.60; Carey £3.61; Newton £4.03. The price is each and the initial quantity is 75 000. You can now plan to meet Carey to tackle the price aspect of the quotation.

This time you decide you will have a say in events. For some reason Mr Blott is subdued but is honest enough to say he made a mess of the first negotiation. Your other colleague, Claire Small, suggests you should all contribute to the planning but says she would be quite happy if you could run the meeting. You all have a look at the costing information and decide to ask the tutor how it was put together. You are told that the material price is based on current market prices which have been falling in recent months. The ink is based on amount used and a well-established price in the market. The folding is time-related on a special machine and the labour is based on £18 per hour. The overheads have been applied at 100% on labour which is believed to be an equitable way of doing it. The profit is a shade over 10%. That is the logic.

Your team decide that when you meet Carey you will explain why the price is so important. It is a product launch and therefore you want to establish where the costs are, and you want to establish the price to guarantee product acceptance. You can then ask how they arrived at a price of £3.61 and, where there are differences, to explain their figures. You will then say that they have an excellent chance of gaining an important contract, providing they get the base costs, and hence, price correct. The purchase will be a long-term need if the launch is successful, and this is another reason why they should play ball. You write all this down and tell the tutor you are ready for the meeting.

When you go back into the main room its set out exactly the same and when you are organized the supplier's representative arrives. She is Joy Archer, who gives the appearance of having done this many times before. You must keep your nerve.

'Thank you for visiting us today to discuss a very important potential contract. You are one of a number who have quoted for the job and the purpose of this meeting is to discuss your offer. We believe the price is too high and we need you to reduce it a little bit.' That is your opening. (Later your tutor tells you that the error has come in the words a 'little bit'. This suggested that they don't have to do a lot on price and therefore you have unwittingly given a clue about your expectations. The rest of it is pretty good and truthful.)

The response is, 'We are grateful for the opportunity to quote and would like the work but we have submitted a competitive price.' (The tutor later explains that this is a subtle test by the supplier to get your reaction but it also contains a clue that they are keen for the order.)

You reply, 'Will you please explain how you arrived at the price of £3.61? It would be helpful if you broke the price down into materials, labour, overheads and profit.' (The tutor later says, well done but having asked the question you should have stopped. You have suggested the form of the answer whereas if you had left it as an open question you may have got more information.)

Joy answers, 'Our material cost is £0.91. Basically the inks are £0.05 and the Board is £0.86. It was purchased eight months ago and will come from current stock.' The tutor points out later that two chances have now presented themselves and you could use your knowledge on current board prices. To be honest you never hear the ink cost because you are only listening to the reply on board! That is why your reply is as follows.

'I hear what you say but we know that the board price has fallen in recent months and the actual cost should be £0.75. We must therefore ask that you use current prices. This would reduce the quoted price by £0.11. Do you agree to do this?' (The tutor says this is a good try and you wait for the answer which isn't what you expected.)

You are told that current stock has to be used and priced accordingly but in view of the circumstances they will reduce the material cost to £0.80, giving you a £0.05 reduction.

'OK,' you say, 'let's look at some other aspects.' (Your tutor later tells you that you did not persist with your demand and snatched off Joy's hand. Actually, you think you have done well but can now see that you must persist.)

'How much is your labour cost?'

Joy replies that it is £0.99. 'Oh, well that seems alright then,' is the best you can do and drop the topic like a hot potato. (Your tutor says that you have given in because their number is lower than yours and you have made no attempt to find out how many minutes have been costed and what hourly rate has been used. This is the case and you feel there is more to negotiation than you previously thought.)

'Are your overheads also £0.99,' you ask.

'No, actually they are £1.15.'

You move in for the kill and tell her that your company would allow them 100% on labour, i.e. £0.99 which would be a £0.16 reduction. Very sweetly Joy says she will agree this, but on this occasion only. You are euphoric and wait for a round of applause (it doesn't come). You ask her is that the best she can do and is she agreeable to a price reduction to———? (Panic sets in because you have lost track of where you are.) Your colleague, Claire, gently whispers, 'It's £2.86 at the moment.'

As you hesitate Joy Archer tells you the new price they will agree to is £3.40 which is a £0.21 reduction times 75 000 which equals £15 750. 'Thank you, we accept.'

The tutor says that there are a lot of learning points here.

1. You lost a grip of the figures.
2. You forgot to challenge profit and folding.
3. You let the seller express the saving as a large number which made you feel good and you lost the logic that you started with.

A better deal could have been obtained here and the first mistake of saying a little bit hadn't helped at all.

This particular exercise ends with the tutor saying that **logical persuasion** is another way to change someone else's views. However you need excellent information about costs, products, markets, the supplier and all other relevant factors. This takes some getting but if you do expend the effort it is, properly handled, a superb way to negotiate. You have already learned a lot and ask the tutor how many other ways there are to change someone's opinion. 'Four more, and we are now moving on to our next exercise to see how you manage another situation.'

Negotiation exercise 3

Doesn't time fly when you are having fun? Teabreaks, lunch, dinner, have never crossed your mind because this is really enjoyable. The tutor had told you that training can be good fun as well as you learning a lot. You agree and notice that by this stage the course is now much more relaxed and the teams are getting very competitive. Time for the third exercise and you wonder what point this will make. Treat it with an open mind; that's what the purchasing manager said.

Your third brief reads as follows.

You are the buyer for Wessex Building Contractors who, for the past twelve months, have been building a new hospital in Grantchester. Throughout this contract you have had major difficulties with the supplier of fabricated steelwork, Tubulara Steel Fabrications Ltd. They were awarded a contract for the fabrication of 120 tonnes of steel and its subsequent erection on site. In the first place they were late with delivery and that delayed the job, stopping other sub-contractors meeting their start dates. Part way through the job, the client changed one part of the specification, causing a redesign problem. All in all it has not been a happy relationship. The contract did not include liquidated damages and the financial position has been calculated. You reckon that Tubulara Steel Fabrications Ltd owe you £46 850 for delays. This can be explained quite simply by the sub-contractors having idle labour for which they had no other work at the time. Equally, Tubulara are claiming from you an amount of £74 000 in respect of abandoned work, downtime, re-design, additional transport and overhead recovery. You have been asked to meet Jim Pringle the Contracts Manager of Tubulara Steel Fabrications Ltd in an attempt to resolve this very difficult problem. There have not been any previous meetings but there have been a few unsatisfactory phone calls because they have submitted invoices which, they say, should be paid.

You all go into the planning room and say, 'Your turn, Claire.'

'I don't know anything about building work. That's not fair.' You tell her that so far as you can see the principles of negotiation are the same whatever line of work you are involved in. The suggestion is that you plan it together and come up with good tactics (another point emphasized by the tutor). If everyone tells the truth, both sides have a point. You have been let down on delivery and that did cause a problem. You did change the specification and that caused them additional cost. The sub-contractors did lose some time and that cost them money. All of that is logical and so you build the tactics around that line of thought.

Back to the main room, same set-up and Claire takes the centre stage! In comes Jim Pringle and immediately goes on the attack. You have certainly not planned for this and the whole team is taken aback. He has gone into power and coercion and the meeting is only seconds old. 'Apart from a slight problem at the start we have done everything possible to meet your requirements. We virtually dropped everything to meet the changed specification. After all that we submitted an invoice which still hasn't been paid. Not only is that unethical it's breaking the contract. When are you going to pay us?' He glowers at Claire who looks flustered.

She responds, 'We are not going to pay you until the whole situation has been discussed, and that includes our claim against you.' (The tutor later explains that Pringle has taken the initiative, has sought to minimize their late delivery and then effectively changed the subject by asking when the invoice would be paid. If you are not careful now you will be diverted from your agenda and the negotiation will be over, almost before it has started.) The response given by Claire is a crucial stage and the reply is revealing.

'We are not even listening to your claim until you settle ours. That is a pre-condition of making any progress. We have been very reasonable in our request for £74 000, so when are you going to pay?' (The tutor says later that this is an attempt to test your resolve and to shut out your needs. If you aren't careful you will get dragged into an argument.)

Claire does very well. Her reply is, 'I am sorry you have responded like that. We have a legitimate claim and it must be discussed. The issue will not go away and we must insist that you accept the fact that you are late with delivery and we can see no reason for that. Our claim is genuine and must be met. When that is out of the way we will consider your point of view.' (The tutor thinks this is excellent because it brings the matter back where you want it to be, and it acknowledges that you will discuss theirs.)

Pringle responds in a way that surprises you all. 'As a gesture of good faith we will reduce our claim by 10%, provided you drop your claim altogether.' Hang on a minute you feel. That doesn't seem equitable. He gives us 10% and we drop our claim! It's too one-sided but at least he gives us something, even though it's not enough. (The tutor's analysis of this is that he has tried it on. Some movement on his part but massive movement on your part.) Events then move very fast.

Claire offers to split the difference. She will concede half of your claim if he will concede half of his. 'No,' is his answer to this. 'I can't do that but I will settle our claim if you will split the difference between £74 000 and £37 000, in other words we will settle at £55 550. All that depends on you also conceding half of your claim on us.' With that he offers his hand to Claire (not in marriage – you will note), and she takes it.

The tutor then begins his feedback saying that your team has fallen for one of the oldest tricks in the book. **Middle ground compromise** is another way to persuade someone else. Be careful, though – you are conceding 50% of your ideal in one go and that can make someone else very greedy. The other thing to learn is that when the numbers start to change you must slow down the pace and know what you are conceding. In this instance too much is conceded without an adequate discussion. I would also suspect that, because the discussion goes very quickly, at the end Claire is stampeded and her lack of experience leads to the unbalanced compromise.

Negotiation exercise 4

You are now in the swing of this and, quite frankly, you can't wait for the next negotiation brief. When it is passed out the tutor tells you that this time your team will be negotiating with one of the other teams. By now, Claire, Blott and yourself are gradually making an effective team. You conclude that it's adversity pulling you together. Anyway, we digress. There is a brief to read.

You are a buyer working for the Howell Medical Company. Your company markets a range of medical equipment under your brand name 'Velure 2000'. The company would like to expand but lacks the capital to do so. There are insufficient funds to invest in research and development, even though your business is profitable. Your marketing department has approached your purchasing manager and has said that they would welcome the chance to add to your range a product called 'Swede-Dress'. This range is made in Sweden by the Procordin Group who try to market it direct. Your estimates suggest they sell about £1 million of product per annum, although marketing believe there is a good chance they could increase this by half. The head of marketing has asked the purchasing manager to negotiate with the UK sales manager of Procordin. You have been asked to undertake the negotiations. There are three items in the 'Swede-Dress' range. They are:

Code XYA-1001   Selling price £2.75
Code YAB-279   Selling price £5.00
Code NOB-2110   Selling price £1.10

You need a negotiation plan before you approach the UK sales manager for a meeting.

Your team start to pool your ideas. This is not a case for power and coercion but there does seem to be a case for some logical persuasion although this doesn't seem sufficient to you. This is a tough case and so you decide to list the points you think should be included in the negotiation. At first it is just a brainstorming and no particular sequence is sought. That can come later in the planning.

Topics to raise

- Our company and marketing   (2)
- Our distribution methods   (3)
- The opportunity for joint collaboration (1)
- Pricing levels and royalties on sales   (5)
- New product development   (4)
- Payment   (6)
- A plan to bring matters to fruition   (7)

The numbering at the side is your final sequence of points for the agenda you intend to follow.

At this stage what you don't know is that the other team with whom you will negotiate are studying a different brief. They are to adopt the role of the UK sales manager for Procordin Group. A summary of the brief reads as follows:

For a number of years you have been trying to sell the 'Swede-Dress' range in the United Kingdom. The total sales levels are currently at £1 million and a loss is being incurred when all costs are taken into account. There is nothing wrong with the product. It is excellent quality but is probably overpriced. Your board of directors in Sweden have said that the ideal would be to find a company who is good at marketing and who have complementary products. If you are approached you have the authority to conclude a deal, providing the manufacture can still be done in Sweden. You should be quite frank in exchanging information, if in your view you can trust the people with whom you are negotiating.

All of the above is unknown to you as you plan. It raises a very important point. There is total common interest here and given that scenario there should be agreement and the negotiations should be amicable. The tutor is now testing how you handle a negotiation where **genuine business objectives** are a very powerful way to settle the outcome of a negotiation. In this case, now being tackled, there is no current relationship and so you must place a major emphasis on your introductory comments. The negotiation begins with Mr Blott as the spokesman for your team.

'Good afternoon, we are very pleased to welcome you to our offices. The purpose of the meeting is to explain that we are seeking a relationship where we can add the "Swede-Dress" range to our existing product range. We have excellent marketing and sales capabilities which we believe will complement what you want to achieve. This means that you can have financial benefits without your current high risk on costs. We have a lot of information to exchange with you and hope you can reciprocate. Do you have the authority to negotiate on behalf of Procordin Group?'

Your tutor says that this is a jolly good opening, which strikes exactly the right note. He gives you full marks for checking the authority to negotiate. This should be a standard question when you begin a negotiation.

'Thank you for the introduction. We welcome your approach, it has coincided with a major product review we have undertaken in the UK. We are receptive to reaching a deal along the lines you suggest but it will, of course, be essential to reach a satisfactory financial resolution. We would not wish to sub-contract the manufacture to yourselves, but you could arrange everything else such as warehousing, distribution, marketing and sales. Going back to the selling prices our margin is currently 30% but we believe the products are not priced sufficiently competitively. We would recommend that the pricing points be changed to £2.49; £4.99 and £0.99. We would also want to review any sales literature you would be putting into the market, prior to its being distributed. Does any of that cause you a problem?' That was the sales manager's response. It builds on everything that Mr Blott raised and now gives you the opportunity to respond and maintain the positive approach to these negotiations.

Cutting a long story short, the negotiation is a great success. An agreement is reached where both sides win. 'There you are,' says the tutor, 'we have seen an excellent example of a **win-win** negotiation and no confrontation. Both sides recognize that there are genuine business objectives which can be reached. Both ensure that they are.' Both teams are praised for their efforts.

Negotiation exercise 5

'Every negotiation is a challenge of some sort,' says the tutor. 'The facts may seem straightforward as far as you are concerned but you never really know how the other side feels or what settlement they will accept. To that end there is a battle of wits, even at the planning stage when you are trying to predict their approach and tactics. We are now ready for the next exercise which will be planned as teams, but this time there will be no role-playing. There may be a few surprises in the way we discuss the following case.'

You are then handed the next brief which reads as follows:

Four weeks ago you were appointed the buyer for the Premier Car Company. They make high-performance cars and have an excellent reputation for quality. You have now taken responsibility for a range of aluminium castings and one of the key suppliers is Driscol Castings who are situated in Daventry. You have checked the past year's history and found that they have only achieved a 92% quality performance and a 94% on time delivery performance. They have persistently asked for a price increase and now threaten to cease deliveries unless you agree to a 3.8% increase within the next ten days. The impact of this would be £56 000 in a full year. The relationship is clearly off the rails and something must be done. You insist on JIT deliveries and pay your invoices in 75 days as agreed in the contract. There is a recent press cutting in the file which shows that Driscol announced a loss of £1.35 million on a turnover of £45 million last year. They have not paid a dividend over the past three years. There have been large-scale redundancies; the workforce has been reduced by 220 in the past eighteen months. You have dies with the supplier for which your organization paid 'part cost'. In other words the ownership in the dies belongs to the supplier. They are a single source of supply and you estimate it would take 4–6 months to create a new supplier. This is the situation requiring your negotiation skills. A meeting with David Stampe, the managing director, has been arranged for tomorrow and it is essential you have an effective plan. You should make a list of the issues and some suggestions for resolving them. That is all you have to do for now.

The issues that you identify are:

8% adverse quality performance;
6% adverse delivery performance;
3.8% price increase request;
delivery stoppage threatened;
supplier making a financial loss;
ownership of dies with supplier;
long lead in for new supplier.

As you study these factors you begin to realize they are **your** issues and so you start to look at it from the supplier's point of view. They get paid in 75 days and that is a long time (yes, you know that some companies take 90 days – but the supplier has probably built in the cost of money to the price). They seem to be having a tough time with more redundancies. Your team's ideas begin to harden towards the view that here is a supplier who could be worth persisting with and with this thought you return to the main room and join the other teams.

A range of views

'Team B, what would you recommend we do?' This team responds that they would not tolerate such a supplier. They would refuse the price increase and find another source.

'Team C, what would you recommend we do?' This team agrees with B's solution.

'Team D, what would you recommend we do?' This team says they would concede the price increase and hope that things would improve. The tutor doesn't think much of this one.

'And what does the A Team think?' Your response is, 'We would open up the negotiations and probe the reasons for the quality and delivery problems. Having heard the response we would offer the supplier some expert help from our quality and production staff. We would agree some improvement plans over a period of six months and tell the supplier we would concede 2% of the price increase when the improvement plans are achieved. We would also have a word with the finance department to check our cashflows and if this is healthy you would offer to settle invoices in 60 days. You would also check how much it would cost to buy out the balance of the dies. If this figure could be agreed this would give the supplier some cash and give you ownership of the dies which could then be moved elsewhere if the position didn't improve.'

The tutor congratulates your team for a very original solution. Your team has however failed to work out precisely what it would cost you to pay quicker and the financial benefits of improvements in quality and production. The most pleasing feature of all this is that you have sought to solve the problem by making **mutually advantageous concessions**. In this case it looks one-sided but if your company retains a supplier by making realistic concessions, then they will tend to make sure you are looked after in the future. We now have five ways to seek to change someone else's opinion.

Negotiation exercise 6

The final case study that is handed to you concerns a problem set in the retail sector. You are again the buyer, responsible now for miscellaneous purchases. These include computer maintenance. The information technology office have spoken to one of the large companies who do this type of work. They have, without reference to anyone in buying, told the supplier that they will award next year's contract to them at a price of £350 000. There is only £300 000 in the budget and you have been asked to pull the chestnuts out of the fire.

Your tutor leaves everyone in the room and asks for a list of possible ways to deal with this situation. The suggestions come thick and fast!

- Sack the IT specialists for exceeding their authority!
- Call in the supplier and give them a shellacking for not talking to buying!
- Bluff it with the supplier and say there is no agreement!
- Bluff it with the supplier and tell them a competitor is cheaper!
- Ask the supplier for a cost breakdown!
- Agree to pay because it is the only honourable thing to do!

The tutor acknowledges these are all possibilities but do not have a great deal of credibility. Bluff is a very dangerous ploy. The first two are power and coercion. Asking for a cost breakdown probably means you will settle at their price. Agree to pay is completely conceding your position. The tutor now makes you aware that there is a sixth way to try and change opinion. This is **attitude change involving emotion**. You are now asked to think of any ideas using this method. These are hard to come by.

- Tell the supplier that the price cannot be paid because the budget is not available and that if they persist someone could lose their job and surely they wouldn't want to be responsible for that.
- Meet the supplier and shake your head, wring your hands, and tell them that there must be a way out of the dilemma and could they help you to find it because you are in deep trouble with the boss. They must have something they can do.
- Tell the supplier that you have your head on the block and the pressure is unbelievable. You have heard they are very reasonable people and please will they find a way out of the mess.

These have a certain ring of desperation about them and the tutor concludes this is an unsatisfactory way of negotiation but, if it is acknowledged, may occasionally have its place. The conclusion from the work you have done so far is that the two most effective negotiation styles are **logical persuasion** and **genuine business objectives**.

Conclusions

This has been a fantastic start to the course and it has motivated you beyond belief. You think this is a fascinating subject that deserves more study on your part. The remainder of the course consists of lectures, role plays, discussions and case studies on the art of negotiation.

The tutor's concluding remarks are worth remembering. 'When you get back to your various organizations you should identify something that needs negotiating. Make sure you have a proper plan and an agenda. Work out how you will tackle the problem and have a go. What you ask for, you might get. What you don't ask for you definitely won't get!'

And finally, remember there are only six ways to influence the other negotiator, provided you've done your homework of course:

1. power and coercion;
2. attitude change involving emotion;
3. logical persuasion;
4. middle ground compromise;
5. genuine business objectives;
6. mutually advantageous concessions.

'Good luck in the future' the tutor finishes, 'and I hope that your careers will prosper. Please try to repay your organizations through reducing costs and improving the contracts that you negotiate.'

MEMORY JOGGERS

41 **Thinking about negotiation**
  - It is a tremendous skill
  - Many buyers have not worked hard enough to develop the skill
  - The seller is usually well trained in negotiation
  - You can always improve your skill level

REMEMBER – negotiation skills are vital in the success of a buyer in all sorts of negotiation situations, do everything possible to sharpen your skill!

42 **Planning for a negotiation**
  - Ensure you have allowed enough time
  - Decide what are the main features of the impending negotiation
  - Think about all the 'angles'
  - Try to anticipate the seller's objectives

REMEMBER – you should allocate sufficient planning time to ensure you deal with the detail of each point that requires negotiation.

43 **Influencing skills**
  - There are only six ways to change someone's opinion
  - Concentrate on positive behaviour
  - Use logic and support it with facts and analysis
  - Listen to the seller's points – you may learn something

REMEMBER – it is the buyer's job to influence the other party that you have a point of view which is valid, you must make the running!

44 **Bringing it to a conclusion**
  - Make proposals to the seller for lower prices, etc.
  - Make sure you deal with all key points
  - Do a summary at the end of the meeting
  - Don't let the seller backtrack on what has been agreed

REMEMBER – the buyer must exert the pressure for an agreement, otherwise the seller will close the sale with the buyer not in an advantageous position.

10 FROM CAPITAL TO PRODUCTION

This chapter takes the reader on from the capital purchasing introduced in Chapter 7 to production purchasing. New concepts are explained such as key/non-key items, red-book targeting, buying using production engineering estimates, open-book negotiations, value analysis and value engineering. Some of the dirty tricks used in tool cost quotations are exposed.

The move to a production purchasing desk was not unexpected, but the change from capital purchasing was at first something of a culture shock. Unlike the capital desk where at any given time you might be handling ten new projects, here the new projects could well be measured in fifties at a time, not as many as you were handling at the consumables desk, but every project vital to the feeding of those omnivorous mass production lines. When you consider that production unit volumes are seldom less than 1000 per day, and that an error of a penny a unit would cost the company (1p × 1000 × 5 × 250) = £12 500 p.a., running a production buyer's desk demands the use of a high level of skill.

Once you have added the skills of the production buyer to those acquired on consumables and capital you are well on your way to becoming a world-class buyer.

With high production volumes, tooling, delivery schedules, inventory control, supplier selection all require very thorough work, added to which is the necessary commitment to maintain/improve cost competitiveness, from both domestic and overseas sources. This is not all. New skills must be acquired, such as value analysis, value administration and value engineering, added to which are cost estimating, the key item concept and the further uses of economic forecasting.

By now many of the tools discussed in previous chapters will have become second nature to you such as:

- know your items;
- know your systems;
- know your policies and procedures;
- know your terms and conditions;

and the use of:

- quotation analysis.
- cost benefit analysis.

- records of
  - meetings;
  - raw materials movements;
  - feeds and speeds;
  - labour and overhead cost movements.

So the new learning breaks down into five categories.

The new learning

1. Supplier research
- use of exhibitions/press;
- embassies/consulates;
- supplier representatives.

2. Source selection
- supplier quality;
- type of tooling;
- financial stability;
- flexibility;
- competitiveness.

3. Cost control
- forecasting;
- key item concept.

4. Price estimation
- Cost estimating;
- VA;
- VE;
- Substitution of materials;
- Rationalization;
- Make v. buy.

5. Price control
- Competitiveness;
- Contractual;
- MLO;
- unit cost.

One major fact which has emerged in the consumables work which underpins the world-class buyer's thinking is the benefits of reduction of the number of suppliers in use for a particular commodity range to the minimum. You will meet buyers who say, 'I like to have several suppliers per commodity.' This is a policy of weakness because the buyer lacks confidence in his or her suppliers. In fact the problem that buyer has is far more fundamental. He/she lacks the skills to select one supplier, the best of what is available, and control that supplier in such a way that the supplier achieves perfection, but can still be kept under competitive challenge.

While true in any buying environment it is absolutely vital in production buying where high launch costs in the shape of expensive tooling are involved.

Another phrase you will often hear from the buyer whose skills are not world-class will be, 'I like to have all my suppliers within a forty mile radius of the company, so that if anything goes wrong I can be there in an hour!' The world-class buyer will buy from anywhere in the world where the best supplier can be found – no company has all the best suppliers in the world less than forty miles from its own front door – and only a nincompoop would think so!

Preliminary costings

In a mass-production environment the processes from initial concept via prototypes to first quantity production follow broadly similar stages when a new or improved product is to be launched. Typically the cycle from initial concept to quantity production takes about 18 months. The new model will have at least a five-year life which, depending on its continued market acceptance, will be extended to 8 or 9 years via face lifts, variants etc.

The company have discovered a niche for a specialist off-the-road vehicle which is codenamed Sandblaster. It will be initially produced at a rate of 500 per day; it has applications as a beach buggy, snow mobile, and has military applications; and sales and marketing have reported confidently that within the first year of production volumes will reach 1000 per day.

The first you hear of it is when a stack of drawings and specifications land on your desk accompanied by a note from the estimating department asking for initial quotations within 30 days from today's date. The drawings are heavily stamped, '**For preliminary cost studies only**'.

The sets of drawings include:

Gear box housing – grey iron casting;
Axle housings (2) – grey iron casting;
Steering gear (BO) – assembly;
Bucket seats (2) – assembly;
Accelerator pedal – steel forging;
Clutch pedal – steel forging;
Brake pedal – steel forging;
Brake assys (4) – fabrications;
Plastic handles (4) – mouldings;
Drop arm – forging;
Hood pressing – steel pressing;
Side panels (4) – steel pressing;
Taper roller bearings (8) – BOF;
Ball bearings (10) – BOF;

Assorted plastic knobs (8) – plastic moulding;
Steering wheel – plastic moulding.

The purpose of this enquiry is to provide broad-brush prices to the estimating department so that they can create an initial costing of the Sandblaster. A brief look at the drawings shows that in many cases design has not been completed – so there is going to have to be a lot of guessing by a lot of people – and not least you!

Handling the cost enquiry

The potential supply sources will be initially drawn from:

1. traditional suppliers (either current or past),
2. suppliers drawn from *Kelly's, BSI Buyer's Guide, Kompass, Engineering Buyer's Guide* or other trade directories;
3. approved suppliers. These are where design engineering have carried out tests on certain manufacturers items and wish to ensure that these items are included in the new project. In such cases the supplier's name appears on the print. Often these are the supplier's own drawings, and confidentiality rules apply, so they must not be sent to any other suppliers.

Enquiry detail

The following information must be provided/requested in order to get the best indicative quotes available.

1. volume required: 500 per day rising to 1000 per day after 12 months;
2. unit price;
3. tool cost: supplier to state if the tool cost quoted is full or part cost; if the supplier is quoting part cost what percentage is being requested;
4. lead-time from receipt of order to production of samples off production tools.

Tool cost pitfalls

With regard to point 3 'tool cost' refers to the special tools, jigs and fixtures required to produce the part. As a rule the supplier is expected to have the relevant capital equipment and no contribution should normally be made.

In some cases suppliers will make the special tools in their toolrooms and in other cases where they have not got an adequate toolroom they will buy them from specialist toolmakers.

Part cost tool costs

Suppliers quote part costs varying from 10% to 90% of cost retaining the balance. This may not be acceptable to the company because the company policy states that tools at suppliers are part of the company's assets, and as such ownership of tools should always rest with the company.

However in certain sectors of industry the practice of quoting part cost is traditional. The reasons given are:

1. By retaining part ownership the buyer does not fully own the tooling and thus is prevented from removing the tooling from the supplier's premises.
2. By part ownership of the tooling the supplier has a greater incentive to maintain the tools in good order.
3. When buyers negotiate paying 100% of tooling it is a wise precaution to stipulate that as part of the contract the supplier as keeper of the tools is responsible for maintaining them.
4. To mislead the buyer. (This is a ploy in which the supplier relies on the buyer accepting the supplier's word that the buyer is paying say 50% of the tool cost, when he or she is actually paying 100%!)
5. To defraud the buyer. (This is a practice which relies on the fact that the buyer subscribes to the theory that the more sophisticated the tooling is, the more expensive it will be, and as a direct consequence the unit cost will be low. It also relies on the fact that non-world-class buyers will snap at low unit costs and neither pay too much attention to the tool cost nor attempt to verify the value of the tooling.)

Assume that you have raised an enquiry for a fairly simple item at a rate of 200 per day, equivalent to 50 000 per annum.

On receipt of the quotes you prepare the quotation analysis shown in Table 10.1.

Table 10.1 Quotation analysis

Supplier	Unit price	Tool cost	1 year Cost	3 year Cost
A	£1.00	£10 000	£60 000	£160 000
B	£0.80	£20 000	£60 000	£140 000
C	£0.99	£11 000	£60 500	£159 000

If unit cost alone is considered then B is the most attractive. Provided B's tooling concept is truly the most advanced then he or she is also most attractive over the three year cost.

But what the supplier **may** be doing is as follows.

Actual tool cost is £10 000. By charging £20 000 they (the suppliers) are able to bank £10 000 providing perhaps 10% interest (£1000). So effectively in order to improve their cashflow they can afford to ensure they get your business by 'funding' their unit price.

If you don't check their tool cost you'll find that after 12 months they'll be claiming a fairly hefty price increase which, although you may be reluctant to pay, leaves you without an alternative because it would mean writing off £20 000 of investment!

The world-class buyer may not be able to assess by visual inspection the precise cost of a set of tools, but what he/she **must** do is to see the invoices paid by the supplier whether or not the decision is to pay either part or full cost.

As your quotations start to be returned by the suppliers you should prepare a quotation analysis as the example shown in Table 10.1 for each commodity in order to establish the one- and three-year cost comparisons. From these you select the most attractive and pass the result back to estimating.

Do not at this stage tell any supplier they have come out best!

There will be a series of activities taking place which will be based on your initial work. Estimating will be working on estimating the costs of the components which comprise 80% of the model cost. They use production engineering techniques to cross check the prices you have obtained. The Sandblaster has 5000 components in it and of those probably 1000 items (20%) make up 80% of the model cost. These items become the key items.

The key item process

The formula to establish a key item is to multiply the number used by the unit cost and rank the usage cost accordingly (e.g. 1000 per day × £2.00 = £2000 per day).

An example could be item AB costs £5.00, item CD costs £1.50, but there are 4 off of CD, so CD should take precedence over AB for cost reduction attention.

Construction of the 'Red Book'

The Sandblaster is divided into sub-assemblies:

Steering unit

> steering gear
> steering wheel
> drop arms
> drag links

Axle unit

> axle housings
> brake housings
> wheel bearings
> brake pedals

Engine unit

> gear-box housing
> clutch pedal
> accelerator pedal

Body panels

> hood pressing
> side panels

From your work and that of the other production buyers, each of the units are built up to establish a preliminary cost. This process is carried out by product cost control, a department with which you will become very familiar.

The Red Book

The Red Book has now provided a vital piece of management information, of which you should have a copy. It details the best price that has been obtained to date. Design engineering now have a first view of the costs of their design, Marketing have a first view of the works cost, sales can now start to test out the dealers who will be selling the product, so that marketing and sales together can decide the selling price that can be obtained in the various markets and finance and accounts can start to assess desirable profit margins, cost recovery etc.

While this process is on-going, design engineering will be refining their design, and will be issuing engineering changes, the revised costs of which must be incorporated in the Red Book, and estimating will be querying the costs that you have provided when they do not agree with the quote you provided.

It is during this period that you can be very effective in discussing with the suppliers ways in which costs could be reduced, researching new suppliers, and researching alternative suppliers to the approved sources recommended by design engineering. This requires you to establish a close contact with the designers to ensure you understand their requirements.

At a certain point in the cycle a decision is made to release the Sandblaster for production. The lead times purchasing have provided have determined the Job 1 date, and it has been decided that the cost of the materials to be bought-out must not exceed a specified bottom line figure.

Thus cost control can be exerted at item cost, unit cost, model cost levels.

Estimating will produce targets based on best production engineering practice which if attained will ensure that the bottom-line cost for the Sandblaster will hit the necessary cost target.

As each full release lands on your desk from design engineering, if it's a key item you request an estimate from the estimator to use as an aid to negotiation – but there's a rock in every snowball – because you must achieve the target!

This means that the entire enquiry process must be started again, and cost reduction exercises established quickly.

Buying against estimate

This is a period where you will be working at very high pressure and all your skills are put to use.

Your enquiry must now not only include the information that was included in the preliminary quotation, but also establish delivery frequency, type of packing, if to be delivered in stillages, the size of stillages (so that material handling are forewarned) ownership of stillages etc. It is assumed that all the suppliers you are using are quality assured, if not they must be quality assured before you can place the order.

On receiving the quotes, a quotation analysis (Table 10.2) has to be prepared and a preliminary selection made which is then compared to the target.

Table 10.2 Quotation analysis: enquiry 500/day for 12 months rising to 1000/day thereafter

Supplier	Unit price	Tool cost	1st year	2nd year
Brown	£16/£14	£20 000	£1.92m	£3.36m
Grey	£15.34/£13	£25 000	£1.84m	£3.12m
White	£15/£14	£28 000	£1.8m	£3.36m

The target has been presented as Job 1 objective £14.00 target £13.00.

The tool cost will be paid (normally) when samples have been approved, off-production tooling. The estimator has stated that the tool cost to support his estimate of unit cost, a tool cost of £25 000, would be reasonable.

The estimate starts with the cost of the raw material, less scrap and waste, and then envisages the creation of the item taking place over 23 operations. Each of the operations is accredited with a certain number of minutes to complete the operation. It takes account of the following.

During the first year there will be a penalty to be paid by the supplier, in an increased overhead to labour ratio; material costs will be higher due to the supplier's not having the ability to buy raw materials at the highest volumes until the following year. (Thus the launch price is targeted (Job 1) at £14 and at a rate of 1000/day the target is £13.)

The cost of a labour minute is normally expressed as the cost of a minute of operators' earnings multiplied by say 180% to account for the overhead content; this is applied to the minutes for each operation. This total is then increased by say 10% for profit and transport and packing.

It will be seen that the quotation analysis shows Grey as the most competitive.

An 'open-book' negotiation

The sales director of Grey is very interested when you tell him that he is under consideration as the supplier for this item. He expresses his willingness to discuss their planned operations sheets with you and your estimator. He also volunteers the fact that if you are able to demonstrate that your target (at this stage you have not disclosed what it is) is achievable he will be willing to consider your proposals.

The psychology of this type of negotiation is based on several premises:

1. an investigation on material cost, minutes of operations, overhead allocations, to assess suppliers' processes of manufacture and costing method;
2. to suggest to the potential suppliers ways in which costs can be reduced;
3. for the supplier to suggest ways in which costs could be reduced by the relaxation of tolerances and design changes etc.
4. to test the unreliability of the supplier's estimate.

(The supplier's estimator has a lot of problems which tend to make the quote unreliable.)

The sales estimator's dilemma

The estimator has to produce several quotes daily. He/she is responding to enquiries which include drawings and specifications, volumes, lead-times, and other requirements, from different customers who present their information in different ways. The problems he/she has include:

1. if the estimator quotes too high the company loses the business;
2. if the estimator quotes too low, they will get the business – but they could end up going broke trying to supply at the quoted price;
3. the supplier's plant has only a finite capacity. What happens if three buyers accept the quotes, and all three involve the use of the only Bloggs 900 machine? This means that inadvertently he's oversold the capacity of this machine. Nobody wants to turn business away; can other less efficient machines be used or must another Bloggs 900 be acquired?

So to avoid these problems a nervous estimator tends to quote high! There are few estimators who aren't so afflicted; so most quotes have a degree of 'fat' in them!

'Yes,' you may say, 'but the quotes I receive are always signed by the sales manager or the sales director – so they must have checked them out before they were sent out.' These are busy men – and while they may spot an error in the estimate if it's more than say 10% – nobody buys a dog and barks himself. So when you are reading a quote it's actually a reflection of all the estimator's doubts and fears! Knowing this the world-class buyer **always** challenges the lowest quote!

At the supplier's works

In order to produce your quote the supplier's estimator envisaged a method to produce your product, and from this calculated the minutes of operation required at each machine, then worked backwards to decide what raw materials would be required.

He/she would establish the costs of the raw materials, then apply a labour and overhead cost to the cycle times of the machines employed. Profit, packaging and transport costs are added and a selling price is arrived at.

So the first step in the negotiations is to compare the machines and their cycle times in the two estimates and identify the points of agreement and disagreement.

A section of your estimate is shown in Table 10.3.

Table 10.3 Estimated comparison of machine cycle times

Operation	Action	Cycle time
Operation 10	Cut ½" bar to length	2 minutes
Operation 11	Machine ends	3 minutes
Operation 12	Gear cut both ends	3 minutes
Operation 13	Mill centre section of shaft	2 minutes
Operation 14	Transport to heat treatment	2 minutes

The cycle times of the machines will be compared to the supplier's operation sheets, and in some cases your estimator has proved to be too keen, and in others the ops sheets may be too slack, so gradually a modified operation sheet will emerge.

The next step is to look at the operator manning of the machines. The significance of this step is due to the costing process which is employed. Assuming that a typical operator earns £8.00 per hour a computation to account for overhead is applied to the hourly rate. Typically the supplier's accountants state that overhead recovery should be, say, 180% of labour hours.

The cost hour becomes (£8.00 + £14.40) = £22.40 which becomes a minute's cost of £37.3p per minute.

Overheads applied to labour minutes

The operations 10–14 total 12 minutes, so that the cost of these operations will be 12 × 37.3p = £4.47 if manned by one operator only.

While the two estimators are comparing estimates you go to see the supplier's buyer. In discussion with the buyer you discover that he gave the estimator an estimate only. When he learns that you can give long-term schedules and that you can recommend a better supplier than the one he is using you discover that the price of the material can be reduced by 5%.

There is another area to investigate, the justification the accountants use to set 180% as the overhead recovery percentage. The list they present shows:

Rent	Rates	Utilities
NHI	Pensions	Staff salaries
Canteen	Consumables	Directors' fees
Indirects	Phones	Advertising
R&D	Transport	Miscellaneous

This will total the sum that they spread over the labour minutes in order to recover their costs. For simplicity, no matter who the customer is, the overhead burden applied to labour minutes remains constant. (Some accountants do vary the overhead burden to the machine, so that their new Heinrich and Wilhelm, for which they paid £250 000 last year, this bears a much higher overhead than the bank of autos they've had for the last ten years.) It should also be noted that they spread their **research and development costs** over all customers. If they are only making to order as far as your requirements are concerned, then why should you pay for R&D which may be used to help your competitors?

(It will be worth using some time in the future – if not now.)

You and the estimator decide to take stock to see how your discussions are coming along (see Table 10.4).

Table 10.4

Cost category	500 daily volume	Reductions	Reason
Material	£5.00	£4.75	Sourcing
Labour 24 mins at £0.133p/min	£3.192	£3.059	1 minute eliminated
Overhead 24 mins at £0.24	£5.76	£5.52	
Sub total	£13.952	£13.329	
Profit	£1.39	£1.33	
Total	£15.34	£14.55	

An unwanted operation

There's still at least 55p to go, you think. Then your estimator says, 'The supplier was asking why we have this end micro-finished. It really isn't necessary, and we could save two minutes.' A quick telephone call to design gets their agreement and the final bottom line becomes:

Material	£4.75
Labour 21 mins at £0.133p/min	£2.793
Overhead 21 mins at £0.24	£5.04
Sub Total	£12.583
Profit	£1.258
Total	£13.84

You then ask for a meeting with the sales director, the buyer and the two estimators (yours and theirs) to present your findings. After the supplier has asked for an adjournment to discuss the matter with his people he calls you back in to the office to tell you that he is prepared to re-quote on the basis of your findings.

But no euphoria yet, please! You say, 'Thank you for that, but we need now to discuss the price at 1000 per day supply.'

The MD asks for another adjournment and when you are both called back into the office he puts the following note in front of you:

For 1000 per day our price will be as follows:

Material	£4.50
Labour 21 mins @0.133p/min	£2.793
Overhead 21 mins @0.16p/min	£3.78
Sub total	£11.073
Profit	£1.107
Total	£12.18

'You will note,' the MD said, 'that for the extra volume we imagine we can reduce our costs at today's prices for the higher material call-off by just under 5%, our overhead takes account of the fact that we only charge half the overhead for night shift activities that we do for day shift activities our labour costs remain unchanged.'

'I take it you will confirm this too in a revised quotation?'

'Yes,' he replied, 'and I shall also add the following clauses to my normal terms and conditions.' They are as follows:

A supplier's terms and conditions

1. From the date of this quotation, this price is valid for thirty days. If you have not placed the order within that time you must apply for a new quotation.
2. Assuming that the order is placed within the next 30 days the price will remain fixed for 12 months with the exception of raw materials. If the price of our steel is increased we will require a concomitant price increase within one month of our request.
3. Eleven months from placing the order if the necessity arises we will raise a request for a price increase. Settlement of our claim must be settled within one month.
4. Payment of invoices. Our terms are strictly 30 days nett.

'I think in view of the open book we have shown you in obtaining the price reductions you were seeking that in the future you should deal with us equally honourably. Therefore these terms and conditions will be given the force of law by our lawyers and, after we have requested you in writing by registered letter after normal discussions have not given us the satisfaction that we believe we are entitled to, we reserve the right to stop production of this item.

'You will appreciate that with an order of some two and a half million pounds commitments in material and labour will cause us to make heavy commitments and we have the right to demand fair treatment from you.

'I should add two points, firstly we are always prepared to negotiate with you on an open book basis, and, before I forget, we shall be buying the tools out so that you will be able to see all invoices.'

As you and the estimator drive back to the office, you say, 'Well, I think we met a good supplier today.'

'Yes,' the estimator agrees, 'he's being pretty tough with his terms and conditions though.'

'Apart from his insistence on thirty days nett, our terms and conditions are very close to what he wants – it's just up to me that we treat him fairly – that's all. But I'm going to write up a minute of what we discussed and send it off in the morning.'

'Good idea,' says the estimator, 'but there'll be smiles all round in product cost control when we tell them the prices we got today!'

The buyer's Black Book

In your discussions with Grey's accountants there was a question which arose with regard to the way research and development was spread all over Grey's customers whether or not the customers required R&D support. In the company's case it was not. So why pay for it? It will often be the case that areas for future cost reduction exercises will appear when for one reason or another the time is not ripe to tackle them. Sometimes it may be a point that you forgot to raise during a negotiation, or something that only struck you afterwards. Or as in this case, a question as regards Grey's allocation of overhead. (This should go into your Black Book – which is a personal aide memoire.) Also there was another entry in the overhead which deserves further study; it was the heading 'Miscellaneous' This also requires looking at in the future.

The world-class buyer always has a Black Book!

The open book negotiation is clearly the most effective form of obtaining the lowest ultimate cost, since it allows the buyer to 'manage' his/her supplier **but** it does not remove the need to be vigilant in negotiation. Very often the buyer ends up negotiating with the supplier's accountants, rather than the supplier's engineers and sales staff.

Negotiation – a form of siege warfare

Because lowest ultimate cost is an ever-moving target the buyer has to stay consistently on the alert for price/cost improvement. But for the same reason the supplier is doing the same thing. The supplier will often conceal his cost improvements.

Two very typical ways are to improve manufacturing methods, reducing staffing levels by attrition; and increasing overheads, by creative accounting. It's not unknown for accountants to keep two sets of books. One for the customers and another for all other purposes.

Suppliers rely on the buyer not carrying out cost investigations, or challenging them with competition.

The sales director of Grey gave you a clear signal that he was likely to ask for a price increase next year. He knows, as you do, that he has got a good long-term contract, by which he can improve his earnings, by proving the need for an extra 2% price improvement here and another 1% there, relying on your inability to uncover the cost reduction schemes he has introduced without your knowledge.

At present you know his operations and you know his material costs, and you know the overhead burden he applies; it is therefore possible to set up a forecast on his likely actions in 12 months.

A forecast

For the first 12 months the usage will be 500 per day for 240 days at £13.84 = £1 660 800.

Including profit, the material, labour and overhead split is:

Material	37.75%
Labour	22.17%
Overhead	40.06%

Your reading will indicate to you in which month the price of material is likely to be increased. You will know in which month Grey reviews the earnings of his workers, and you can assess the likely price movements and timing of the overhead items the accountants showed you on your discussion with them.

If you have forecast that during the next 12 months:

Material will increase by 3%
Labour will increase by 2%
Overhead will increase by 1.5%
Then Grey will ask for   (3% of 37.75% of £1 660 800) = £18 808.
                                          (2% of 22.17% of £1 660 800) = £7363.
                                          (1.5% of 40.06% of £1 660 800) = £9,964.8.

Giving a total of £36 135.8 or 2.1%

If in 12 months' time the supplier was to request a price increase (which you in fairness would agree) to restore his profit situation Grey should be awarded an increase of 2.1%.

But having forecast what action the supplier is likely to take it is now your responsibility to see how to, at least, offset the price increases he is likely to ask for, which on the face of it appear just.

Savings planning

The tools listed under the heading of **The new learning** at the beginning of this chapter included value analysis, value engineering, substitution of materials, rationalization, make v. buy, competitiveness/competition and contractual.

Each one of these methods can be used in order to offset potential price increases and in fact to maintain a constant policy of cost reduction.

Use of value analysis

In Chapter 4 the decision to reduce the number of bolts used in certain assemblies resulted in the designer having to examine the necessity of having so many different bolts in use. While this was treated as a rationalization exercise it was a value analysis exercise too, as the designer had to ask him/herself, 'Is this part truly needed?'

The fundamental question is, 'This item fulfils a specific purpose, is there anything incorporated into the design which does not assist in the function or can be achieved more simply?'

In this case, should you decide to go for a VA cost reduction exercise you need to form a committee with the following representation.

The company

The designer
The estimator
Buyer

The supplier

Manufacturing manager
Estimator
Sales manager

Normally the company buyer should take the chair and set the agenda. It may well be that the supplier will say, 'This exercise including making experimental models and tying up members of my staff suggests that you will make profit out of this, and because of our contribution we should be allowed to keep half of the saving that we jointly achieve.'

Since your aim is to get to the lowest ultimate cost then this can be conceded with safeguards including putting a term (say a year) in which the supplier can enjoy this extra profit contribution.

The supplier, however, should be aware of the fact that he is under threat from competition and if VA doesn't have the desired result – then he could lose the business.

Value analysis can often be combined with value administration. This takes a wider view of the supplier's operations from two points of view, many of which the buyer can show will help the supplier improve profitability with their other customers.

Use of value analysis combined with value administration

It will be remembered that the operations sheet gave ops 10–14 a 12-minute cycle which at 37.3p per minute cost £4.47p.

It is possible that by machining the shafts at two at a time instead of the planned one at a time to halve the cost of ops 10–14, the resulting saving paying for the extra tooling required. Once the supplier has recovered the cost of the extra tooling by you paying an unchanged price, the cost reduction can be implemented and a POA issued at the new price.

Another aspect of value administration is in an objective study of the supplier's organization. This can cover all or part of the supplier's organization and methods aimed at improving productivity. The benefit to the supplier is that if you are able to show that they can produce your product more economically they have the opportunity to increase their profit with their other customers although the reductions which they are able to make with your guidance reduce your prices. The forum is the same with the exception that the company team is supplemented with a production/planning engineer.

Value engineering

If after a couple of years a new product is being considered, and Grey have now arrived at such a peak of efficiency that they outstrip their competition, then their team can be invited to work with the company's designer to design a product which can be manufactured most simply – always provided Grey are prepared to negotiate 'open book'.

Make v. buy

There are very few companies who do not recognize that their skills are concentrated in a few areas of expertise which are usually known as their 'core skills'. Occasionally they become drawn into activities which are not where they see their expertise. An example is where a core item is required to be painted before shipment. They are then faced with either shipping the item to a painter, or setting up their own facility. The decision will be made on a cost benefit study – but despite the fact that their core business is not in painting they now have to dilute management skills, capital, and other concerns which, had they stayed out of painting, they would not have had to do.

The **make v. buy** decision will often work in the opposite way too where work which is **core business** gets sourced outside due to the buyer's not really being aware of what his/her company's skills actually are.

As a general rule if the item to be bought has features which suggest that it could be made-in then in addition to enquiring on the outside the buyer should place an enquiry with the planning and production engineers. The benefits to the company are:

1. no profit to be paid to the supplier;
2. extra work passing across the company's machines reduces the overhead burden on **all** the products passing over those machines;
3. greater productivity by all staff and labour involved provided no extra heads have to be employed;
4. even if extra equipment has to be bought provided it is still in the core business sector it may still be beneficial to make-in.

Similarly there may be parts currently made-in which could be purchased less expensively from a supplier.

However, if for example there are ten different items made on a production line it is worse than useless to put out one item only – even if this produces a unit cost saving. Because it would still have been contributing to the general overhead, and by moving it out, the other nine items bear a heavier overhead, and company profit is reduced. In a case where an item is uncompetitive when made-in the enquiry placed with the potential suppliers must include **all** the items produced on that line. The question then to be solved in the make v. buy study is: should the whole production line's output be bought-out?

All the foregoing techniques can be deployed as offsets to the forecast of the supplier's next prospective price increase. During the 12 months after you have placed the order with Grey you must plan how you are going to continue the price control you've started.

Some buyers will say, 'I write a contract which is tied to an index such as BEAMA or a specific part of the National Digest of Statistics, or one of the other commonly used formulae.' The weakness is that a formula gives the supplier a right to demand a price increase annually. Any buyer who gives their supplier a key to the company safe with instructions to help themselves (according to a formula) is just a rubber stamp!

Controlling the supplier

In the 'siege warfare' of production buying there is one surefire way of challenging a supplier's projected price increase. You have forecast that the supplier will want to claim a 2.1% increase in 12 months. The suppliers that you enquired from before were not as good as Grey, so now is the time to revisit *Kelly's*, *Kompass*, the BSI's *Buyer's Guide*, etc. but also to start looking at foreign sourcing. Many embassies produce booklets, or even directories via their trade delegations which will give you an excellent guide to the potential suppliers in their countries. So, by the time Grey writes or calls requesting a price increase you can tell him that at his **present** price he is uncompetitive and explain that you cannot afford to buy at an uncompetitive price.

While in this chapter we have been concentrating on price there are other aspects which carry equal weight and have to be driven and controlled just as closely.

The other areas are quality, delivery, quantity, flexibility. The buyer has a right to demand zero quality defects, zero late (or early) deliveries, quantity as scheduled and appropriate supplier reaction to changes in call-off.

The contract with Grey would be based on the blanket order/schedule principle. The schedule would be structured on a stockholding which would be the minimum safe holding considering the frequency of deliveries. As an example, because the value of a day's inventory is £13.48 × 500 = £6740 the stock day's value becomes an important consideration, and consideration should be given to a just-in-time delivery cycle. A cost benefit study which balances the borrowing cost of a stock day versus the cost of delivery of a stock day provides one leg of the equation, for example:

borrowing cost for one day is £200.

And if a further three stock days could be delivered for £200 due to the size of the vehicle JIT is not a particularly cash attractive option. However as Grey are going to be manufacturing every day, two days' stock held and topped up daily would appear to be the most attractive option. This means that if the daily delivery is made in the morning the stock is three days and the stock is down to two days by the time the next delivery is made. Customarily an agreement on this delivery cycle would be part of the contract and from this the number of stillages required are computed, and the company and the supplier share the cost of the stillages.

Satisfaction criteria

The supplier then has only to maintain his deliveries to schedule in order to satisfy a zero faults record with regard to delivery and quantity. But if he becomes irregular in either aspect it could threaten your continuity of production. In your contract with Grey you would have to establish performance criteria which would constitute unsatisfactory performance, such as eight hours late on a daily delivery or more than 10% short on a single delivery.

Your clause here would read, 'should either deliveries be more than eight hours late or contain less than 90% of a full stillage Grey will be warned to improve. Should this situation then fail to be eradicated the company may at its discretion resource.'

Production stoppages due either to quality problems or stockout problems might also bear a consequential loss clause.

Your clause for percentage quality problems would be, 'In the event of Grey's failure to provide 100% quality in any delivery Grey will be warned that further failures may provoke the company at its discretion to resource.'

Records must be maintained by quality control and progress as to Grey's performance in both areas and any failure reported to you for action.

It may well be that at times you will be required to obtain special orders which require Grey to produce more than have been officially scheduled. A good supplier will bend every effort to ensure that the extra quantity is provided quickly, a bad one won't!

So in addition to your price records you should have records by individual batch delivery of quantity and quality and delinquencies if and when they occurred. Coupled with your notes on flexibility you have the equipment to assess your supplier's performance objectively.

These statistics will also help you to resist Grey's request for a price increase, if all the other exercises discussed in this chapter come to naught. But all the exercises in this chapter are cost-reduction exercises which the world-class buyer employs to ensure that his buying prices go **down** every year, and just resisting a price increase is the bare minimum.

MEMORY JOGGERS

45 **Finding world-class suppliers**
- Read a good cross section of business journals
- Contact embassies and high commissions
- Interview representatives of existing and potential suppliers
- Visit trade exhibitions

REMEMBER – it is the buyer's job to find new sources of supply who can meet world-class standards.

46 **Tooling costs**
- Check how the supplier arrived at the price
- Is it full or part cost?
- Check the life of the tool, ideally expressed in quantity
- Get competitive quotations for tooling

REMEMBER – the expenditure on tooling is a critical on-going cost and it must be controlled and negotiated just like everything else.

47 **Forecasting skills**
- Get the economic city pages in the press
- Seek help from financial colleagues
- Check labour and material cost movements
- Read what the contract says about price movements

REMEMBER – the ability to forecast possible movements in any aspect of cost is a tremendous help with forward planning of selling prices.

48 **Open book negotiations**
- Use open book to eliminate unnecessary cost
- Permits the seller to make a constructive input
- It may uncover estimating errors
- Imposes an ethical code upon the buyer

REMEMBER – this is a new style of managing a supplier's costs and many are not ready for this dialogue.

11 INCREASING THE BUYER'S EFFECTIVENESS IN SOURCE SELECTION

This chapter gives various techniques for improving the buyer's effectiveness in selecting sources. Time savers are introduced together with an explanation of the function and use of the information contained in the Tooling Questionnaire and the Commercial Audit Questionnaire. The development of approved sources is also outlined.

The negotiations and discussions with Grey, in the last chapter had caused a lot of time to be spent, which in a busy period was hard to find. The fact that Grey was an established supplier to the company reduced the time taken to do the task.

When researching suppliers, the major criteria in source selection is often price – but in fact only one element of a successful purchase is price, because you only get what you pay for. What you need to know is what are you getting for your money! As has been stressed many times in previous chapters the buyer's aim must be lowest ultimate cost, part of which depends on how effectively use is made of the working hours available. If you can conduct two effective negotiations where formerly you only conducted one, then you have doubled your effectiveness.

Asking the right questions

The world-class buyer asks the right questions, and listens carefully to the answers. It is in this part of the process that you establish precisely what other contributions the supplier is offering, which aside from price, offer the best value for money, in other words – the lowest ultimate cost. There is a lot of time that can be saved here.

In Chapter 1, discussing the tools of the trade, the enquiry was discussed together with the importance of creating a situation where each potential supplier was given the same information against which to quote. In return the buyer received a price, a tool cost, and a lead time, and on this information made a preliminary sourcing decision. Many questions had to be answered later, and some no doubt would be forgotten in the heat of the moment, only to raise their ugly heads at a later and more inappropriate time.

There are a considerable number of refinements which can be introduced at the enquiry stage which save time later and at the same time save you from driving 'full bore' up a cul de sac.

1. Always ask for a plant list. This is a list of the capital equipment owned by the supplier, and is a powerful mechanism in source selection.
2. Always ask for a copy of the supplier's latest annual report.

By a few simple checks you can determine their profit margin before tax, and compared to the previous year whether they are doing better or worse, whether they are recruiting or shedding staff and so on. Take care, though, because the information is somewhat dated.

Of course these annual reports are usually 'prettied up' versions of reality but with practice you will learn to read between the lines.

There is then a list of questions which you need to put to the supplier to determine whether they have actually understood your enquiry (remember Grey's estimator?) and are actually offering you what you want.

You are about to raise an enquiry for 2000 per day for a plastic moulding you judge should cost around 0.75p ea. (The pay-back period is three 240-day years.)

Clearly the suppliers will quote for a moulding tool cost which will have to be designed and made. The complexity of the tool will determine the lead time. The same principle applies, be it a casting, pressing, forging, machined item, a sintered item, assembly, packing materials or whatever. Probably the only exceptions being catalogue items or proprietary items.

It is axiomatic that the quality of the tooling dictates the quality of the finished product. The two biggest threats to continuity of production are tooling irregularities, or where the capital machine on which the tools are designed to run breaks down, the supplier does not have a second machine suitable to accommodate the tooling.

Tooling considerations

If the supplier buys this tooling from a specialist toolmaker the repair of tooling has normally to be carried out by the specialist. Any problems in material feeds, injection cycles, cutting speeds, forming problems (which are almost bound to happen from time to time) necessitate the tools being taken out of production and the supplier's buyer having to get the repair done. Of necessity an arm's length problem may have the tooling unavailable for several days.

Many suppliers have their own toolmakers, equipped with their own tool room, who are company employees. This arrangement normally provides for faster attention in the event of tooling difficulties.

In either case of course, the tooling is manufactured to run on a specific type of capital machine but in the latter case the in-house toolmakers will be more familiar with the machine/s in use and will almost certainly reduce the likelihood of problems.

There is also a pricing question. The probability is that the bought-out tooling will be more expensive than the made-in tooling.

Against this there is a possibility that the company that make its own tools will be less innovative than the specialist with a much wider experience base.

Experienced buyers are sharply divided here, some buyers will not buy from suppliers who buy their tools out.

Coupled with the requirement to know who will manufacture the tooling there are two other aspects the buyer needs to explore.

The enquiry is for a supply of 2000 plastic items per day. A determining factor in the unit price is the number of impressions in the moulding tool. If the tool is a four impression tool the unit cost will be possibly twice the price of an eight cavity mould's product but the cost of the eight impression tool will be more than twice that of the four impression tool. The product however will be produced in half the time.

Tooling to produce multiples is usual in pressings, castings, mouldings, machining, etc. It goes without saying that the higher the number of multiples produced at one 'hit', the higher the tool cost. The important point here is that the faster the cycle time – the lower the unit cost, and the greater the supply security.

The second aspect that the buyer needs to know is that quite frequently – and always at the wrong time – capital machines breakdown. Many suppliers will claim that they practice 'planned maintenance' so that wearing parts, such as bearings, electrical parts etc. are replaced before they wear out – and that machines never break down. However many maintenance engineers will say, 'We wait until a machine breaks down, then we plan how to maintain it!' The problem is that with bearings on perhaps a 16 week delivery you could run out of material before the replacements arrive – and that does the buyer no good at all.

If, in the event of a machine breakdown, the tooling can be immediately placed on another machine of a compatible type then production continuity is not affected.

Sadly, some suppliers will have a range of equipment which is not compatible. Suppliers tend to build up their stock of capital equipment over many years and in certain cases each machine has been purchased to fulfil a different purpose and to transfer tooling from Machine A to Machine B means extensive modification to the tooling which can take as long, and cost as much, as acquiring new tooling.

Not very long ago the writer was visiting a supplier with an impressive machine tool shop full of numerically controlled machines and the manufacturing manager took him to one corner of the plant where a machine the writer had never seen before was standing.

'How old do you think that is?'

The writer confessed ignorance.

'It's a vertical borer that's been in constant operation since 1909 – and it's still the most effective tool we've got for some operations – sadly the company that made it went out of business forty years ago, so when it eventually packs up we'll have to find a different way to do that job.'

The writer felt he was having his leg pulled, but as he watched an operator with a small stillage of work walked over to the nearly 90-year-old machine and began to set it up!

The writer wondered if the buyer, whoever he or she was, knew on what a slender thread the buyer's continuity of production rested.

This is perhaps an extreme example but it makes the point that when the supplier's estimator quoted, that machine's operation would have been the one included in the quote, and that you must know if there is an alternative machine capable of running your expensive tooling if there is a machine breakdown.

If the supplier does not have ready alternatives then to source from him or her is endangering your future supplies. Yet every time a buyer sources on price and lead time alone they either ignore the risk, or even worse, are ignorant of the danger.

Ten questions

Often buyers will claim they have no technical expertise, although every capital machine in use today, through boring, drilling, grinding, gear cutting, hobbing, shaving, pressing and casting, was invented between 1846 and 1896, and with their associated tooling determine the cost of the product. Use of the questionnaire shown in Figure 11.1 sent out with every enquiry will make sure you don't fall into the trap of ignorance.

In responding to the accompanying enquiry could you please respond to the following questions:

1. Please provide a brief description of the special tooling planned. Also please state if multiple or single unit tooling.

    . . . .

    . . . .

2. What machine/machines will the above special tooling be mounted on?

    . . . .

    . . . .

3. What is the hourly production rate planned?

    . . . .

    . . . .

4. Are there alternative machines that the special tooling can be mounted on, without modification of the special tooling?

    . . . .

    . . . .

Figure 11.1 Capacity Tooling Questionnaire

5. Does the supplier work a single or double shift?

    . . . .

    . . . .

6. What is the lead time for the acquisition of the special tooling?

    . . . .

    . . . .

6b. Will the special tooling be made in or bought out?

    . . . .

    . . . .

7. What is the lead time for the acquisition of the appropriate raw material?

    . . . .

    . . . .

8. What is the normal transport you will employ to deliver to this plant?

    . . . .

    . . . .

9. What is your preferred delivery frequency?   . . . .

10. What is the normal transit time from your plant to ours?

    . . . .

    . . . .

Figure 11.1 *continued*

Analysing the ten answers

When you get your quotes back accompanied by the Capacity Questionnaire you will naturally start by preparing a quotation analysis (see Table 11.1).

Table 11.1   Quotation analysis

Supplier	Unit cost	Tool cost	Lead time	Raw material acquisition
Jig	0.75p	£50 000	2 months	3 months
King	0.76p	£35 600	3 months	2 months
Tare	0.73p	£78 800	3 months	2 months

The responses from the three suppliers are given in Table 11.2.

Table 11.2   Response to Capacity Questionnaire

Question	Jig	King	Tare
1	4 Imp	4 Imp	6 Imp
2	Bloggs 250	Jones 300	Bloggs 1000
3	160/hr	200/hr	300/hr
4	Yes	Yes	No
5	Double shift	Double shift	Single shift
6	2 months	3 months	3 months
6b	Made in	Made in	Bought out
7	3 months	2 months	2 months
8	Road	Road	Rail
9	Weekly	Daily	Weekly
10	2 days	1 day	1 day

Based on a three-year pay-back basis **there is no difference between the price, including tool cost, between the three suppliers**. Tare has produced the most attractive unit cost, but the tooling investment is much higher than the other two. The tooling is bought-out and there is no alternative machine should the Bloggs 1000 break down. The supplier expresses a preference for weekly delivery by rail.

If the decision to source had been based solely on the Quotation Analysis Tare might well have been the selected source, but supply security is also marginal since over an eight-hour day the supplier can produce 2400 so that his maximum surplus produceable is 400 which may or may not be sufficient to cover unscheduled call-offs.

Both Jig and King operate a night shift providing a maximum daily output of 2560 and 3200 respectively. Both suppliers make their own tools, and have alternative machines that can be used, so that both offer better supply security than Tare.

Final assessment

While the buyer is able to determine the delivery method and frequency required, the delivery preference indicates the price for transport that was included in the price. Varying the transport method and frequency will alter the transport cost. It should also be noted that the material delivery quoted by all three suppliers varies from 2–3 months. This is an indication of the coverage the supplier will need to have in the schedules to ensure that there is forward authority to procure the raw material.

It will be seen that although King presents the highest unit cost, in every other respect including tooling investment, King is the most attractive source. The buyer should therefore invite King to look again at the unit price, and the tool cost. The probability will be a willingness to modify the price, which will make the pay-back over three years the most attractive.

The questionnaire has saved a great deal of post-quotation discussion, and helped to avoid selecting a source which would not be the most suitable. It also helps the buyer to select 'horses for courses' when next the buyer is looking for another similar component.

The commercial assessment

In the course of your working month, part of your time should be spent in supplier visits. These can be for research purposes, or price discussions, or for other business reasons.

Buyers are often heard to say, 'I'm far too busy to go to see new suppliers, or go to exhibitions, or read technical journals!' Such buyers will never reach world class, because the successful buyer is always aware of competition, and recognizes that some suppliers are more successfully managed and led than others. Often it is the skill of the management team which makes the difference, in others their strength is in their design team, with others it is their manufacturing skills, or their financial controls. Sometimes one key person leaves, or dies and the company immediately starts to crumble. In order that you can assess what strengths your supplier has and be able to compare them with other suppliers it is necessary to quantify their skills. Whenever you visit a supplier, if you have not already completed a commercial assessment you should complete one. If it was done some time ago it should be updated, and without fail one should always be completed every time a new potential supplier is visited (see Figure 11.2).

1. Supplier name and address	Telephone Number Facsimile Telex
2. Company structure	Plc Privately owned etc.
3. Management structure and names	Chairperson Managing Director

Figure 11.2 The Commercial Audit

	Sales Director Engineering Director Purchasing Director
4. Number of factories and locations	Brief description
5. Associations with other companies	Ownership Sister companies
6. Founded	History
7. Factory: (a) area of plant (b) extension opportunity (c) structure (d) ownership, i.e. rented	
8. Condition of buildings	Brief description
9. Employees	Staff Hourly paid Production/non-production
10. Processes carried out: (a) state: capacities (b) obtain plant list (c) facilities	
11. Major customers > 2% of supplier's turnover	
12. Quality control approvals AQUAP. BS5750 etc.	
13. Wage review anniversaries	
14. Industrial relations history	
15. Financial status Annual report? Do they accept open book negotiation?	
16. Prepared to hold stock?	
17. Payment terms.	
18. Carriers. Own/other	
19. Toolmakers. Own/other	
20. Internal scheduling system	
21. Internal Purchasing resources	
General notes	

Figure 11.2 *continued*

Understanding the 21 answers

The interpretation of the commercial audit is partly comparative but it also gives important information upon which to make judgements. One company producing the same product as a competitor may present more attractive features than another, perhaps in the way they manage quality and after sales service. The answers to your questions also help to establish that the company you are surveying meets certain vital criteria in order to become a supplier to you.

1. The supplier's address

Clearly location of the supplier geographically presents transport questions which need to be thought about. In certain parts of the world, and one of the writers has twice had this experience, factories (both potential suppliers) were built alongside major rivers. In the monsoon period the factory was flooded annually for several weeks, to the extent that the factories were out of commission for part of the year. Reasons for actually considering the supplier's address may not be as dramatic as that, but even in the UK there are areas where at certain times of the year supply can be interrupted due to bad weather so that consideration has to be given to increasing the stockholding at certain times of the year should you decide to use this supplier.

2. Company structure

This question links with numbers 3 and 5. The management of any business is an affair of dominant and recessive personalities which blend to make a corporate personality which is unique. The type of 'corporate personality' varies too with the size of company. With the smallest type of company you are likely to deal with the managing director who has often built the company up. These MDs are often autocrats. The people who work for such an MD are little more than puppets who do not dare argue with the boss. All decisions flow from the MD so if you source with this company and you later have a difference with the boss, there is no court of appeal.

In a second-generation, privately owned company, the MD's son – who seems invariably to be called by the rest of the company, 'Mr John', to distinguish him from the founder – is now the MD, and his father is now the chairman.

In such a company 'the family' will still make all the decisions. Such family-run businesses will sometimes look on the professional buyer as little better than a 'shyster', should the buyer suggest open book negotiations. They are obviously not all like that – but be warned!

Once the plc reaches a reasonable size it can recruit good professionals as heads of the main disciplines, and here you should make sure that you can meet at least the four personalities listed on the commercial audit form. The impression you should hope to get is that of a team of keen people who are willing to work with their customers and have ability. If the team seems to be a group of mediocrities – well again you have been warned!

Where more than one site is managed from a central location you must find out how the activities of the various sites are co-ordinated. This is far from idle curiosity because your material, should you source with them, will be made at a different site than the one your orders and instructions go to. This means that there is another layer of players you must get to assess.

If the board members you are dealing with are a local board then you must establish what degree of local autonomy they have. As an example of where the local board may not have enough local autonomy, one of the writers had on one occasion the need to increase production of a component he was buying by a factor of ten. The local board were most enthusiastic and quickly came up with prices, timings and improved manufacturing processes. But they needed some expensive new capital equipment. To obtain approval to spend the money they had to raise a capital approval request to their main board who refused to make the cash available because they were over-extended due to a sister company in an entirely different line of business being in difficulties.

This means that when you get to **question 5** you establish how their company structure relates to the sister companies, i.e. if one goes down, do they all go down?

Questions 7 and 8 are self-explanatory.

Question 9

The ratio of staff to hourly paid is important to know from two points of view. Firstly, staff costs are applied to overhead, whilst hourly paid costs go to labour, and this is useful information in negotiations. Secondly, ratios vary from one industry to another, but if for example staff was in the ratio of say 3:1 this would indicate they were not a lean mean company.

Question 10

The core business processes are easily established and with a plant list you can quickly gain a good general picture. What is often more interesting are their facilities which may make them particularly attractive to you.

A company with an identifiable core range of activities is a likely supplier to you since they have specialized in achieving excellence in certain manufacturing processes, but sometimes their very specialization limits their use to you. For example, you may require a component which needs heat treatment, then a welding operation, finally some sections painted. If your chosen supplier has to obtain the welding, heat-treatment and painting from sub-contractors the material has to pass through the hands of suppliers that are unknown to you, and although the original supplier accepts responsibility for their work pipeline problems are never far away and so your supply line is vulnerable. So, learning the facilities they have which are ancillary to their core business is useful.

Question 11

Major customers representing greater than 2% of the supplier's business. It is vital that you know the range of customers and the spread of business that the supplier has with them. It is useful at this point to consider for a moment the ideal sourcing policy that a buyer should pursue. In the ideal world the business that you have with a supplier should be sufficiently large to ensure that you are a most important customer to the supplier but not in a position whereby your amount of business is of such a size that you are in the supplier's hands, and open to coercion only a little short of blackmail.

There are subsidiary considerations too, for example, if you have placed so much business with the supplier that if you were to take the work away, the supplier would be bankrupted; this, apart from being bad for supplier relations, gets you a very bad press! Also this knowledge inhibits your buying freedom. On the other hand placing too little business with any supplier to command the attention you require causes you to fritter away your purchasing power in penny packets which is definitely not world-class buying.

As if these considerations are not enough there is the question of who are the suppliers' other customers? Imagine that their major customer is your most dangerous business rival. Is it a good idea to place work with them? You could be vulnerable to the rival putting pressure on your supplier to stop your supplies. In previous chapters there have been references to policy aspects of purchasing and in the field of the share of a supplier's turnover you allow to be your work there is a great need for a policy statement.

A sourcing policy

A customer is significant if they represent more than 2% of the supplier's turnover, since they will certainly be in the top 50 customers. A supplier could probably survive if they lost up to 30% of their business overnight, but certainly would fail if the loss of business exceeded this by much. Therefore the extremes are set ideally being more than 2% but less than 30% of the supplier's turnover.

Between these two extremes the higher the figure you can award the supplier the more your leverage increases and the more effective the use of your buying power. Equally, the supplier finds it more convenient to deal with a smaller number of customers. The supplier's marketing problem then changes to diversification. If you are in, say, the automotive industry which is subject to significant market swings they will seek to find a foothold say in pharmaceuticals, or defence or some other business sector, which also helps you in not having to share capacity with a rival, and also allows the supplier a more stable environment.

Therefore the answer to question 11 hits directly at your policy sourcing intentions. Of course, the supplier may not want to be too dependent on your work because of a fear of too great an exposure to one customer. But this aspect of the supplier's marketing and selling policy will emerge in your discussions.

Question 12

Each of the quality approvals listed shows that the supplier commits to provide material which conforms in all respects to the customer's quality requirements. You should ask to see the relevant documentation. If they do not hold any of these certificates then you should ask the supplier if they are prepared to accept a quality assurance study from your company, which if they do not gain outright approval means that you cannot place business with them until such time as they do gain your quality approval. Arising from the quality assurance discussion they have to be appraised of your policy on consequential loss, and/or liquidated damages.

Supplier responsibility

Very simply, if they warrant that the material will be satisfactory on receipt at your works, and will survive the warranty period when the material is in service, then they must compensate you and hold you free from any cost resulting from bad quality to the extent of fighting law suits and paying fines.

In this regard, if the supplier has made an item to your drawing and your design, and this fails in service the supplier is not liable. If the item is a fully proprietary item the whole cost associated with the liability should be the supplier's, and in such case you must ensure that your contract is specific on this point.

While on the subject of supplier responsibility the position on product liability has to be discussed. This concept originated in the USA and has spread into Europe, though in a more reasonable form. Basically the American definition of product liability is that if a product is so designed that it can be misoperated, no matter that the handbook says, 'Do not turn handle B when Valve A is in the off position', then the manufacturer is held liable in law for damages for any loss or damage resulting from the misoperation. Further if a second accident occurs then in the second case the plaintiff will also be awarded punitive damages which are designed to punish the manufacturer for not rectifying the fault on production, that is with customers in the field. It becomes most important that now all possible steps are made to ensure that suppliers carry their own insurance against product liability claims. It is the buyer's responsibility that all proprietary items where the supplier is selling a 'black box' are covered against such eventualities.

Question 13: Wage review anniversaries

The purpose of this question is twofold:

(a)   to establish the timing of potential price increase requests;
(b)   to provide an indication as to when a strike over wage bargaining might arise.

Question 14: Industrial relations history

Strikes and the duration of past industrial relations problems are a useful guide to likely future performance. A bad past record does not bode well for the future!

Question 15: Financial status

It has been stressed several times that you should always obtain a copy of each year's annual report. Apart from gaining a view of their profitability it is useful to compare one year with another to see if business is expanding or contracting, if new equipment is being purchased, and if labour is increasing or decreasing in numbers. All these factors provide you with information useful in negotiation.

In the last chapter a description was given of an open book negotiation with Grey. In earlier negotiations the yardstick of the material, labour and overhead costs were used to determine a fair price. Some suppliers will say that their price is fixed at the time of the quotation and they do not negotiate, no matter what. Unless you ask the question 'up front' you run the risk of not finding out until too late!

Question 16:   Prepared to hold stocks?

There are several reasons for needing to know this information early in the buying process. Firstly there is the economic batch (or bulk) quantity problem. You may be wanting a regular weekly supply of, say, 500 pieces when the supplier finds that for selfish purposes they need to make in batches of 5000. If you have to accept the whole batch in one delivery your inventory costs will rocket. So buying from this supplier may not be economic, unless they are prepared to hold the stock.

Secondly, there is the situation where the supplier can produce at 500 per week but at certain times and at short notice you will need urgent delivery of an extra 1000, but you don't want always to have to carry an extra 1000 in inventory. If the supplier is prepared to hold 1000 in stock at all times against this eventuality the problem is solved. Possibly storage space is a genuine limitation but you have space where they have not. In such a case the supplier may perhaps agree to supply a stock to be held at your works, or even a neutral warehouse to be held in bond for which you do not pay until you 'break bond'. Once bond is broken you pay immediately for the goods and the supplier replenishes the bond stock as part of the next production run.

Thirdly, there is the question of raw material stocks. It may be that the schedule you can give the supplier is two months firm, renewable monthly, but the raw material is on three months' delivery. So a solution has to be found for this.

You can give authority provided that you know the item you will order has a long life for the schedule to contain a tentative portion which is the authority for the supplier to acquire raw material on the understanding that the material is not converted to finished product unless schedule authority is given. If however the schedule authority is not given, then the raw material becomes your responsibility to pay for. Often this is not a problem as the raw material can often be sold back to the raw material supplier, used for something else or sold to another supplier. The supplier may say they are prepared to hold stock even without tentative schedule cover as he knows he can always dispose of it. It is very necessary that this stock arrangement is explored early on.

Question 17:   Payment terms

It is an important part of business operation that cashflow is always positive. This means that at any given time there is a positive balance of cash coming into the operation that is greater than that being paid out. In order to ensure positive cashflow the accounts will hold up due payments to suppliers so as to compensate for large sums which are having to be paid out. This is a piece of chicanery which is devised to keep borrowings down. Suppliers who have forecast that they will be paid for deliveries made in the past suddenly find themselves without the income they had forecast. If your accountants make a habit of this they are breaking the agreement you have made with the supplier on payment terms and not to put too fine a point on it, **swindling** the supplier. The result is that the supplier will react by not trying quite so hard to satisfy your supply requirements, then put you on 'stop' which means no deliveries will be made until the account is regularized. If the supplier is treated to this performance more than once or twice they react by demanding payment for each delivery on arrival at your works. If accounts can't or won't pay then you are looking urgently for another supplier.

Clearly you have to stay on top of the accountants to make sure your suppliers are being paid on time. There is a positive side to this however. If the supplier is prepared to accept payment at longer than 30 days nett, say at 60 or 90 days or in certain cases even longer then the company cashflow can be assisted.

This is because in the case of 90 days payment terms, in the first year of operation of the order you only pay for 9 months' materials in the first 12 months and this is a very effective way of supporting the company's cashflow legitimately. But in agreeing payment terms you are giving your **personal** word that the agreement will be honoured.

Your word is your bargain

In a world where some accountants lie by numbers, some marketeers can't spell truth and some engineers always blame others for their own blunders, there is one area in which a 'promise' is still honoured. If your supplier promises that a delivery will be made at a certain time the supplier will move heaven and earth to ensure that the delivery arrives on time. Any promise a good supplier makes will be kept at almost whatever the cost. The world-class buyer values very highly this attribute in a supplier and makes every effort to ensure that any promise given is equally kept. If you become known as a 'word-breaker' suppliers won't trust you and a buyer who is labelled untrustworthy won't reach world class.

Of course there will be a few occasions where through events beyond your control you find that you will be unable to keep your given word. You must then contact the person you gave your promise to, explain and apologize, but don't do that too often either – it will look suspiciously like just another ploy!

Question 18:   Carriers

This question is designed to establish who will be responsible for delivery of the goods to your specified destination. It may even be that the supplier wants you to collect the material from the supplier's plant. In which case, should you agree, his price must be ex-works and not delivered to your works as your terms and conditions state. If the supplier you are talking to is an overseas source then in addition to determining the actual method of transport you must also agree the Incoterms you will employ.

Question 19:   Toolmakers

As has been previously discussed it is very important to know if the supplier will make their own tools or buy them out.

Question 20:   The internal scheduling system

What you are looking for here is an efficient system which covers the following processes:

(a)   To whom do your orders/schedules/instructions/panic calls go to?
(b)   Who is responsible for ensuring that raw material is available?

(c)   How are the production areas instructed to make your requirements?
(d)   Who is responsible for progressing your requirements through the supplier's works.
(e)   Who is the normal contact?
(f)   Who is the normal contact's boss?

From these questions you should be able to decide if their systems are ones which can work with yours. If this supplier's system is unable to react to rapid change – because its rigid and hidebound and your buy fluctuates like mad – well, you have been warned!

Question 21:   Internal purchasing resources

You will remember that in the last chapter Grey's buyer told you he'd only done a rough estimate for the cost of the raw material, but then when you challenged him he was able to get a better price for the first year's quantity and the second year's bigger volume requirements. You will have your own opinion of his work – but one thing was obvious – he was a bit on the lazy side. Imagine if your product was stopped due to the need for a panic material – would you sleep well knowing that your company's livelihood was in his hands? Probably not. Most likely you would phone him to see how he was getting on and start progressing the panic yourself! You would if you were world class!

The supplier's buyers are an important part of your supply chain and you will meet some bright-eyed and bushy-tailed men and women buyers at your suppliers – but you will also meet those who are unqualified, inexperienced or just plain stupid. If they fall into the latter categories, then it tells you something about them but it's a good guide to the type of management of the organization you are surveying.

To carry out such an audit will take several hours to complete, sometimes by the time you've got half way, you will know that it's a waste of time to continue – so your general notes need only read, 'Audit discontinued, directors in conflict with each other!'

If on the other hand the supplier appears satisfactory to you then you have saved many hours of fruitless labour in the future banging out enquiries to suppliers in whom you have no confidence because you have found a good one!

Uses of the commercial audit

With some suppliers when you announce that you want to do a commercial audit they will say, 'Leave it with us, we'll fill it out and send it back to you!' The reader's own conclusions will suffice here without any comment from the writer.

Some buyers reading this will say, 'A commercial audit is all very well, but I don't have the time to audit my existing suppliers, leave alone potential sources!'

To which the reply must be, 'How much time do you waste raising enquiries to suppliers you don't know, placing orders on suppliers who don't have an internal scheduling system worthy of the name, chasing such suppliers till you are blue in the face? Certainly more time than half a day a week and in a year that would give you fifty sources surveyed of which half at least would be known, secure sources.'

Secure sources who meet all the audit criteria take the minimum time to administer.

Also because you have audited the supplier your ability to **manage** them has improved to the extent that you can then start to build up your own experience basis which stands you in good stead in internal meetings. Imagine if the production manager says to you, 'We need to treble our output of this product, which means that we must get the components you buy not only at three times the volume but painted and welded as well – and I need to know if it can be done!'

Your audit report will enable you to respond when it can be done (tool capacity report) material lead time, and approximate timing of increased delivery volumes. You also know if the supplier's facilities include welding and painting – now this is real world-class buying.

When you have finished an audit you will find that it falls into one of three categories:

1. a supplier that commercially you approve, and will place them on your enquiry list;
2. a supplier that you would put on your enquiry list if the supplier would improve certain aspects – these could be anything from any one of the 21 questions that you felt needed improving; you could also add in such a case that when the recommended improvements have been put in place, and you had verified them you would put them on your enquiry list;
3. suppliers who do not meet the standards that you require.

In each case you must inform the supplier, although there is no point in spending much time on the real washouts.

Approved sources

As you progressively audit your current and potential suppliers you will steadily establish a cadre of three or four suppliers in each commodity range. These suppliers are the ones that you place all your enquiries on for that range of commodities which means that every enquiry you place is going to a supplier in whom you have confidence that whichever one supplies the lowest quote will meet the high standards you have set. Normally, since you need to concentrate your 'spend' on a minimum number of sources, more than three or four maximum approved sources will tend to cause dispersion of your buying power. So if you find a better approved source as a result of later audits then you must eliminate the least satisfactory of the approved sources by competition.

The selection of the right sources has other benefits. The right sort of supplier once informed that he or she is an approved supplier wants to keep that relationship and will normally demonstrate this in a willingness to go the extra mile in order to satisfy your requirements.

The approved suppliers too will feel that they are an extension of your business, as indeed they are and will want to know how your business is going. This policy of approved sources often leads to the annual approved suppliers' meeting where management brief them on future company plans.

Thus you build up a business relationship with your suppliers based on the mutual profitability basis – but never confuse it with personal friendship. When you move on and someone else sits at the buyer's desk they will take on your mantle.

The buyer's attitude

All the advice in this chapter has been aimed at maximizing the use of time to increase the buyer's effectiveness in achieving the lowest ultimate cost. This requires the buyer to strike a personal note where he/she should:

- be empathetic to the supplier's needs;
- be tenacious in negotiation;
- be energetic in pursuing his/her objectives;
- be efficient in all dealings with suppliers;
- develop a firm personality so as to lead your colleagues and the suppliers to achieve the 'seven rights';
- always display integrity and where necessary courage.

MEMORY JOGGERS

49 **Issue a professional purchase enquiry**
- Supply accurate information
- Send the contractual terms and conditions of contract
- Ask for relevant information such as cost breakdowns
- Identify non-recurring costs, such as design and tooling

REMEMBER – The quality of your purchase enquiry will convince the seller that there is a competent buyer handling the enquiry and that is a help!

50 **Visiting suppliers**
- Do a commercial audit
- Do a quality audit
- Meet the key people and some of them will not be the directors!
- Have a look around the offices and factory

REMEMBER – the effective buyer will visit key suppliers on a regular basis and will plan for this activity – the truth is at the supplier's premises.

51 **Sourcing policy**
- Use only qualified suppliers
- Take risk of supply into account when making decisions
- Don't put all your eggs in one basket unless there is good reason
- Think about supplier rationalization programmes

REMEMBER – an effective sourcing policy lies at the heart of a buyer's strategy; the right balance of suppliers is essential.

52 **The ideal buyer**
- Has integrity and courage
- Deals with queries promptly and efficiently
- Is not a 'clock watcher'
- Believes in satisfying the client's needs

REMEMBER – a dedicated buyer stands out a mile with colleagues and commands respect from suppliers.

12 A SUPPLIER STUDY IN MAINLAND EUROPE

Based on an urgent need to resolve a vital question of supply strategy this chapter describes and explains a major negotiation and brings in to play the operational application of many of the tools and techniques introduced in earlier chapters: quotation analysis and cost benefit analysis, blanket order/scheduling, competition, open book negotiations, the Tooling Questionnaire and the Commercial Audit Questionnaire.

It is just after 6pm and you are thinking of going home when the internal phone rings; picking it up, almost against your will, you hear a voice say, 'Come and see me now, will you?'

It is the purchasing manager. You go along to his office – it is an invitation you can't refuse.

The message to Garcia

'Do you know the story of the message to Garcia?' he asks.

You shake your head, wishing you'd gone home five minutes earlier.

Well, it appears that in 1916 there was a revolution in Mexico, led by one Garcia. The Mexican Government requested help from the US Government to put down the Revolution, who obliged by sending a strong military force to Mexico. After some months it became obvious that the best that could be obtained was a stalemate, so the two governments decided to send a message to Garcia to set up a meeting to discuss some form of accommodation.

A Mexican cavalry colonel rode off into the hills carrying the message. The following day the colonel's horse returned with the colonel's body tied to its saddle. Another messenger was sent; he came back like the colonel – dead! Several other messengers were sent – all with the same result.

Meantime in Washington, DC there was growing concern over the failure to bring this matter to a conclusion, and the Foreign Secretary was becoming impatient, so one day he called one of his Bright Young Men into his office and scribbled a few words on a piece of paper, folded it in four and passed it over the desk to the BYM.

'Take this message to Garcia, will you?'

Two weeks later the Foreign Secretary was not in the least surprised to receive a cable from Mexico City.

'Message delivered. Meeting with Garcia next Wednesday.'

'Now,' says the purchasing manager, 'I have a "Message to Garcia", for you!'

(This sounds ominous: it is obviously one of those occasions when careers are put up in lights – or irretrievably wrecked.)

'Puckeridge and Broke have been the traditional suppliers of our main gearbox castings for over ten years and we are single sourced with them.'

A strategic decision

The purchasing manager continues, 'Jim Crockett the sales director of P. & B. told me this afternoon that they are being taken over by Close and Lane who, as you know, are our biggest competitors. Now Close and Lane are a very competitive lot. You might almost say predatory, and it's not the first time they've taken over a competitor's major supplier – and then, after a few months, the deliveries to the competitor start to deteriorate, and then the new management of the supplier demand a thumping great price increase. By the time the competitor has woken up to what has happened they're faced with a six or more months re-tooling problem, with some other source, and in that time Close and Lane have strangled their supplies. It will often take a company several years to regain its lost reputation after such an event, and they have fatally weakened several competitors by playing that game! Now Jim Crockett tells me that it will take about six months for Close and Lane to take full control of P. & B. – and that's all the time we've got to move in. Rest assured, the only reason that they've taken over P. & B. is because they think we're getting too powerful.

This means that to knock Close and Lane's plans firmly on the head, we've got to find an alternative source fast and have supplies coming in within the next six months. The difficulty is that, apart from P. & B., there are only three other foundries in Europe who can make castings of the size and complexity we require. Tooling-up will take the best part of six months, so that means that we must select the source we're going to move to in the next two to three weeks, then be tooled up and be supplied before Close and Lane can start putting on the pressure. The three European Foundries are:

LeRoy (Lille, France);
Humboldt (Hamburg, Germany);
Bertoldi (Milan, Italy).

He reaches for a folder and opens it.

'Here are your flight tickets. You leave for Lille tomorrow afternoon. You have appointments with senior directors of all three firms at two-day intervals, and here are the names of the people I have arranged for you to meet. Now I want you back to me in the next two weeks with the following information:

1. recommendations for the source we should tool up with;

2. unit and tool costs;
3. lead times;
4. delivery cycle;
5. draft contract;
6. reasons for your choice.

'If you consider it necessary you may issue a letter of intent but **not** instructions to proceed!

'You've got tomorrow morning to pick up your drawings and specifications', and with that he passes the file across the table – 'So off you go! By the way,' he smiles, 'you've just received your first message to Garcia.'

Sleep is hard to get that night. Apart from anything else, what is the difference between an ITP (instructions to proceed) and L of I (letter of intent)?

Your CIPS notes supply the answer to that one.

Instructions to proceed

A verbal or written instruction to a supplier to proceed with contractual work, issued prior to the formal contract. Often referred to as an ITP it does create a legal relationship between the buyer and seller.

Letter of intent

A communication from the buyer to the seller informing the latter that it is the intention to place a contract for that which is the subject of a quotation. **If correctly worded it does not create a legal relationship.**

By the time of your flight to Lille you have prepared the following:

1. three sets of enquiries complete with the appropriate drawings and specifications;
2. current unit prices;
3. commercial audit forms;
4. capacity tooling questionnaires;
5. current inflation rates;
6. current exchange rates;
7. a brief view of the national governments.

On the day of your trip to Lille the situation is as shown in Tables 12.1 and 12.2.

A short assessment of future economic movements

France

If the orders are placed in France prices would not be likely to contain much if any of a price increase component for inflation in the foreseeable future – but with the franc strengthening against the £ stg, there could well be some pressure for future price increases driven by the strengthening franc, if the trend continues.

Table 12.1 Inflation and exchange rates relationships

Country	Inflation rate	Exchange rate	Strengthening/ weakening v. £1 sterling
France	1.9%	8.47FF	Strengthening
Italy	4.0%	2395It L	Weakening
Germany	3.4%	2.47DM	Strengthening
US $	2.4%	1.5$	Weakening

Table 12.2 Interest rates

Country	Interest rates	Unemployment
France	6.22%	12%
Germany	5.83%	8.9%
Italy	8.19%	10.3%
UK	5.16%	9.7%

Italy

With inflation at nearly double that of the UK a price increase of 4%, twelve months after placing the order could well be a possibility, but this could be mitigated somewhat if the Italian lira continues to weaken against the £1 stg.

Germany

With inflation significantly higher than in the UK and the DM strengthening against the £ stg, price increases seem highly likely after 12 months from placing the orders.

National politics

If these were not stable democracies this study would have to be done in much more depth, but while in all three countries there is an element of political and social turmoil there are no positive contra-indications to the view that supply should be as secure in any of these countries as it would be in the UK.

The three components in your sourcing operation are shown in Table 12.3.

Table 12.3 Components in sourcing operation

Part number	Description	Unit price	Annual quantity
237–481	Gear box	£40.00	50 000
237–998	Axle housing	£25.00	40 000
237–1001	Steering housing	£33.00	60 000

Having by now progressed some way with your French studies, but having no Italian or German, you take the precaution of establishing the names of the components in all three languages (see Table 12.4).

Table 12.4 Names of components in French, Italian and German

English	French	Italian	German
Gear box	Boite vitesses	Cambio velocita	Zahnradgetriebe
Axle housing	Trompette	Carcasse-assale	Achsehäuse
Steering housing	Boitier-direction	Carcasse-sterzo	Lenkgehäuse

Modus operandi

With little time to spare you decide to use the commercial audit method to isolate and identify the differences between each of the companies and also to establish the differences between them and similar UK companies' conditions and practices, while the supplier's estimators prepare quotations. This will be on your first visit, the second will be to receive the quotations and discuss/negotiate as necessary.

A visit to Lille

Arriving at LeRoy Fonderies SA you are shown into the office of the Sales Director, M. Levebvre. He speaks very good English, and while you explain that you are considering resourcing the castings he is studying the drawings. You also explain the urgency for quotations.

'Yes', he says, 'we could make these for you.' Then he rings for an estimator who appears almost immediately, and in rapid French tells him the quotes are required in four days. The estimator grimaces, picks up the drawings, specifications and enquiry forms and goes out again. As he leaves you wonder if French estimators suffer from the 'estimator's dilemma', that you've encountered when negotiating with Grey (Chapter 10). You decide they do!

'Now,' says M. Levebvre, 'I am at your disposal, what do you wish to know?'

Taking a commercial audit form from your briefcase you start to work your way through the 21 questions (Chapter 11). LeRoy Fonderies is a *société anonyme* (SA) which indicates that it is the equivalent of a UK (plc) although there are two management boards. The first, exactly like a British board of directors, the second where the board discuss their plans with the *Syndicat* (Union Members' Representatives) before implementing their plans.

'Do the Union Representatives have a full say in approving the main board's plans,' you ask.

'That is part of the social contract,' Levebvre replies, 'but no, we tell them what we think they need to know.'

All the replies are very positive until you got to question 11, when you ask, 'Could you tell me who are your major customers?'

Lefebvre asks quite sharply, 'Why do you wish to know this? We do not normally reveal the names and share of our business that represent our major customers, certainly not without their prior agreement.'

'How strange,' you remark, 'I should have thought that you would be proud to name your customers!'

'But of course we are, but it is sufficient for you to know that we are suppliers to all the main constructers in France and in the rest of Europe.'

'The major reason for our asking this,' you persist, 'is that if you have customers more important than we are they will take priority over us, if we are competing for capacity, and secondly to be sure that you can cope with orders of the size we are discussing. It is after all worth something in the region of four and a half million pounds per annum.' (You don't want to give him the actual price £4.98m as you want to give him something to aim for.)

'You need have no fear of that,' he replies, 'provided you pay us at the agreed interval, which certain British customers do not, and your schedules are received by us at agreed monthly intervals, you can be sure that we will produce to schedule. We do not have to use expediters to hasten French suppliers because everybody behaves in the same way. Our purchasing headcount is lower within France than in the UK for this reason. However, we have to employ expediters whom we call "relanceurs" when we buy from certain other countries, notably Italy and UK. But I am willing to tell you that our major customers in France are Citroen, Peugeot and Renault; Mercedes in Germany; we also have good business in Italy with Fiat, and Ford in Belgium. We also deal with certain major British companies. I can assure you they would not deal with us if they did not have confidence in us.'

Question 12 also produced some discussion. 'The French customers have all given us top approvals, and so have Fiat and Ford,' and he points to the framed Ford Certificate on his office wall. 'Naturally if you want to put your quality assurance people into our works we will give them every co-operation. Also you must understand that we are also members of the French Foundry Association which also governs our quality performance.'

He passes a copy of the document to you and as you read quickly through it, one clause catches your eye:

Castings are to be inspected to meet the customer's metallurgical and dimensional requirements, and are to be 'fettled' as specified by the customer. No visible faults should be passed to the customer. As regards non-visible faults, such as interior blow holes, these may not be discovered until the customer has part machined the item. In such a case the machinist is to return the casting to the foundry for replacement. Members of the FFA do not hold themselves responsible for recompensing the machinist for the labour costs incurred before the 'blow hole' was uncovered, since the random blow hole in a batch of castings may be considered unavoidable.

'We expect to receive all our castings in a fit state to be machined, and we would certainly expect to be recompensed for our lost machining hours were we to find a hole half way through machining,' you say.

'We can negotiate something, I feel sure,' says Lefebvre, 'that will satisfy you, but it will be an extra cost.' (No, it won't! you think stubbornly.)

The wages review situation (question 13) is remarkably similar to UK conditions, except if a union negotiated nationally an increase in earnings the newspapers report each grade's new earnings. For some grades not only do they receive national awards, they can also receive merit awards. Of course, both management and employees pay much higher National Insurance benefits.

The industrial relations history (question 14) shows that three years ago there has been a four-week strike but since then there have been no significant labour problems.

The financial report (question 15) shows that they made 9.5% profit before tax which seems reasonable so you move on to the sub-question, 'Are you prepared to participate in "open book" negotiations?'

'We are prepared to share with you the cost of the raw materials, and our labour costs – but we will not go into detail with our overhead. We will not reveal to any third party such details as our directors' salaries and payments we may or may not make to, for example, political bodies – but our other major customers do not seem to have a problem with this, so there is no reason why you should. Now' he continues, 'why do you ask if we are prepared to hold stocks?' (This is question 16). 'They are expensive and as you can see although this is a big plant, we do not like to fill up our space with heaps of castings going nowhere, and for which we have not yet been paid. We would prefer to offer, say, a 10% increase in your schedules, if you are worried about the reliability of your schedules which you could pay for and hold at your works as a safety net. However you should know that we build into our tooling at least a 20% tooling margin and guarantee to deliver anything up to 20% extra within two weeks of receiving your schedule revision. You see we believe in supplier flexibility is what the customer of today requires above all!'

'Thank you,' you say 'Now how about payment terms?'

'We are willing to accept payment by bank transfer 30 days after receipt in your works,' Lefebvre states.

'But our order will be worth over £4 000 000 per annum to you,' you protest, 'I had hoped you would offer something nearer to 120 days!'

'French law does not permit us to go more than 90 days. However I am prepared to offer 45 days, but bearing in mind, despite the fact that you will have to pay part cost for the tooling, that we will also have to make a big investment, I think 45 days' credit after the materials arrive at your works is as far as I am prepared to go!'

Question 18 is straightforward. LeRoy already uses a major French carrier who delivers daily to the UK crossing from Calais to Dover, and Lefebvre agrees to quote CIP (carriage and insurance paid to destination).

The toolmaker (question 19) is easily resolved; they use their own toolmakers exclusively.

Questions 20 and 21 require that you gain an understanding of the internal scheduling system and assessment of the internal purchasing resources. Lefebvre leans back in his chair. 'I think it is time for you to meet the two who are responsible for those departments, and so I have asked them to join us here.'

The two managers who are responsible to the sales director are Mme Evelyn Marchand in charge of production control, and Pierre Colbert, the purchasing manager. Mme Marchand speaks excellent English and as soon as she says, 'We have been using MRP2 for the last four years,' you realize that this lady is very much on the ball. She explains how orders and schedules are received and processed, and you realize that she is also someone in whom the customer can have a great deal of confidence – but if you want to argue with her over deliveries or schedule figures, you'd better be sure you've got all your facts straight – it doesn't look as though she suffers fools gladly!

Pierre Colbert's English is not much better than your French, but when after a few minutes he uses the phrase, 'the lowest ultimate cost', you begin to feel that he too is a good professional. After a few minutes more of discussion you turn to Lefebvre and say, 'I'd like to thank you very much for your help and co-operation in this study. I will be back here in four days' time to collect your quotations and have at least a preliminary discussion with you at that time.'

'Very well,' says Lefebvre, 'and where are you off to now?'

'I'm going to Hamburg, and then Milan.'

The three French people exchange looks, then he smiles and says, 'Well, *bon voyage!*'

As you leave the plant you realize that they have worked out exactly why you are going to Hamburg and Milan – then you think, 'Well, the fact that they know I'm also doing the same job with their competitors ought to get them on their toes!'

That is another lesson for the *ab initio* world-class buyer – the world-class suppliers know their competitors very well. Recognize this fact – and use it to your advantage!

A visit to Hamburg

The following day finds you entering the foundry of Humboldt AG. It seems bigger than LeRoy and is located on the edge of the ship-building sector, and certainly the buildings that you can see look more modern than those of LeRoy.

Once in Herr Doktor Professor Humboldt's office you are grateful to find that he speaks almost accentless English, although it is disconcerting to hear him talking to his secretary in German of which you do not understand a single word. He tells you with evident pride that he is the great grandson of the founder Heinrich Humboldt and the company has been in the hands of the family for 120 years. They started off in shipping and diversified into commercial castings after the Second World War.

'So you will see,' he says, 'we are well equipped to fulfil your orders.'

After you have explained the urgency of your mission he quickly scans the drawings and specifications you have given him, then calls his secretary to pass them to estimating. 'They can be made at these works easily and you can be sure the quotes will be ready in four days. Now what can I tell you?'

The commercial audit proceeds quickly up to question 5, which refers to their association with other companies.

'Why do you wish to know this?'

'If, for example, you owned or were owned by companies which in some way might be a threat to our business relationship.'

'We are starting up a company in what was East Germany which will have a similar product line to the ones that your company produces.' he admits, 'It is right that where possible successful industries like our own provide jobs for the less fortunate members of our society – but I can assure you now that we have the view that our customers are our livelihood – and that is why Humboldt has survived so long – rest assured my friend you have nothing to fear.'

(Well you've found out something unexpected there by asking the right question – you wonder briefly how marketing and sales would take the news when you report back.)

Questions 7, 8, 9 and 10 are all straightforward. For question 11 he provides a list of his top customers, Volkswagen, General Motors, and various well-known aircraft concerns, as well as shipbuilders etc.

With regard to quality approvals he is perfectly relaxed about having QA in his works although he does say in a slightly superior way that it would be completely unnecessary because he holds approvals from all his top customers.

The normal wage review situation is little different from that of France or the UK – but when it comes to question 14 which is to do with industrial relations he is a little uncomfortable as he replies, 'You must realize with German inflation running at 3.4% German labour unions pressing for wage increases and our borrowing rate high compared to most of Europe plus the fact that the Mark is strengthening against some significant currencies, we have some difficulties in retaining our competitive edge in certain markets. Naturally we are taking firm management action to keep prices down in order to hold our export markets. I cannot guarantee that we will be free of labour problems in 1996.'

His reply to the question, 'Are you prepared to hold stocks?' is that they scrupulously honour customers schedules (provided that schedules are not varied at intervals less than two months ahead) and that therefore he sees no necessity to hold stocks. In his view stocks are wasted money and energy. Apart from anything else rapid change and high stocks make the labour restless.

Payment terms? Humboldt gives all customers the same terms, 45 days from receipt at the customers' works. The reason is that financial order is one of the reasons for Humboldt's survival over the last 120 years.

The question about carriers is easily answered. Humboldt carriers serve the whole of Europe, and supplies to UK would present no difficulties.

The question about toolmaking provokes the response that normally they make their own, but if the toolroom is under pressure they would buy out tooling.

The Herr Doktor Professor is very willing to discuss questions 20 and 21 which deal with the internal scheduling system, and the internal purchasing resources.

This is an area in which he takes a strong personal interest and he has amalgamated the two departments under a materials manager, Herr Fiedler, 'who unfortunately doesn't speak English, and as you do not speak German I have not invited him to this meeting'. He goes on to describe the MRP system they use, and that under Herr Fiedler there is a group of customer liaison personnel, many of whom do speak English. The purchasing department is 12 strong and in the opinion of Herr Humboldt are second to none.

You thank him for his help, arrange to return to discuss his quotes with him in four days and take your departure.

A visit to Milan

Arriving in Milan the following morning you go straight to the Fonderia Bertoldi SPA. This is a public company with 80% of the shares owned by the Benedetti family, who have a big say in the way that the company is run. Having visited two world-class foundries in as many days you are beginning to be able to form impressions of the similarities and differences between the three. The Bertoldi plant is the smallest of the three but not by a great deal – the work tempo varies considerably. In the German plant there is absolute order.

The British Standard is that work should be at the equivalent rate to walking 3.5 mph; Germans seem slower, the Italians much faster. The effect of this higher tempo seems to result in a less orderly appearance – although, you reason, with many tons of molten metal being handled hourly no-one can be disorderly for long.

The sales director is Sergio Morin and although he speaks some English, he has Maria Vespucci his secretary, acting as interpreter. She seems to be translating your questions and his answers faithfully enough – but what worries you is if the nuances that are inherent in language are getting through – you resolve there and then that since the four main languages in the Community are English, French, German, and Italian, if you are going to become a world-class buyer you are going to have to pay a great deal of attention to getting more languages under your belt.

It is also a worry that although the 'front office' people speak English it is impossible to cross check what they say with the 'workers' – and that means if they care to, the 'front office' can tell you any old thing.

The question and answer process goes well, however. They are major suppliers to Italian and French industry, and they supply just-in-time to Fiat; they are always prepared to consider JIT to other customers and are also prepared to hold stocks; in fact until you get to payment terms Bertoldi have seemed the most attractive of the companies to date, particularly as they are prepared to accept 'open book' negotiation without quibble.

Then Sergio via Maria says, 'You should understand that we can only permit 30 days' maximum credit, and we will want a 50% contribution to tool costs prior to starting work. You will see that our financial report for the last three years' records an annual loss. A high proportion of our work in the motor industry has been in the doldrums for this time which is why we must be very careful with our forward investment. With regard to carriage, because of our location all our transport has to go through the passes in the Alps, and fog and snow do become a hazard for a few days each winter. Our French customers prefer containerized rail deliveries from Milan to Paris for which we allow 24 hours' travel time, and which is totally reliable. Incidentally the French customer works on no more than five days' stock being topped up every 24 hours.'

'Do you have customers in the UK?' you ask.

'Yes,' comes the reply, 'and we allow 48 hours transit time by road. In the winter we agree to build up their stockholding (at their expense) to one month's value and this has always proved to be more than adequate to cover our weather problems.

But I must signal you that rail and container service is cheaper and can be more direct and faster once the Channel Tunnel is working – you should consider this. However at your request we will quote for delivery by road (CIP).'

Sergio and Maria then take you down to the administration block where purchasing and production control are situated. The heads of both departments speak some English – but again when you ask the production controller about how individual call-offs are treated – you have to explain what a 'call-off' is. Once he understands the question his answer is just the one you would hope for, but the language difficulty is very real and time-consuming.

Well, you have made sure that the enquiries have got to the right places, you've carried out commercial audits, collected financial reports from all three sources, and for a moment you wonder if the Italian purchasing manager would have done as well as you have done up until now, if he had had this job to do. It was impossible to forget his answer to your question, 'Where do you buy most of your materials from?'

'We buy nothing outside Italy, and 95% is bought within our own region – that is within 100 kms of this factory.' He says this with an air of great pride. Then you remember that not so long ago you would have felt that he was right to do this and applauded him for it – now you feel he is shortsighted and unimaginative.

Back at your hotel you decide to draw up a comparative score sheet (see Figure 12.1).

A comparative assessment

There is one other thought to put into the equation and that is the likely price inflation once the order has been placed. It looks as though LeRoy would be looking for 2%, Humboldt for 4%, and Bertoldi for 3%. Humboldt relies on the fact that once a customer has tooled up with him you do what you are told; the French are prepared to discuss price on a semi-open book basis, and Bertoldi is prepared to be open.

It is clear that technically all three ought to be able to produce the products but in each case there are areas where the supplier has revealed aspects that are unacceptable to the company.

The areas of disagreement with LeRoy are:

1. their reluctance to be sufficiently open about their major suppliers – is there something on that list of customers they don't want us to find out?
2. the French Foundry Association's strictures on blow holes being found on machining operations were not to be compensated for with regard to the machinist's lost time;
3. their total unwillingness to hold stocks – although their flexibility offer was almost as good if they could prove it works;
4. their lack of willingness to negotiate full 'open book'.

The areas of disagreement with Humboldt are more serious:

Question number	LeRoy	Humboldt	Bertoldi
1. Name, address, fax, etc.	Recorded	Recorded	Recorded
2. Company structure	Public	Public. Run like family firm	Public. Benedetti family own 80% shares
3. Management structure	Management board. Syndicat board	Management board	Management board
4. Number of factories	1	1	1
5. Association with other companies	None	Setting up competitor to buyer's company in what was East Germany	None
6. Founded	1925	1874	1945
7. Area	640 000 sq. m.	800 000 sq. m.	550 000 sq. m.
Extension area	Yes	Yes	Yes
Structure	Brick	Concrete	Concrete, light structure
8. Condition of buildings	1930s type	1950s type	Post 1945/mixed
9. Staff	150	102	130
Hourly paid	900	1000	850
10. Processes	Continuous cast	Continuous cast	Continuous cast
	Grey iron	Grey iron	Grey iron
	Cu & Ali	Ali	Gun metal
	Welding, painting. Good lab	Welding, painting. Excellent lab	Welding
			Painting. Good lab
11. Major customers	Renault, Peugeot, Ford	Volkswagen, GM and Ford	Fiat
12. Quality control approvals	All major customers	VW and Aircraft manufacturers	Fiat
13. Wage review anniversaries	Annual in May	Annual in September	Annual in June
14. Industrial relations	Last strike 3 years ago	Expecting trouble	Last strike 2 years ago
15. Financial status	Profit 9.5% before tax	Profit 6.5% before tax	Loss considerable
Turnover	1 300 000 000 FF	190 000 000 DM	200 000 mil L.lt.

Annual report	Enclose	Enclosed	Enclosed
Accept 'open book'	Partial	No. Believe competition is buyer's measure	Yes
16. Prepared to hold stocks	No, but offer flexibility	No, very rigid	Yes, if paid for. Offers JIT type supply
17. Payment terms	45 days	45 days	30 days
Tooling	PTC after sample approved	FC after sample approved	FC 50% up-front
18. Carriers	Hired transport	Own vehicles	Offer container, rail or hired transport
19. Toolmakers	Own	Mainly own	Own
20. Internal scheduling system	MRP2	MRP2	MRP2
21. Internal purchasing resources	Good	No indication	Not too impressed

Figure 12.1 Score sheet: LeRoy v. Humboldt v. Bertoldi

1. This competitor they are setting up. How to be sure that by sourcing with them you won't be opening the door to providing them with free and invaluable industrial information?
2. The inflexibility of scheduling arrangements. It would be impossible not to vary the schedules outside a two-month horizon.
3. Humboldt's personal attitude is inflexible too, which is a worry.
4. They are worried about economic effects on their prices – which worry you!
5. Total refusal to justify prices – saying that competition is the buyer's measure. Clearly a buyer is in a very difficult spot if having paid a very large sum for tooling he or she is faced with a big price increase from a supplier who is effectively saying – 'you don't like my price?' Then the advice is to pay up and then take your work elsewhere!
6. There are potential labour problems in the offing too.

The areas of disagreement with Bertoldi are different again.

1. They have made a loss for the last three years and 80% of the shares are owned by the Benedetti family – but if they take their money elsewhere it might not be possible for Bertoldi to survive. Which means that if you are going to source with Bertoldi you'd have to get some sort of contact with the Benedetti family that they wouldn't 'pull the plug' without giving say, six months' notice.
2. Because of their weak financial situation they are asking for payment in 30 days and 50% of the tool cost up front. This is not a happy situation because assuming the tooling takes six months' they might go belly-up, in which case the 50% tool cost would be lost – but also with P&B being taken over by Lane and Close, the company would be right up the creek without a paddle! Clearly the Benedetti family would be the key to any business one is going to do with Bertoldi.
3. They don't have too much experience of shipping to the UK which is a lower level concern – which is resolvable.
4. Finally their purchasing manager is a pretty parochial soul – but then you haven't been allowed to meet the German materials manager!

On the basis of the study so far it appears that your first preference would be LeRoy; the second, provided you could get the Benedetti family on board would be Bertoldi and running a not very close third is Humboldt.

As you get on the plane at Milan to fly to Paris en route for Lille you think of that unfortunate Mexican colonel who has tried to deliver that famous message to Garcia and think, it won't be the Garcias that'll assassinate me if I come back with the wrong message, it'll be the purchasing manager!

MEMORY JOGGERS

53 **Going overseas to buy – the minimum you need**
- Credit cards, passport, travellers cheques, etc.
- Your terms and conditions of contract
- Understanding of the culture
- Commercial audit documents
- Tooling or other special questionnaires
- Dates of public holidays, religious festivals, etc.

REMEMBER – the conventions of your country are most unlikely to prevail elsewhere and therefore you must take account of this when visiting overseas suppliers.

54 **When you are negotiating**
- Don't let them pressure you with time or language
- Ask for privacy if you have to do complex calculations
- If you don't understand any phrases, ask for clarification and persist until you do understand
- Don't assume words mean the same in each country
- Maintain your ethical beliefs – no matter what the temptation

REMEMBER – overseas negotiations will be quite different and you must adjust to the different practices, timings, culture, etc.

55 **Provisional contractual agreements**
- There may be no contract but you can reach agreement in principle
- Dig in on major points – don't feel inferior if you don't understand the language
- Know the difference between letters of intent and instructions to proceed
- Write down the salient points in such a way that you can later understand the detail

REMEMBER – you may wish to reach provisional agreement pending final confirmation of a contract when you return to the office, make that absolutely clear to the other party.

13 A DIFFICULT NEGOTIATION – MADE EASIER BY THE USE OF TECHNIQUES

This chapter continues the tactical application of the techniques covered in the case in the previous chapter, building on the techniques covered in the rest of the book. It includes final source selection, raising a letter of intent and developing a contract. It demonstrates the practical value of the six classic negotiation techniques covered in Chapter 9.

The flight seems interminable. What complicated matters is that although it is the same three items you are dealing with, the texture and character of the three negotiations are so different. One moment your mind is in Lille, then in Hamburg, and then in Milan. To bring this set of negotiations to a successful conclusion is going to demand the effective use of all the lessons you have learned to date. If there were time you would receive the quotes at your desk, prepare a quotation analysis, then a cost benefit analysis, make a preliminary choice, then send SQA in to give their verdict. Then conduct a final negotiation. As the 'spend' is so high you would then push the recommendation 'up the tree' and wait not too anxiously for it to come back again 'approved'.

But this time there is nobody to share the blame with, you are on your own, and under considerable time pressure. There is a week left in which to have the whole job done. Well, first things first, get your ducks in a row! Reaching for your pad you start writing.

The tactical plan

1. Receive each quote at the supplier's works.
2. Ask for an adjournment in a private office so that you can study the quote.
3. Compare quote with current prices.
4. Discuss/negotiate quote with supplier, taking careful note of all agreements. (The agenda for the discussion can only be prepared after quote analysis.)
5. For your own guidance you have to have at your fingertips:

(a)   terms and conditions (Chapter 1);
(b)   construction of a schedule (Chapter 2);
(c)   contract construction (Chapters 3 and 8);
(d)   negotiation skills (Chapters 9 and 10).

6. After you have completed your discussion you have to get each potential supplier to sign up to a draft contract provisional on your placing the work with them, because you would not know who you are going to award the work to until you have completed your negotiations.

7. Getting to the lowest ultimate cost would be the first task because the only yardstick you have is the current UK supplier's price, which has been negotiated over a number of years. As is usually the case, long established prices tend to be below current market rate, so you would have to work very hard to make overall savings, but with £4.5m per annum on offer, suppliers should be willing to compete very hard to get the business. If they aren't prepared to compete, then you are talking to the wrong sources.

8. Even if a supplier quotes a really attractive price and you can't achieve a satisfactory draft contract, then again, you can't use the supplier, and you wouldn't know what the best deal would be until you have completed the cycle of visits.

9. And finally when you have decided the source, if it were possible to give the successful supplier a letter of intent, bearing in mind the purchasing manager wants to have a final say, it is the time to try for one last concession, and you are unlikely to know what that is until you have seen what the unsuccessful suppliers has to offer.

The agenda for the formation of the contract is largely established. The terms and conditions are printed on the back of the enquiry document, and are repeated on the back of the purchase order, so taking a blank order form from your bag, you note down the salient features you have to resolve to form the basis of an acceptable contract.

The basic essentials

The obvious first point is to define the parties to the contract. After this come the following.

1. Terms of payment

(a)   Company minimum standard 45 days from receipt of goods.
(b)   Foreign currency or sterling?
(c)   Electronic exchange? bankers draft? bank exchange? other?

2. Quality

Supplier to assure quality. Establish rework and reject routines.

3. Confidentiality

Vital, particularly with Humboldt who are setting up a competitor to your product in the eastern part of Germany.

4. Intellectual property

All design and reproduction rights vested in the buyer.

5. Terms of quotation

Must be CIP – delivered buyer's works, all charges paid (see **Incoterms** in Appendix C).

6 and 7 Tooling payment

Supplier to define full cost. Where part cost only is involved, percentage to be paid for by buyer to be defined. Tool costs will only be paid for by buyer after sample approval, and first preproduction run has been delivered and accepted. Samples must be from production tooling (tooling questionnaire must meet requirements with regard to reserve capacity, and flexibility with regard to ability of supplier to use more than one capital machine in case of breakdown).

8. Samples

Sample submission dates must be strictly adhered to.

9. Sub-contract

No part of the work associated with this contract is to be sub-contracted without buyer's authority in writing.

10 and 11. Quantity variation

The instrument of the contract/blanket order will be computer generated schedules. Variations will appear in both the fixed and tentative portions of the schedule. Only the current month will normally not be subject to change. The supplier must react to these changes and inform the buyer if the new change is not achievable within the span of time indicated by the schedule and state at what time the change shall be instituted.

Supplier flexibility is measured on a percentage basis, and failure to achieve these norms may result, after discussion, in the buyer cancelling the contract.

12. Price variations

Requests for price increases will normally not be considered at intervals closer than on the annual anniversary of the placing of the order/contract. One month prior to this date the supplier may submit a price increase request which must contain a full explanation of the influences causing this request. The buyer reserves the right to accept/refuse or modify this request. With regard to currency fluctuations the order/contract will be placed at the exchange rate ruling on the day. Variations of 5%, say, either way will not be considered as significant by either party. Beyond this, both parties may renegotiate a different exchange rate.

13. Packaging and shipping

To be negotiated. The preferred method is that the supplier delivers in returnable stillages owned by them, or at worst the buyer contributes 50% of cost to be agreed for the stillage population.

14. VAT. This to be shown as separate item on invoices and monthly statement.

15. Letting the order

This order is placed subject to the buyer's terms and conditions, plus any agreed amendments submitted by the supplier. Where the buyer's terms and conditions of contract vary from the standard conditions, the contract conditions shall take precedent.

16. Force majeure

Standard terms and conditions apply.

17, 18, 19 and Invoices

(a)   Invoices are to be provided with each delivery showing quantities and prices of items in the batch.
(b)   Where prices vary from the prices on the order invoices will not be paid.
(c)   The invoice month is from the 25th of month 1 to the 24th of month 2.

20. Consequential losses and product liability

(a)   Consequential losses: The launch date for production quantities is specified at the head of the contract based on milestones agreed with the supplier. Quantifiable production losses will be sustained by the buyer if these dates are not met. If these dates are not met tool cost payment will be withheld at the rate of 5% per week or part of a week up to 50% of the price of the tooling.
(b)   Product liability: The supplier will save and protect the buyer from any claims or legal actions brought against the buyer resulting from faults in manufacture not attributable to design or specification information given by the buyer.

21. Tooling

Tooling is to be retained in good order by the supplier, until given release to dispose of the tooling by the buyer.

22. Cancellation

This order/contract is placed 'For the life of the models on which the items in the contract will be fitted' with the following provisos:
(a)   Supplier meets quality performance specified.
(b)   Supplier meets delivery performance specified. (Supplier will receive monthly statistical reports showing performance against zero defect norms.)
(c)   Prices remain competitive compared with available competition. Failure to meet this requirement, after discussion, may result in contract cancellation. This will normally result in six months' notice being given.

23. Applicable law

English Law shall apply. Note: French suppliers will often want law according to the courts of Paris, and Italians and Germans will want their own, but you are the buyer. International lawyers will often tell you that in certain cases you would be wiser to accept foreign law before English law as it gives the buyer more latitude. American law is an absolute minefield of state laws and national law, and if ever you are tempted to use American state and national law, be very careful! One way round this problem is the use of arbitrators who use natural justice as their rule. If you decide to take this route the supplier and you must agree at the inception of the contract. Finally you should remember that going to law makes fat lawyers and thin clients. If you do have to go to law, you as a negotiator have failed somewhere!

The tactical plan in operation

Well, you're as ready as you will ever be, which is just as well, as you are now walking into M. Lefebvre's office, and there on his totally clear desk is a large brown envelope!

'Welcome,' he smiles as he holds out his hand. 'I should imagine the last few days have been quite hectic for you jetting around Europe. How did you find Hamburg and Milan?'

'Very interesting,' is your reply. You are determined to give nothing away. 'Are those my quotations?'

'They are indeed,' he says, handing the envelope to you.

'I wonder if you could lend me an office where I could read your quotations, then perhaps we could discuss them further?'

'But of course, I have to have a meeting with Pierre Colbert the *Chef d'Achats*, sorry, our chief buyer, and I shall be gone for about an hour, so please use my office, and should you require anything please ask my secretary.'

As soon as he closes the door behind him you open the envelope. Stripped down to its essentials it reads as shown in Table 13.1.

Table 13.1

Part number	Description	Unit price	Part tool cost
237–481	Boite vitesses	364.21 FF	508 200 FF
237–998	Trompette	177.87 FF	338 800 FF
237–1001	Boitier-direction	287.98 FF	440 440 FF

Lead time for submission of samples.
Item 1, 5 months. Items 2 and 3 four months.

Pre-production and/or production could follow immediately sample approval was given. The exchange rate they've used was 8.47FF/£1 stg, and they'd quoted

CIP. The next thing to do is to convert their quote to sterling and compare their prices with the UK current price (see Table 13.2).

Table 13.2

Part number	Current price	LeRoy price	Annual volumes
237–481	£40.00	£43.00	50 000
237–998	£25.00	£21.00	40 000
237–1001	£33.00	£34.00	60 000

The bottom line calculations are given in Table 13.3.

Table 13.3

Part number	Current annualized cost	LeRoy quotation annualized
237–481	£2 000 000	£2 150 000
237–998	£1 000 000	£840 000
287–1001	£1 980 000	£2 040 000
Totals	£4 980 000	£5 030 000
		+ Part tool cost £152 000

Lefebvre knocks at the door. 'Can I come in? Well, what do you think of our prices?'

Which approach now?

A direct question! What, you ask yourself is the best tack to take? Thinking back to the negotiation course you've been on, you review your six options.

1. **Power and coercion.** No – you need his co-operation.
2. **Attitude change involving emotion.** No – dramatics would be inappropriate.
3. **Search for a middle ground compromise.** No – because until LeRoy's prices are attractive to you there is nothing to compromise about.
4. **Trading mutually advantageous concessions.** The concession is: if he gives you the best quote you would give him business. Nevertheless it is worthwhile underlining the point.
5. **Logical persuasion.** Perhaps.
6. **Genuine business objectives.** This is the one. A big turnover, more than £4m per annum for at least five years, and if he is competitive there is the possibility of quoting for the rest of your foundry work. This must be where their interests lie!

Lefebvre sits down at his desk. 'Well,' he prompts.

You've decided to lead on (6) and follow with (4). 'Thank you, first of all for your rapid response to my request for quotations, but I have to observe that your prices are not attractive, and unless they can be reduced we are missing the opportunity to enjoy a genuine business objective which from your point of view is worth more than £4m per annum for at least the next five years and lose the opportunity of quoting for all our foundry business. In order to get to this position we must negotiate. If not this opportunity will be lost to you.'

'Certainly, I am willing to discuss prices, how far out are we?'

Truth or dare?

(Now here is another dilemma, Lefebvre certainly asked direct questions, but what should you reply?) If you say you want £3 off the gearbox, the axle housing is OK and you want £1 off the steering housing you could (perhaps would) be limiting the amount he could reduce by, but also it would be desirable if his prices are sufficiently below 'current' to pay-back the cost of tooling inside a year. If you give him an impossibly large sum to reduce by, he would know you were stringing him along and the negotiating atmosphere would be irretrievably destroyed. You could of course give him a figure to reduce the bottom line by, to apply where he found it most convenient, but he might take more off the axle housing, leaving the other two still uncompetitive even though the bottom line was acceptable, and this could cause problems with the Red Book (Chapter 10).

You decide to tell him the near truth. 'If the gear-box was £4.00 less, the axle housing £1.00 less and the steering box £2.00 less, then we could say that you are competitive with our current supplier. If you were able to agree to this you would be in the running to gain in excess of £4m business per annum. So I would suggest it would be worth your while to make these reductions.'

'Well, of course you would,' he smiles, 'but what do we get in return if we supply at lower margins than we have estimated?' (Suddenly, the grimace the estimator has made when Lefebvre gave him the estimating job to do, and the knowledge you picked up about the estimator's fear of quoting too low, crosses your mind. The thought occurs to you that Lefebvre isn't dead certain of those quotes, so there is undoubtedly room to manoeuvre. You resolve to keep 'selling' your point of view.)

A fair trade

'I repeat, M. Lefebvre, that I will be ready to place blanket orders for these items inside the next two weeks for delivery within six months – the contract will be for the life of the model, and with spares, facelifts, etc., perhaps several years longer and with the way the motor industry is behaving this work must be invaluable to you. We are not affected by the peaks and troughs of the motor people.'

'Five years at least,' he muses. 'Would you give us a guarantee of that?'

'Yes, the contract would read, "For the life of the model, subject to our criteria on supply, quality and price competitiveness." These criteria would be built into the contract.'

'Let us say provisionally that my colleagues were to accept your price proposals, you say that you would be requiring bulk supplies in six months.'

'Yes, but we would want samples and pre-production batches in five months.'

'That would be possible if you could give me an order this week.'

(Another poser – because the PM and the legal eagles would want to run their eyes over the draft contract, and at minimum that could take quite a few days. So once again you decided to tell the truth.)

'I couldn't guarantee an order this week, even if you were to meet the price indications I have given you – as you know, I have to return to Hamburg and Milan – but if you do provide the best quote I could certainly provide you with an official order/contract in two weeks, even if there were some minor details still to be resolved.'

'Very well,' said Lefebvre, coming to a decision. 'I will provisionally agree to your prices – I will hold them for two weeks provided I have something official by then. If I have heard nothing then we must be free to sell our capacity elsewhere and this deal will be off. Now proceeding on the assumption that you do give us the order we need to talk about the terms and conditions you left with us. Presumably they are your standards.'

You note down the prices you have been given compared to the current price (see Table 13.4).

Table 13.4

	Current price	*LeRoy 2nd quote*
237.481	£40.00	£39.00 (330.33 FF)
237.998	£25.00	£20.00 (169.40 FF)
237.1001	£33.00	£32.00 (271.04 FF)
Bottom line	£4.98m	£4.67
Tool cost		£152 000
Grand total		£4.822m

Pay back within a year! (You gave no sign of this achievement to Lefebvre!)

'Before we start to discuss the draft contract, would you be good enough to ask your estimator to complete this tooling questionnaire as it will save us a lot of discussion at this stage – and if he will return it completed while I'm here – provided it's satisfactory we can add it to the draft contract.'

Lefebvre looks through it quickly, then calls his secretary to pass the form to the estimator.

Then together you work your way through the points you have listed based on the terms and conditions while you were on the plane. After two hours there is a draft contract on the table.

The provisional contract

1. Terms and conditions of payment

(a)   The company will pay at 45 days from receipt of goods which will be priced according to the attached price schedule CIP.

(b)   Payment will be made in sterling.

(c)   Payment will be made by bank transfer.

(d)   Prices on price schedule are at the exchange rate 8.47 FF/£1.

(e)   Exchange rate banding clause A 5% band is applied so that while the franc/pound sterling remains between 8.05 FF – 8.89 FF no action will be taken by either party. Movement beyond this band will necessitate a renegotiation.

2. Quality

(a)   LeRoy Fonderies warrant that their materials will conform to the Company's drawings and specifications.

(b)   The Company operates supplier quality assurance and LeRoy Fonderies agree to giving the Company's quality personnel permission to carry out quality audits on LeRoy's premises as required by the Company.

(c)   The FFA regulation with regard to 'blow-holes' is annulled with regard to this contract. Any faults discovered in the machining cycle are to be returned for replacement, and the Company will be compensated by LeRoy Fonderies for waste machining time.

(d)   The Company operates a statistical analysis of quality performance. Monthly reports are issued to suppliers. Quality faults exceeding .025 per batch are adverse and the supplier will be warned to improve. Failure to improve may result in cancellation of the order/contract.

3. Confidentiality

No drawings, specifications, models, samples or other information will be revealed to any third party.

4. Intellectual property

All drawings, specifications, models, samples, etc. are the Company's property.

5. Terms of quotation

Valid for two weeks. The offer lapses unless instructions to proceed or other firm instructions are received by LeRoy Fonderies prior to this date.

6, 7 and 8. Tooling payment

Payment for tooling will be made by the Company under the following rules:

(a)   Samples will be submitted by LeRoy Fonderies off production tools according to the attached schedule.

(b)   On receipt of sample approvals LeRoy Fonderies will dispatch 100 of each of the items shown on the attached schedule for pre-production machining trials.

(c)   On receipt of approval of pre-production quantities LeRoy Fonderies are to submit tooling invoices which will be paid by bank transfer 45 days after receipt of invoices.

(d) The part tool cost (50%) is firm at £152 000 (1 287 440 FF) at an exchange rate of 8.47 FF/£1 stg.

Any modifications requested by the Company are to be costed by LeRoy Fonderies and referred to the Company prior to implementation.

9. Sub-contract

LeRoy will not sub-contract work without the Company's prior authority.

10. and 11. Quantity variation

(a) Schedules will be issued by the Company by the 24th of each month which will project the next two months' firm requirements, and the following three months' tentative requirement. The tentative content is for planning purposes only.

(b) Firm requirements are displayed as weekly requirements.

(c) From time to time variations to stated requirements will be required. LeRoy agree that, provided any given week's required increase does not exceed a 20% uplift, the extra will be delivered in two working weeks from receipt of the request.

(d) In the event that LeRoy Fonderies are unable to meet a requirement in full they will inform the Company and advise when the deficit will be made good.

(e) Measurement of delivery performance will be based on a requirement for 100% adherence to schedule. Monthly the Company issues a statistical analysis of supplier performance. Should the performance persistently exceed half a per cent above or below scheduled quantities cancellation of the order/contract may result.

12. Price variation

(a) Price variations will only be considered at annual anniversary dates from the issue of the order/contract.

(b) Variation requests are to be submitted one calendar month ahead and must include the following data:

(i)　price movements in materials costs post the last settlement;
(ii)　price movements in labour costs post the last settlement;
(iii)　price movements in overhead costs post the last settlement.

(c) These movements will be compared with the Company's information and the supplier's claim will be processed accordingly. The Company reserves the right to negotiate, modify or reject the claim subject to discussion.

(d) This excludes exchange rate modifications as detailed in Clause 1.

13. Packaging and shipping

Delivery will be made in 6 × 4 × 3 steel stillages. The population of stillages will be agreed after a separate study takes place. Costs will be shared on a 50/50 basis and a separate contract will be raised to cover this aspect.

14. VAT rules

The rate for materials will be applied by LeRoy Fonderies and documentation will be that appropriate to allow reclaim under EEC rules.

15. Letting the order

The order is let under the conditions of the contract which overrides the standard terms and conditions where the two are in conflict.

16. Force majeure

The Company's standard terms and conditions apply.

17, 18 and 19. Invoices

(a) Invoices are to accompany each delivery.
(b) Monthly statements are to be received by the Company not later than the 20th of each month.
(c) Payment will be made by bank transfer on the 45th day after receipt of the monthly statement.
(d) Invoices which vary from the order/contract price will not be passed for payment unless supported by a purchasing order amendment.

20. Consequential loss and product liability

21. Tooling

22. Cancellation

23. English law

The last four clauses are exactly as you have defined them on the plane and you add these unchanged onto the contract. The addenda of the tooling details are added in the form of the completed tooling questionnaire adding the cost details below:

> 100% cost £304 000 (2 574 880 FF)
> 50% contribution £152 000 (1 287 440 FF)
> *Tooling capacity 50% greater than normal weekly requirement.

Lefebvre and you sit back.

'Well, that's our preliminary contract then,' he says as you both sign and date it. 'I'll take a photocopy of this to show my colleagues and to our legal people and I presume you will want to do the same thing. Now I've agreed all this, but I still have to get final agreement from the rest of my board. You've run us very tight in certain areas, now what can you give me to help me convince my people of your good faith?'

A sign of good faith

'You will appreciate that this is a competitive study I am undertaking and it will be another two or three days before I will know who has been successful. But I will promise that if you are the successful supplier I will undertake to send you a letter of intent before I go back to the UK.'

'What does that say?'

'It states that we've decided that at some time in the future we **will** place our orders with you – which allows you to make a start on planning, if you wish to – but there is no engagement as to when we will place these orders. It does not give you the right to commit any resources which can be expensed to us. If my management accept my final recommendations, it may still take a while before I can issue a formal order supported by the final contract but I will send you a fax, followed by a letter which will give you instructions to proceed. Now, this has the same validity as an order, and you can commit resources against it.'

'When will I see your ITP then?'

'If you're successful – before the end of next week,' you say.

'Well, I look forward to hearing from you then before the end of next week!'

You shake hands and then you set off for Hamburg.

Summation

Summing up as you drive to the airport there is a nagging worry eating at you. The agreement you've reached is very good – but can you be sure Lefebvre will get the agreement to those prices? He sometimes seems a little less than fully confident, and then there is the fact that the offer only has two weeks' validity. Why? Is it that another customer is getting close to placing an order? Well, whatever; it means that you are going to have to get the best deal you can with the others in case LeRoy turns out badly.

The German experience

Herr Doktor Professor Humboldt greets you formally and passes over to you his quotations. Following your practice in France you sit in a vacant office to analyse Humboldt's quotes (see Table 13.5).

Table 13.5

Current	LeRoy	Humboldt
1. £40.00	£39.00	£44.00 (108.66 DM)
2. £25.00	£20.00	£19.50 (48.165 DM)
3. £33.00	£32.00	£35.00 (86.5 DM)

Tool cost: £400 000 (988 000 DM) 100% cost to be borne by customer.

The bottom line is:

Current £4.98m; LeRoy £4.67m + £152 000 compared to Humboldt's.

1. £44.00 × 50 000 p.a. = 2 200 000
2. £19.50 × 40 000 p.a. =   780 000
3. £35.00 × 60 000 p.a. = 2 100 000

    Total: £5 080 000 + £400 000.

Humboldt has used the exchange rate of 2.47 DM/£1 stg.

When you have completed your comparison you return to Humboldt's office ready to open negotiations and this time you are certain of your opening remarks. You've decided to use **genuine business objectives (No. 6)** with a dash of **trading mutually advantageous concessions (No. 4)**. It has worked well with LeRoy; it should work well with Humboldt. But Humboldt's reply to the benefits you could offer meets with a slightly aggressive response which surprises you.

'Obviously you consider our prices too high!'

'Well, yes I do, we are offering more than £4m of business annually for at least the next five years and in view of the size of the business we are talking about we would expect that prices should be sufficiently attractive to persuade us to change our source of supply to you.'

'As I told you we will react, should we choose to, in line with market conditions. This approach presumably means that you have competition prices better than ours!'

You nod.

'Tell me what they are, and we will consider matching them,' he says shortly.

'No, I will not reveal competition prices – other suppliers have provided their best prices and I believe you should do the same.'

'Then how am I to believe you when you say you have better prices?'

Fighting fire with fire

'That's easy,' you reply, snapping your briefcase shut and standing up. 'I'll leave now!'

(Note Humboldt is using **power and coercion** (1) and you respond with **attitude change involving emotion** (2).)

'Nehmen-sie platz!' he roars. 'Sorry, you do not speak German. Please sit down!'

Grudgingly you sit down – demonstrating through your body language that you are still sizzling.

In a more conciliatory tone he says, 'I would be prepared to reduce our prices by 10% – but that is our last word. That would make our prices:

237-481 £40.00 stg.
237-998 £18.55 stg.
237-1001 £31.50 stg.

You quickly calculate the bottom line:

1. £40.00 × 50 000 = £2 000 000
2. £18.55 × 40 000 =   £742 000
3. £31.50 × 60 000 = £1 890 000

Bottom line = £4 632 000.

'That's an improvement,' you admit, thinking that the bottom line is that, excluding tool cost, Humboldt's annual cost is better than the current or LeRoy quotes.

Trading proposals

'Do these prices satisfy you?' Humboldt asks.

'Well, I'd like to see another £1 off the price of 237-481' you say, 'but more importantly there is this tool cost. It is higher than I would have expected, and also I see that you expect us to pay the full tool cost. If you had said that we would be paying a part cost which is customarily what we do I would not press for a further reduction on the unit price.'

'I have already made clear that I would not negotiate further on unit prices and as regards part cost of tooling it is quite customary in Germany too, but as I explained at our last meeting we have problems here in Humboldt. We made only 6% before tax last year, inflation is up, the labour is beginning to request higher wages, and our borrowing rate is too high. Consequently, we must keep investment down. But consider this, if you were to pay 50% of the tooling cost and we were to retain 50% we would have to recover that portion in our unit prices which of necessity would have to be higher to accommodate that contribution. With UK borrowing rates lower than ours this is a good deal for you.'

So Herr Doktor Professor Humboldt is not prepared to negotiate further on either unit cost or tool costs – but the prices are better than current – and if the French can not hold their tentative offer this might be the source you choose, so you will have to try to develop a provisional contract here too.

Compared to Lefebvre, Humboldt is not prepared to nod his head at anything; every 'i' has to be dotted and every 't' crossed. But eventually you work your way through the clauses.

Failures to agree

But there are some 'sore thumbs'. For example, the following clauses.

1. *Terms and conditions of payment*
   Clause 1 (v) If the exchange rate varies by more than 2½% either way the price was to be re-negotiated.
2. *Quality*
   Any rejects found have to be returned to Humboldt for credit at buyer's expense, and no allowance will be made if faults are found part way through the machining process.

10. and 11. *Quantity variation*
   Schedules must be firm and unchanged; variations will not be accepted by Humboldt unless indicated in the third schedule month.

13. *Packaging and shipping*
   Stillages are to be supplied by the customer at no cost to Humboldt.

20. *Consequential loss*
   Not accepted by Humboldt who will deliver on time and in line with customer's quality requirements, therefore this clause is irrelevant. In regard to product liability, Humboldt can see no reason for them to be involved in cases of this nature.

22. *Cancellation*
   Humboldt accept that failure to attain quality and delivery requirements could eventually result in cancellation, but should the buyer wish to cancel on the grounds of Humboldt being cost uncompetitive, Humboldt must see documentation showing that competition was in all ways superior before accepting cancellation.

Summation

Clearly clauses 2, 10, 11, 13, 20 and 22 are not acceptable to you and you will have to take advice from finance and legal before going any further. Your buyer's instinct tells you that the chemistry is wrong between your company and Humboldt, but you agree that if he's got the business you will send him a letter of intent before going back to the UK. But if they, Humboldt, are under cost pressure in a difficult cost controlling period they will be very likely to demand a hefty price increase at the first opportunity and the evidence is that they will not negotiate. As you leave Hamburg you find yourself hoping that Humboldt does not become your supplier!

The Italian job

Once in the offices of Bertoldi in Milan you make your way to the office of Signor Sergio Morin who greets you warmly saying, 'I will speak English today, I have given Maria the day off.' He presents you with his quotations and leaves the office while you analyse them (see Table 13.6).

Table 13.6

Item	Current	LeRoy	Humboldt	Bertoldi	Total
1.	£43.00	£39.00	£40.00	£40.00	£2 000 000
2.	£25.00	£20.00	£18.55	£26.00	£1 040 000
3.	£33.00	£32.00	£31.50	£31.00	£1 860 000
Annual totals	£4.98m	£4.67m	£4.632m	£4.90m	

Bertoldi has quoted 100% tool cost which they suggest a part cost contribution of 50%, i.e. £175 000 so first-year costs become LeRoy £4.822m, Humboldt £5.032m and Bertoldi £5.075.

The exchange rate is 2395It.L/£1 stg.

A change of approach

Before returning to Sergio Morin's office to commence your negotiations you consider which of the six options to use. It is noticeable that the choice of a blend of options 4 and 6 has worked well with Lefebvre – but it seems to annoy Humboldt.

Then how is it best to get Morin's mind focused onto your objectives – rather than putting him into the defence mode as has happened with Humboldt. Then you remember hearing that power and coercion need not be as brutal as sending in the tanks and the bombers – but can be a gentle, almost airy suggestion that you have knowledge the other does not possess. The indication that you have this intriguing piece of knowledge can be camouflaged in a pleasantry.

You walk into Morin's office and at his invitation sit down. 'I thought Italian foundry engineers were supposed to be the best in Europe.'

'So we are,' replies Morin, with a smile, 'but it does not mean that we are necessarily the cheapest!'

One up to him. You grin in spite of yourself, and riposte, 'Well, at these prices I can't see you getting much business!'

'Come now,' says Morin, 'there is an old Italian proverb which in English says simply, "one hand washes the other." You are here because you are looking for a supplier, I am here because I want your business – and what else have we to do for now but to see how this can be arranged?'

'The fact is, Signor Morin, your quote is the highest of the four foundries that are most specialized in the type of work I am looking for. Unless your quotation is considerably reduced we have nothing to discuss. The other competitors have given me their best price and I need the same from you!'

(Morin is a friendly individual and you are getting more confident. In fact you are beginning to understand that world-class buyers don't pussy-foot around, but came quickly to the point. Time is a very valuable commodity to be used effectively.)

'Well,' says Morin, rising to his feet, 'give me ten minutes, I will go and see my chief estimator, and my works manager. I will see if there are any reductions we can make to costs – but we have quoted for this most carefully because I do assure you we want your business.'

He leaves you on your own.

You wonder if Morin is really having a meeting with his people or waiting somewhere for ten minutes to heighten the tension with a piece of theatre.

It is exactly twelve minutes by your watch before he returns.

'My two principals have again gone over this carefully, constructing quotations once more – and by making some big changes and some serious economies we can offer at the exchange rate we used previously the following:

Item 1   £38.00
Item 2   £24.00
Item 3   £30.50

'We have decided that we can reduce the unit costs of items 1 and 2 by making our tooling more sophisticated but that adds another £10 000 to the tooling bill making the 100% tool cost £360 000. On item 3 we will reduce our margin to an almost unsupportable level in order to reach our absolute bottom price.'

Quickly you evaluate the effect of these changes (see Table 13.7).

Table 13.7

	Current	LeRoy	Humboldt	
1.	£43.00	£39.00	£40.00	
2.	£25.00	£20.00	£18.55	
3.	£33.00	£32.00	£31.50	
Annual totals:				
	£4.98	£4.67	£4.632	£4.69m
Tool cost contribution		£152 000	£400 000	?

Morin waits expectantly while you hammer away at your calculator.

'Well, that's better isn't it?'

'Yes,' you allow, 'but I am very confused about the tool costs. You said in the quote you gave me this morning that the sterling cost of 100% of the tooling was £350 000 and this last decision adds a further £10 000 making the 100% cost £360 000. Further your quote suggested that we make a 50% contribution. Now what actually do you mean?'

'It means that if we are to settle on this arrangement we want you to pay £180 000 with order, and £180 000 when we have satisfied your quality and pre-production requirements.'

An impasse

'Then I am sorry, Signor Morin, I regret that we cannot do business. I came here today prepared if you met our requirements to construct a provisional contract for the next five years' work – but you are not helping yourselves:

1. 'With regard to tool costs we would never normally pay "up front" for production tooling. Particularly in the case where the supplier has been making losses for the last three years. With such tooling until it has been proven we can be wasting our money.

2. 'I might have some justification for asking my management to offer a much smaller sum "up front" if your unit prices were really attractive, but while competitive – they are not extraordinary.'

An approach to the shareholders?

'Now you told me that the family Benedetti own 80% of the shares of the Fonderia Bertoldi, and that they were exerting pressures on you to contain your spending. If this is the reason for this quotation I could perhaps persuade them to relax the purse strings in order to agree not to ask for "up front" tooling money and to share with us on a 50/50 basis the total tool cost. Perhaps we could arrange a properly notarized agreement to that effect.

'If we could arrange that, I would be willing to continue negotiations. Perhaps I could bring to their attention an old English proverb – "You've got to speculate to accumulate!" Investors always speculate – buyers very seldom do!'

Sergio Morin has been looking at you very closely through this last statement and then he says, 'I am a member of the Benedetti family, my wife Anya is the daughter of the founder and she holds 51% of the shares. With her vote I can always get my way in family matters. I am prepared to concede the following:

1. 'We will agree to absorb 50% of the tool cost.
2. 'Of your 50% we will only ask for half of that with order. So that you will pay £90 000 with order, and £90 000 when sample approvals have been granted.
3. 'And this is our absolutely last word. We will shave our price of item 2 down from £24.00 to £23.50.'

Your calculator rattles again. Compared to LeRoy, Bertoldi's final offer is:

	LeRoy	Bertoldi
1.	£39.00	£38.00 (£1 900 000)
2.	£20.00	£23.50 (£940 000)
3.	£32.00	£30.50 (£1 830 000)
Annual cost:		
	£4.67m	£4.67m
Tool cost:		
	£152 000	£180 000
To be paid after approvals		50% paid with order

It is so close and it has been a Herculean task to push Morin so far. He's obviously fired his last shot. You decide to tell Morin that the final sourcing decision will have to be made in the UK but you want to proceed to develop a provisional contract (as you have done with the other two) to save time should the final decision be in favour of Bertoldi.

A sea of 'contras'

But the 'contras' start to mount up.

Payment terms

Thirty days mandatory.

6. and 7. Tooling payment

Part cost but 50% with order. Balance after sample and pre-production approval.

12. Price variation

Because of the inflation rate in Italy and the weakening lira, Bertoldi require to increase prices at each cost impact which affect their profit. Thus if the price of pig iron (a basic raw material) goes up they want the facility to uplift the price increases to be a monthly event. This is apart from currency fluctuations where Bertoldi will not agree to more than a 5% band without re-negotiation.

(Clearly this had been Bertoldi's reason for accepting 'open book' negotiations.)

13. Packaging and shipping

The Company is to supply all stillages free of charge to Bertoldi.

20. Consequential loss

Bertoldi offer 'best endeavours' only and will not accept any agreement on compensation payments should they be late on provision of samples or pre-production batches.

You and Signor Morin work your way through the clauses and it becomes obvious to you that wherever Bertoldi can meet your requirements they will bend every effort to do so – but the cash strictures applied by the shareholders mean that Bertoldi is less attractive than you have hoped.

Summation

At bottom the choice is simple provided LeRoy confirms the provisional agreement – but if the French deal falls through then the choice is between Humboldt where the chemistry is wrong, or Bertoldi where the chemistry is right but the cash situation is not without risk.

A final try

'Look,' you say, 'you've got a copy of the provisional contract we have developed. You know that you do not satisfy our requirements on clauses 1, 6, 7, 12, 13 and 20. I've also told you where I need improvement. I do not have to make up my recommendations for another day or so. If you could meet my requirements you'd be in with a very good chance of getting the order – but otherwise it's most likely the business will go elsewhere.'

Morin thanks you for the offer – but says they have done their best.

You go back to your hotel with mixed feelings about Bertoldi and decide you will keep them on your enquiry list for the future.

The verdict

Back at the hotel you put in a call to Lefebvre of LeRoy. It is a choice of evils if LeRoy falls down.

'*Allo, Lefebvre, qui parle?*'

'Good afternoon,' you say, 'I take it that your colleagues agreed all the details on the provisional contract we raised two days ago?'

'Yes, they accepted it all.' (Phew!)

'Good, then as I promised I will fax you a letter of intent but there is one small snag, all the competition has been lower than you on item 3.'

'By how much?'

'At least a £1.00.'

There was a moment's silence then . . .

'Very well, the price for item no. 3 will be £31.00 – you can confirm that on your letter of intent if you will.'

'Thanks.'

'Now, when will I be receiving your letter of intent?'

'I shall be sending it off via the fax from Italy within the hour.'

'I shall look forward to receiving it, and thank you,' said Lefebvre and hung up.

Well, that is a load off your mind – and you sit down to compose your communication (see Figure 13.1).

You send the fax off. For a moment you toy with the idea of sending the purchasing manager a fax too on the lines of 'message to Garcia delivered – source selected – letter of intent issued'. But then you think, would a world-class buyer be so frivolous as that? 'Well maybe,' you concede, 'but then other buyers have different purchasing managers!'

The next flight from Milan to London is in two hours – you decide to be on it.

The final assessment

On the flight you list out your answers to the tasks the purchasing manager has set you, and calculate the speed of payback of the tools which is:

1. £39.00 × 50 000 = £1 950 000
2. £20.00 × 40 000 =   £800 000
3. £31.00 × 60 000 = £1 860 000

Annual total = £4 610 000.
This is compared to the current source at £4.98m.

So the annual saving is £370 000. Against this the tool cost has to be set off of £152 000 which gives a payback after 4.8 months of production. That demonstrates that, contrary to belief, the current supplier has not been put under challenge against his competitors as he should have been. But then, if you'd been sitting at your desk shuffling enquiries and quotes, you too might have concluded that from the original quotes for LeRoy, Humboldt, and Bertoldi there wasn't much in it.

FAX

LeRoy Fonderies,
Lille,
France

For the attention of M.J. Lefebvre, Sales Director

Reference your original quotation dated .... and our discussions at your works of the .... resulting in a preliminary contract dated ....

For the following items:

1. 237-481   £39.00 Stg
2. 237-998   £20.00
3. 237-1001   £31.00 (price agreed today's date)

Tool cost

Part cost £152 000 to be paid after sample approval and pre-production batch approval.

Delivery

Samples and pre-production to be delivered within the next 5 months. Scheduled deliveries to be commenced immediately after approvals.

Exchange rate 8.47 FF/£ stg.

This signifies our intent to place orders in the near future. It does not entitle you to commence any work which may be expensed to us.

Regards

Figure 13.1 Letter of intent

So there is another lesson learned. Although you have had to use a range of techniques – because of time and pressure and the fact that the suppliers are overseas – that you haven't applied that way before – isn't it a technique that could be used at home as a pro-active system of getting to the lowest ultimate cost?

The stewardess is coming down the aisle towards you pushing the drinks trolley. You decide a small celebration is in order, so you choose a G&T.

56 Negotiating overseas – more pointers

- Use an interpreter if you need to, don't struggle to the point of no return
- Maintain a pace that you are comfortable with
- Beware of commercial data sent by you to the office, it may be read
- Your timescales are not theirs, so don't be impatient
- Think about the payment methods and know how they work
- Check the political situation
- Be aware of the inflation rate and its history
- Don't accept excessive hospitality
- Observe the customs of the country
- Be sensitive to loss of face when 'winning' a major point
- Do not reveal highly confidential data of other suppliers
- Never sign anything in a meeting
- Recap all major points and make sure there are no misunder-standings

REMEMBER – you cannot return to the country to tie up the points you missed the first time around – get it right first time. That demands high-level planning.

14 APPLICATIONS OF STRATEGY

This chapter looks at training and developing buyers for world-class performance. It begins to look at the strategic applications of the lessons from the book, showing how buyers can match product ranges to overseas manufacturing specialities and develop economic forecasts relating to their industry which can successfully refine savings targeting and aid the selection of feasible objectives.

'That's a very good performance,' says the purchasing manager, as you finish your report on the reasons for your choice of LeRoy. 'Now get an ITP off to them today, and then get legal to complete the contract. Make sure you've got the order and contract away to them by the weekend. By the way, drop a note to Bertoldi and Humboldt thanking them for their interest but telling them they have been unsuccessful on this occasion. It's a courtesy which a lot of buyers do not observe – but it's a valuable indication to the suppliers which indirectly helps the buyer – because it serves as a guide to help the supplier do better next time.'

Some ideas for buyer training

After the events of the last few weeks things seem a little flat until the chief buyer sends for you.

'The purchasing manager has asked me to give him some ideas about buyer training – apparently he's hopeful that soon after the financial year we'll get two recently qualified people coming into the department. Personnel have asked him to present a paper showing how they will be trained. Apparently, the new people will be around twenty years old, with either BA Business Studies, or the CIPS Diploma – or perhaps both. What are your views?'

'Well, of course, there are the basics, "know your items, know your systems" (Chapter 1) but I found what hampered me was that I didn't know how the business worked! I didn't know what the departments actually did, and I couldn't entirely see how the buyer's role fitted in. It wasn't really until I went on the Farrington course that I realized how much power a buyer has, and that each skill you acquire forms the basis to develop another skill. I really wonder how you can teach a person like the two you've described to become skilful buyers most quickly.'

'So what do you think the objectives of purchasing training should be?'

'Well, how about world class in three years?'

'So, you think it could be achieved in that short a time? Then how would you start?'

'I don't believe world-class buyers are born – but there are not that many people who've got the right mix of personal qualities to be absolutely top flight. I believe there are nine essential qualities a student buyer has to have.'

The nine essential personal qualities

The potential buyer needs:

1. to have common sense;
2. a strong moral sense;
3. an aptitude for planning both short and long term;
4. the ability to 'see' the cascading results of any action;
5. be capable of expressing themselves well, and have the ability to 'walk with kings, but not lose the common touch'.
6. to be determined, but not pig-headed;
7. to be imaginative, but able to keep their feet on the ground, with an analytical frame of mind;
8. to be mobile, willing to travel at the drop of a hat and willing to put whatever it takes into a job to bring it to a successful conclusion;
9. to be self-starters – but capable of being equally effective when working alone or as part of a team.

'Yes,' agrees the chief buyer, 'but hopefully the recruiting process automatically selects people who have these qualities – so what then?'

'I've met buyers, and I expect you have too, who are completely lacking in one or more of these qualities – but assuming personnel can give us some good material who are well academically qualified the student buyer needs to put their academics temporarily on the back burner. Their training will be priceless once they've mastered the practicalities. When I joined the company I found the factory, the systems, the different departments an impenetrable jungle, and I wasted months learning the difference between accounts and finance, planning and production engineers, quality control and inspection. I believe that if the newcomer was taught the roles of the various departments, and how they interface with purchasing, people could progress a lot faster.'

Practical training

Students often become demotivated and bored because some senior people believe that they are trained by giving them long lists to compile, and computer tabs to analyse. We all have to do that sometimes, but we know why we're doing it, and the resultant information has a meaning – but for them it's meaningless.

'So as soon as possible they've got to be given work which combines training with work which is making a visible contribution to the company.

'I think we should be aiming at what is effectively a vastly accelerated apprenticeship. I'd give them a spell as an expediter to start with, where they learn to control suppliers, count items, chase panics, deal with the shopfloor folk and learn their way about the factory. That way they learn how important supply is.'

'Yes,' said the chief buyer, 'I agree with that. When I came into purchasing, no matter what your qualifications you started off as an expediter. The training theory was, that unless you developed into an efficient and effective expediter then you would never be promoted to buying. Well, what would you do next?'

'Well, after six months' expediting I'd put them with either the estimators or the planning engineers for a three-month spell to learn something about costing through practical examples. Then finally an overview of the workings of finance.'

'How about marketing, accounting, quality and design?'

'Their time in expediting would bring them into contact with accounts, inspection and quality – so perhaps a fast overview of marketing and design should also be provided.'

'This would mean then that the student wanting to enter purchasing would not be anywhere near the department they want to enter for a year.'

The buddy system

'I've read of an American system that covers that objection. When the student enters the company he/she is attached to an operating buyer who gives the student regular tutorials aimed at linking in the trainee's mind the knowledge acquired with its eventual application. Then after the first twelve months the student starts buying training on a "sitting with Nelly" basis with the person who was their buddy.

'The training process consists of an ever-increasing and stretching set of objectives to be achieved. During this period they should attend at least one off-site negotiating course.'

'So,' commented the chief buyer, 'the student buyer would have a set of MBOs which they wouldn't know how to tackle at the beginning of the second year.'

'That's right, at first the buddy would be guiding the student very closely, but at the end of the year the buddy's influence will be reduced just to counselling when required.'

'So, who would you propose as the buddy?'

'Well, it could be the chief buyer or the purchasing manager but I would very much prefer the buddy to be an up-and-coming buyer because it would help the buyer to think through the subtleties of their job and to learn how to guide, lead and advise juniors.'

'Yes,' said the chief buyer, 'I like that – anything else?'

Post-training development

'After the second year I believe that the buyer should move at regular intervals on to different commodity ranges and types of buying. This is to widen experience. I notice that you and the purchasing manager are equally at home with any commodity we cover, and I know that as just one example, if I'd not been on capital, I wouldn't have been half so effective on buying tooling for production items. So experience increases the buyer's effectiveness as a direct ratio to the number of different commodity ranges covered.'

'I suppose you would also include foreign language and advanced negotiation training too.'

You nod agreement, and then add, 'I'd like to see the policies and procedures more user-friendly too. After policy and procedure number 4 they get progressively more woolly. For example, what are the rules on make v. buy? When I was doing my foundry study I saw all three foundries were doing extra work to castings they were supplying to other customers. They had transfer lines where they were machining castings, the Italians were actually assembling complete gear boxes. In fact they were capable of doing everything our machine shop does. I didn't ask them for costs because I didn't know if I would have been wasting my time, and I wasn't sure if I could propose such a radical cost reduction proposal. After all if bought-out costs were favourable it could result in large-scale redundancies in the factory.'

'If you made such a recommendation it would not be your decision as to the action resulting – it would be a board decision. You should never ignore an opportunity to make recommendations. I agree that we do ask our buyers to "wing it" too often. I'll take that on board too.'

It is later that week when the purchasing manager calls you into his office. He hands you a small brown envelope and asks you to open it.

It is the biggest raise you've ever had!

You are about to thank him when he holds up his hand and stops you.

'Over the last three years we've put you at all the jumps we could think of – some you've cleared without even noticing they were there, others you've scrambled your way through, and others you've cleared effortlessly. So this raise signifies our satisfaction with your work. This also constitutes an improvement in grade – you are now a senior buyer. But there's a rock in every snowball so I've got a couple of tasks for you.

'Firstly, I want you to do an economic study on the possible UK economic movements for the year 1995–6. I want to present a paper to the board with a view of the economic battle facing us. I should add that management want us to reduce prices by 5% on prices ruling on at the start of the financial year.

'Secondly, I want to see a paper from you, on the savings possibilities of starting a campaign of overseas buying. We might have to try to make our 5% following this route as I think we'll have difficulty in hitting management's target, if we don't follow this line.

'The mark of the world-class buyer is to start off with a strategy and I need some options. I'd like both reports within two months.'

So that is a thought-provoking strategy! Well, the question is where to start?

A forecast of UK economics

Basic data

The Government's intentions (frequently stated by the Chancellor) are to keep inflation below 4%.

OECD Growth Report, June 1994

Forecast growth, 1995: 3%.

It should be remembered that the Government statistics list a range of commodities which include everything from fruit and vegetable prices to mortgage costs. Movements are measured from 12 months back, so that if the price of mortgages come down, this reduces the bottom line of inflation although some other commodity prices may have lifted. The National Digest of Statistics records the raw movements of costs in representative industries but does not take into account the economies that an individual company may make to offset these recorded increases. So effectively the buyer has to do a study which is tailored specifically to the company or companies that the buyer is considering.

The aim must be to decide what costs pressures will bear on to the supplier network, and as a result what price increases the supplier will ask for using the economic impacts to justify the size of the claim. Timing of the presentation of the price increase would normally be the anniversary of the previous price movement.

Once this part of the forecast is completed this is a reasonable representation of the price increases **if there were no purchasing department present.**

The second part of the forecast is to plan the methods at supplier and commodity level, detailing the ways in which these potential price increases will be off-set. This second part is the savings forecast; by applying the one to the other, it can be seen what the actual forecast for potential price movement over the period under review will actually be.

The buyer who makes a practice of this exercise will have their own set of economic indicators such as the following.

Current indicators

1. Many reports from such bodies as the CBI says that prices at the suppliers are being constrained by the fear of losing business if they attempt to restore profit levels by increasing prices to customers (**pent-up prices).**
2. Considerable number of reports in the press of companies profits down. (This bears out (1).)
3. A growing number of accounts of increased militancy and strike action where employees are seeking to, and succeeding in, breaching the Government's unofficial guide line of 2½%. Some increases being claimed are up to 10%.

   (As a wise precaution the buyer should contact his suppliers and ascertain their labour/management situation. If industrial relation problems are on the horizon then the buyer should ascertain the possible duration of such disruption and bring in extra stock to cover the duration of the strike.)

4. Increased taxation and progressive VAT costs will increase labour and staff pressure for wage increases.
5. Relationship of £ stg. exchange rates. This includes the US$/£ relationship. Most internationally traded commodities are traded in dollars of which oil is just one example. Due to the poor trading going on worldwide, prices of such commodities have been traded at a lower price than costs would justify, which means UK buyers have not felt the full impact of the fall in the value of the £ vis à vis its trading partners currencies.

A widely reported set of actions are the movements of OPEC to increase prices. Despite the unit costs being $x per barrel if there is a glut then world trading brings the price below the $x price. In order to offset this the OPEC suppliers are limiting output in order to drive prices up. If they succeed, oil prices will rise amplified by the weakness of the £ stg. against the US$.

Just these five indicators show that there is a significant inflationary sword of Damocles suspended over the buyer's head.

If these indicators are applied to the MLO ratios then we see the following.

Materials

There are few materials used in industry at the raw stage which are indigenous. As a rough estimate the £ stg. has fallen in value by something in the order of 10% (average) + over 20% with the US$ since it was 'floated' – this has helped exports and the full impact has yet to be experienced on imports.

Labour

Due to the high unemployment position wages have been relatively stable – but recent tax and VAT increases are leading labour to request increases higher than the unofficial 'norm'.

Overhead

Energy costs due to taxation increases put pressure on suppliers who are heavy users of energy.

The trigger for a considerable move in inflation will be as demand starts to rise. If an increase of 3% as forecast by the OECD in output comes to fruition then this will be the trigger for increased inflation.

A reasonable assumption could be 5% increase in imported raw materials, a 4% increase in labour costs, and say an increase of 3% on overheads.

To assess this impact you must now look at specifics.

Dollar related materials

This includes all materials where oil is used as the feed stock:

- paint
- plastics
- lubricants
- oil
- synthetic rubber
- motor fuels

Energy related

Notably aluminium, iron and steel.

Direct imports from European suppliers

From finished high-tech components through raw materials down to timber etc.

Labour costs

Among your domestic suppliers you will have some with more powerful work-forces than others. There will be some suppliers who are specialists with little fear of suffering the effects of competition. These groups are much more likely to breach the 'norm' by a considerable order of magnitude than the lean business facing tough competition. Also some geographic areas where suppliers are located are less active in seeking large increases than others. Your departmental records and buyer's knowledge should be able to tell you who these various categories of supplier are. This should enable you to 'shade' labour increases more precisely.

Overheads

The trends in rates, heating, lighting, water, NHI, VAT, staff salaries, transport are nearly all upwards. This area is the most difficult to forecast because of the different accounting allocations which each supplier puts to overhead. However a good guide is to discuss with your own accounts department, the effect on overheads in your company and apply the resulting percentage to the forecast you are doing on suppliers.

To test your assumptions you should take, say, a plastic item with a current price of £1.00 which the buyer tells you is:

70% material
15% labour
15% overhead

If the material price (oil based, dollar/pound vulnerable) increases by 5% then 3.5p is added to the price, with labour moving by 4%, then the price grows by 0.6p and if the overhead grows by 3% the price due to overhead growth moves upwards by another 0.45p. Thus the total growth becomes 5%.

Your price which, was £1.00 at the beginning of the financial year could become £1.05 by the year's end.

Carrying on the check test, take a steel item where the price is also £1.00. Here the movement may be:

60% material. Increase due to energy, transport, VAT and NHI = 4%

15% labour. Say due to pressure put on the supplier who is planning for 3% growth and decides to concede 4.5% in return for industrial peace.

25% overhead. Supplier also pays 3% extra.

The increases that the supplier will have to face are 2.4p on material, labour 0.675, and overhead impact 0.75p. This means that an increase of 3.825% could be requested by the supplier. The average supplier aims at a profit margin of some-where between 7 and 10%, and unless they could make management savings their profit margins risk being approximately halved, which is a powerful incentive to fight hard for a price increase.

Estimating the potential impact on the total turnover in the department.

By taking a representative item from each category of items purchased you may end up with a list of say, 30 different categories of potential price movements.

By then 'weighting', according to annual forecast spend, it is then possible to arrive at a bottom-line figure of worst case economic movement, e.g.

total forecast spend – plastics: £2 000 000 @ 5% = £100 000
total forecast spend – steel items: £5 000 000 @ 3.825% = £191 250.

Thus on a total forecast turnover of £7 000 000 you could concede £291 250 = 4.16%. This percentage would represent the 'full year', or index change, year on year. If you assume that all increases would be paid at mid-financial year then the 'fiscal' increase would be half that of the index, i.e. 2.08%.

Thus your considerations letter would incorporate your views on the likely impact of inflation on the buy; and an estimate (if all increases were paid) of 2.08% (fiscal) and 4.16% full year.

Assuming the purchasing manager agrees with you, and with a turnover actually of £100 000 000, then the department stands to have to pay out a sum exceeding £4 000 000 – effectively for nothing!

The next step

Each buyer is then requested, using your models, to complete a forecast on his or her own buy, plotting in the increase as though paid a year from the previous increase. This allows the true fiscal effect to be calculated.

A savings forecast

As the buyer plots the likely cost effects of a price increase he/she prepares a plan to (at minimum) offset the increase the forecast indicates as likely. This is also worked on a fiscal and full-year basis, timed from the point at which the buyer estimates that the saving will occur. Assuming the buyers collectively are able to say that they can produce savings of 2.08% fiscal and 4.16% full year, then inflation has been netted off.

The purchasing manager is not going to be satisfied with that – so he or she will be going through each buyer's forecast to improve the nett year end balance, encouraging buyers to negotiate later settlements in order to reduce the fiscal effect. Buyers will find new targets emerging on products for rationalization, resourcing, resistance, substitution etc. – and it's back to the drawing board on savings planning.

Overseas sourcing – some thoughts on a twin-track strategy

Clearly the purchasing manager is not feeling confident about netting off inflation at 4.16% plus an additional saving of 5%, making 9.16% to be achieved; which is why he's asked for an exercise to be done on overseas sourcing. Getting your own ducks in a row is the first step. On a turnover of £100 000 000, 5% represents £5 000 000.

To source out the whole £100m at a 5% saving would be logistically impossible in a year. Of course you could consider £50m at 10%, or £25m at a 20% saving. Or £10m at a 50% saving could produce the desired £5 000 000 saving.

One thing is certain: to make this target, or even approach it, some of the overseas markets are going to have to be very competitive.

Another issue is which commodity groups and families within groups should be studied?

A study has been done by one of the other buyers; it shows that in the 5000 items regularly bought there are 1000 items which constitute the highest spend on the unit cost × usage formula. This exactly coincides with the Pareto ratio that 20% of the items purchased represent 80% of the cost and 80% of the items only represent 20% of the cost.

Plainly the key items offer the biggest potential; further, because great strides have been made in rationalizing whole families of items, both key and non-key items are obtained from the same supplier. So if a new supplier is found, the offer could include not only the key items but the associated family of non-key items too, simplifying resourcing actions.

Research

Firstly, you need to know in which families the key items are. They fall into eleven categories:

bearings	castings	turned parts
instruments	forgings	pressings
electrics	plastics	wheels
oil seals	wiring harnesses	

The eleven categories break down to four manufacturing skill levels:

* **high tech** – instruments (electronic), electrics;
* **specialists** – bearings, wheels;
* **general engineering** – turned parts, pressings and oil seals.
* **labour intensive** – castings, forgings, wiring harnesses and plastics.

Quite probably some of the manufacturing skills would migrate into another category but it is at least a place to start from.

What countries should be explored?

A good start is the list of members of GATT (General Agreement on Tariffs and Trade) which list some 80 or more countries who give each other preferential treatment in trade and economic affairs. This lists among others those least developed countries who could be possibles. You list these. There are areas too like the new countries which have emerged out of the breakup of the USSR who should be capable of good quality engineering work. There are countries hungry for hard currency that might well offer an excellent price in return for payment in hard currency. Two prime examples come to mind with Poland and Brazil.

On the high-tech items you decide not to include the Western Europe nations, Scandinavia or North America in your first study, but try to get more information about:

India	South Korea	Tai Wan
Malaya	Singapore	Hong Kong
Poland	Romania	Hungary
East Germany	Brazil	Mexico

There are many other countries which look interesting as far apart as China and Czechoslovakia; these two head your second list to try if the first do not seem productive. Two countries on your first list are perhaps doubtful starters, because, although South Korea and Hong Kong have expanding engineering based economies, South Korea is having problems with North Korea and Hong Kong will pass under China's control which might be a problem later on.

Sales advice

Sales have said in a recent communication that they are encountering resistance in certain Second and Third World countries because the local customers (often the government of the country in question) are complaining that within the company's product there are components that they can make themselves, and they would be much happier if part of the product they are being asked to buy contained a percentage of locally manufactured content. So a visit to sales produces a list of countries to add to your own list.

Embassies and legations

By a combination of letters and visits to the commercial attaches you are able to obtain lists of suppliers who manufacture items in your product ranges. Many countries provide export incentives to their exporters, through the GATT agreements in many cases import duties are either non-existent, or very low, and in some cases labour rates are very low.

They are able to discuss shipping costs, and air freight costs in general terms. The British High Commission is also able to give advice in some areas.

Shipping

Next you make a call on the company's shipping agent to get an idea of costs. This is not as easy as you have thought. Incoterms (see Appendix C) was a great help but basically she starts by explaining the costs which add to price from an ex-works delivery:

- export packing;
- insurance;
- road transport to quayside;
- lift/lifts onto ship;
- stowage aboard – this was costed on a variety of factors, cube size and weight, deck cargo or hold;
- lift/lifts from ship to shore and quayside to vehicle;
- import duties where applicable;
- delivery from quayside to customer.

Her advice is that you should obtain your quotes DDP (delivery duty paid). Looking at the list of countries you are proposing she adds that she doubts that in some cases the suppliers would be able to do the costings – in which case you are to tell them to quote ex-works and then ask her to give an estimate of the shipping costs applicable.

You have started mailing enquiries immediately you have returned from your swing around the embassies and you have in fact asked for DDP and ex-works quotes for a different reason than the shipping agent has given. You have asked for the quote both ways in order to find out what the basic unit cost would be.

A pile of quotations

You find as the quotes flood in that there are some extremely interesting prices coming in, as well as percentage of 'no quotes' and ones that are completely out of court, but what does emerge is that there are opportunities to make savings in all the countries you have enquired from.

The dilemma is what to do next. Most, indeed all the quotations need a lot of refinement, qualification and negotiation before you could consider raising orders and making contracts. There is more than a faint possibility that in some areas savings, including transport costs of 20%+, are attainable. Your presentation to the purchasing manager is hedged about with words like 'possibility, potential, probably' and so on.

After he's studied your report and your findings for a few days he comes out of his office to say, 'You know, if we could source just £2 000 000 of our turnover, saving 20% that would contribute £400 000 to support the efforts on the new savings plan. If we can source £2 000 000 overseas this year perhaps in the following year we might be able to move £4 000 000 out. However, we might not have to go as far as that.' You look askance.

The twin-track policy becomes a triple track

'The majority of our suppliers have in their contract a clause which says that if we tell them they're under competitive challenge they will endeavour to meet the competition price. Now with these ex-works prices we can offer the existing suppliers realistic competition prices which they must meet or get as close to as they can, otherwise we may well choose to resource.'

'Surely,' you say, 'this is a massive con trick you are proposing to work on these overseas people?'

'Certainly not. If after negotiation with the current supplier the overseas supplier is still competitive he'll get the business. But before we make the change over we've got to be absolutely sure of the new supplier, and that's going to need every bit of negotiation skill, and supplier assessment support we can apply.'

Operating the triple track negotiation

It looks as though the purchasing manager is steering towards a process that is going to be a real administrative headache for somebody.

1. Overseas buyer does partial negotiation with a foreign source.
2. Sends quotation to domestic buyer.
3. Domestic buyer negotiates with current supply source.
4. If current supplier can meet competition or cannot meet competition overseas buyer has to be informed.
5. If overseas supplier is uncompetitive supplier is informed accordingly.
6. If overseas supplier is competitive overseas buyer completes negotiation.

But there are questions that will cause a lot of problems if this route is chosen.

What if the domestic supplier is only able to halve the difference between the current price and the overseas quote? Will the overseas source be invited to requote?

Who will administer the overseas supplier once he becomes the supplier? The domestic buyer who has the line responsibility, or should the overseas buyer retain control because he has done the negotiation?

Although it is only an extension of what the buyer does every day, some very tight procedures will have to be written.

You go home musing.

It seems these days that you just cannot keep out from under the purchasing manager's feet. Only a week later you are in his office again!

'Personnel like the ideas you and the chief buyer have put together on an accelerated apprenticeship for new buyers and we've decided to adopt it with the two new people we've got coming in. I've decided to make the chief buyer their "buddy." '

'You are a little disappointed and perhaps it shows on your face because he hastens to add, "You would have been the natural choice for that role except that I've another job in mind for you." You told the chief buyer that you thought the policies and procedures need revising. I would like you to list out say a half dozen policies and write them in the way you would like to see them, and the attendant procedures to go with them.

'It's very good training for the aspiring world-class buyer to think through the linkage between the policy and the appropriate procedure – but I disagree with your point that buyers have to "wing it" where they run into a situation the procedures don't cover. Provided they act in line with the policy, they are not "winging it" but interpreting policy. Frankly, I expect my buyers to be able to do that standing on their heads.'

You realize you are getting a rocket for not using your head, but he hasn't quite finished. 'You should have learned by now there is only one species of animal on the earth that can change its environment to suit itself – and that's us humans – and I would have expected you to provide some examples of how you wanted to improve your environment before you went off half-cock!'

Barely have you got back to your desk and sat down but who should materialize in front of you like the Demon King in pantomime but the purchasing manager!

'How are those French suppliers of yours getting on,' he asks. 'It's about time they were coming on stream, isn't it?'

'They passed sample inspection two weeks ago, the preproduction batch passed through the transfer lines without a hitch last week and they will be able to start supply from next week!'

'That's splendid,' he exults. 'Look at this letter.' (See Figure 14.1.)

'So my strategy and your tactical implementation of it really paid off.' Then two of the biggest grins ever seen in the purchasing department spread over your faces as you envisage the purchasing manager's letter of reply.

Close and Lane Foundry
(Formerly Puckeridge and Broke)

The Purchasing Manager

Dear Sirs,

Subject: 1.   237-481
           2.   237-998
           3.   237-1001

We have recently completed a study on the profitability of certain items, and we find that the above mentioned items are grossly uneconomical. From the first of next month our new prices are as follows:

Current price	From first of next month
1. £40.00	£70.00
2. £25.00	£55.00
3. £33.00	£64.00

Unless we receive your acceptance of these prices by return regretfully we will have to cease production after the 'firm' quantity on your present schedule has been delivered.

Yours faithfully,

Close and Lane

Figure 14.1   Letter from Close and Lane Foundry

Policies and procedures revisited

As you sit down to think about policies and procedures you realize they link with strategy and tactics. Really, if you could get the strategy right, the procedures, or most of them really fall into place.

You've used policy no. 5 (Chapter 2) to warn a requisitioner that they are planning to spend more money than is necessary. But this only nibbles at the problem – so you decide to start with a policy statement that clearly defines purchasing's role in the organization.

Despite the work that purchasing is doing in battling to achieve the lowest ultimate cost, certain internal departments are doing much more to bring purchasing's work to naught than all the suppliers put together.

The problem really stems from company employees being allowed to make commitments without any reference to the procurement specialists.

The people who take it upon themselves to make these commitments fall into several categories:

- **Design engineers** who select a proprietary item and specify its use. When the buyers find out what has been done, the supplier knows the buyer cannot resource or even negotiate successfully because design has completely disarmed the buyer.

  So the company has a supplier that the buyer cannot control.
- **Managers** who are proud that they can sign contracts exercising their 'machismo', committing the company to the most horrendous conditions. If asked, they would argue, 'How could a mere buyer assist the great almighty me?'
- **Directors** who feel that if they have got authority to build a new building they can select their own architects without reference to the procurement specialists.
- **Planning and production engineers** who are convinced that they know all about the procurement of tooling and facilities and do everything they can to present purchasing with a *fait accompli* in order that they can represent themselves as the 'people with the power' to the market. They too would so commit the company to a supplier that purchasing has no room to negotiate.
- **Foremen and secretaries** who contact a supplier and specify a particular supplier's product and don't even ask for an order but ask for the material to be delivered to their office and then raise a cheque request to pay for the goods.

Apart from the appalling waste of company resources both in cash and in time with unqualified buyers spending time that would be better spent doing their own job there is the very real suspicion that they are bent!

Why would a director select an architect that later proved expensive and incompetent unless the director has been persuaded by the offer of a free holiday in the Bahamas?

Or why should the planning engineer spend so much effort in trying to keep purchasing out of the picture when looking for a new machine tool unless he or she is really working to have a new kitchen installed in their home?

Unless the whole process, from the preparation of a neutral specification followed by a set of identical enquiries and a quotation analysis, is transparent then the initiator is liable to be accused of taking bribes to choose the source that has been chosen.

Of course many of these actions are carried out by other departmental members out of ignorance – but not all – so to protect the innocent and the just plain stupid, as well as to root out the guilty, a very clear and unequivocal policy must be put in place.

Policy no. 5

Purchasing are responsible for all procurement activities from preliminary research for a commodity or service. Under certain conditions purchasing may delegate certain aspects of the research prior to the selection of a supply source to the requesting department, but source selection even in these cases rests finally with purchasing.

No commitment made by any company servant will be honoured by purchasing unless the appropriate procurement processes have been carried out by purchasing.

Procedure no. 5

Any company member authorized to specify requirements of any nature which will eventually result in company expenditure is henceforth to conform to the following:

- proprietary items;
- machine tools;
- process machinery.

Before contacting any suppliers a specification is to be raised which does not favour anything currently on the market but describes the function. This is to be issued to purchasing who will, in liaison with the requisitioning department, conduct research to select the best source and to negotiate the best conditions of price and supply.

Services
Professional services } As above
Sub–contractors
Consumables not covered by existing blanket orders   As above

This would undoubtedly make more work for purchasing but the internal procedures would remain unchanged. Except that:

1. the buyer should consider each new requirement as a rationalization opportunity;
2. the buyer must respect the requisitioner's technical expertise but ensure that the buyer's commercial expertise is equally respected.

Policy no. 6

Make v. buy and buy v. make. It is the responsibility of all company employees to be alert to possibilities of achieving lowest ultimate costs through the application of the above techniques.

Procedure no. 6

All such recommendations should be directed to purchasing who will obtain present costs and compare the fully absorbed internal costs with the bought-out costs. This will include the involvement of finance accounting and the appropriate engineering departments.

A report will be made by purchasing to the board if the action recommended provides rapid payback of investment and is considered by all departments participating to be achievable.

Policy no. 7

Extra-territorial purchasing: as a company selling worldwide it is the responsibility of purchasing to buy wherever in the world items, materials, services can be obtained at the lowest ultimate cost in a worldwide context.

Procedure no. 7

Purchasing must maintain a positive comparison by vigorous enquiry action of current prices against those available from both domestic and overseas competitive sources.

Each family of items should be 'turned over' i.e. put out to competitive quote at least once per year. Where better prices or other LUC advantages are uncovered the holding supplier is to be informed that competition is available and must be invited to requote giving their best price. Depending on the result the buyer takes the appropriate action.

Prior to resourcing overseas the following must be carried out:

- the overseas supplier must be quality assured;
- full commercial audit carried out;
- face-to-face negotiations must be carried out.

Currency banding must be wide enough to ensure that it is sufficient to embrace the currency swings that have occurred over the last three years.

Normally quotes should only be accepted on DDP terms. Where other Incoterms are accepted shipping must establish all costs applicable to the buyer to ensure that projected savings can be achieved.

All prices must be converted to pounds sterling.

Policy no. 8

Contracts: **all contracts entered into must be prepared by the company.**

Procedure no. 8

Where suppliers offer their own pre-prepared contracts it must be explained that company policy does not permit these to be accepted.

Purchasing will draft a mutually agreed contract with the supplier and pass the draft to legal for finalization.

The next procedures you consider are as follows.

Policy no. 9

Shared ownership of costs of packaging and stillages with supplier.

Policy no. 10

Ownership of tooling, jigs and fixtures at suppliers: where full cost is paid the tooling should be on the company's asset register and identified as the company's property.

Policy no. 11

Methods of payment available to overseas suppliers.

Policy no. 12

Communication with the press and media.

Another message to Garcia

You've just decided that it is time to go home when the internal phone rings. You know who it is before you've picked up the receiver. It is funny the way the PM always seems to call you into his office just as you are about to declare a 'cessation of hostilities' for today and go home.

In a moderately philosophical frame of mind you make your way down to his office.

'I've been looking at the overseas study that you finished a couple of weeks ago, and there are some most interesting trends in it. For example you've got very good quotes for General Engineering Components from India, Taiwan, Malaysia and Hong Kong. There are opportunities for wheels in India and Korea. There are oil seals in several countries, notably Taiwan and Hong Kong.'

'Yes, that's right, and I have quite a lot more good quotes since I put my report in.'

'Interesting,' says the purchasing manager, changing the subject abruptly. 'I've been going through your records – and you've done well on every desk you've served on. You saw right from your earliest days how the top-class buyer controls the market he/she is in, and manipulates it to achieve the lowest ultimate cost in pursuit of the company's advantage.

'You absorbed all you could on manufacturing methods, costing and accounting procedures; you learned as much as you could about the law as it affects us in our profession; you've developed very good negotiating skills and your knowledge of contracting is good. You've produced good plans for buying training and a good working example of an economic forecast. I understand you've achieved A Level in French and now you've applied to learn German.'

'Yes,' you said, 'but I've had some good training.'

'It's taken us three years and a bit to get you to the stage where we could be confident that in any set of circumstances I could foresee you would behave as a world-class buyer.'

'I know I've changed. Some months ago I was talking to an Italian purchasing manager who proudly announced that all his suppliers were within fifty miles or so of his factory. When I started in buying I would have agreed with him – but when he told me that, I was quite shocked at his short-sighted parochialism.'

'Well, I'd have felt the same way if he'd said that to me,' the purchasing manager replied. 'Now, I've got another message to Garcia for you. I would like you to contact this list of suppliers you identified in India, Taiwan and Hong Kong and arrange to visit them.

'Take the drawings and specifications of the families associated with the key items they quoted on, and negotiate the best ex-works and landed costs you can get and telex them back to me as soon as you've got them. If the current supplier can't meet your price and you are satisfied that the supplier meets all our commercial audit requirements, I'll send an SQA inspector out to you. If they get a clean (or near clean) bill of health I'll ask you to place a trial order. If that's OK we'll single source on your supplier. Obviously we'll have to set up some fairly elaborate supply protection routines. But in certain cases I'll keep the option open to split source with the current supplier – but that will depend on your report. You should be able to get to the stage of raising draft contracts in four weeks if the suppliers are any good – so I'll expect you back in a month.'

He can see you are thinking furiously and he adds, 'Since the day you started working with Mrs Ferguson you've travelled 1000 miles in buying terms – and how she sung your praises – and now you're starting on the next 1000. Your career reminds me of one of the proverbs of Lao-Tze – a journey of a 1000 miles begins with one step. Good luck!'

APPENDIX A: MEMORY JOGGERS

1 **The buyer's rights**

- Purchase the right material
- At the right time
- At the right quantity
- At the right place
- At the right price
- At the right quality
- At the lowest feasible inventory

REMEMBER – These are essentials and cannot be compromised ever!

2 **The buyer's motivation**
- Buy better than anyone else
- Make my company competitive
- To be a world-class buyer
- To keep production moving
- To hit deadlines

REMEMBER – If other buyers are better than you, guess who goes out of business – you!

3 **Cost v. Price**
- Seek competitive quotations
- Know your markets
- Challenge prices
- Establish the basis of cost
- Do the bid analysis

REMEMBER – You should create and control the competition – use your skills!

4 **Know your items**
- What is the raw material?
- How are they made?
- Where are they used?
- Are they standard or a special?

- What is the lead time?

REMEMBER – If you don't know your items you will surely pay too much!

5 Terms and conditions of contract
- Know them inside out
- Make sure they apply to your purchases
- Know what they are for
- Know what they protect
- Have a good reason to change them

REMEMBER – They are to protect your company's interests – use them!

6 Policies and procedures
- Develop key policies
- Define the procedures
- Make them work
- Tell others what they are
- Change them when they can be improved

REMEMBER – Policies and procedures give you direction – without that you are lost!

7 Beware the amateur buyer
- Buying is second priority to them
- You know the market
- You have the knowledge and skills
- Buying is your job
- You have the contacts

REMEMBER – You are trained with special skills. That's why you are a pro!

8 The min-max system
- It's not always the best way
- Stock less than mean improves profit
- Bonded stock may be possible
- Savings on stock add to profit

REMEMBER – Excessive stock is a drain on working capital!

9 Competitive enquiry
- All suppliers to have the same information
- Provide a good specification
- Ask for supplier's suggestions
- Create competition
- Create level playing field

REMEMBER – Good purchase enquiries lead to an effective purchase!

10 **Manage your in-tray**
- Check it daily
- Don't ignore tough purchases
- Don't let it manage you!
- Set priorities
- Stick to them

REMEMBER – You should be the master of the in-tray – it's good practice!

11 **Quotation analysis**
This is designed to compare the various bids for:
- Price
- Delivery
- Tool cost
- Other non-recurring items
- Payment terms
- Quality information
- Financial status
- Contractual compliance or otherwise

REMEMBER – this is an organized way to ensure that all factors are evaluated.

12 **Dealing with the supplier no. 1**
- Don't lie
- Be fair
- Be businesslike
- Give due consideration to what has been said
- Specify what you want

REMEMBER – it's your job to test and check what you are told.

13 **Dealing with the supplier no. 2**
- Listen to what is said.
- Don't let the seller control the meeting
- Listen for negotiating signals
- Don't be afraid to ask for what you want

REMEMBER – the more the seller controls you the less chance there is to negotiate. Why do you think they want control?

14 **Dealing with the supplier no. 3**
- They want the maximum price
- You want the lowest cost
- You must find the 'bottom line'
- Use competition
- Maintain enough pressure to get what you want

REMEMBER – the seller is at the most vulnerable when it is realized you are looking for one last concession and then the order is theirs.

15 The one-off buy
- Don't buy off the price list
- Ask for a discount
- Check if there are any price breaks for quantity
- Are there future orders in the pipeline which could be used as a lever

REMEMBER – sellers make good profit from one-offs, therefore the price can be challenged.

16 Lowest ultimate cost
The lowest ultimate cost will involve many factors depending on the nature of the purchase but will probably take into account:
- Unit price
- Storage costs
- Maintenance costs
- Warranty provision costs
- Energy costs
- Life of product spares support costs
- Likely technology change costs, i.e., computer software replacement/enhancement

REMEMBER – all these costs must be quantified for make v. buy studies and for a major purchase. They must be proven by a cost benefit analysis.

17 Product rationalization
- Get your ducks in a row before firing
- Who will resist your efforts?
- What reasons for change will you give them?
- Can you obtain high level support for your actions?
- Start with something that looks readily achievable
- Make sure you find credible sources of supply.

REMEMBER – product rationalization is an excellent way to lower costs but it needs an organized approach as you select the commodity groups for action.

18 Supplier quality assurance
- Make sure your quality standards are appropriate
- Check the supplier's level of approval, e.g. BS 5750.
- Send them a QA questionnaire.
- Make a visit with QC personnel.
- You want defect free deliveries.
- Get samples of workmanship – take up references.

REMEMBER – SQA is a total approach involving you and the Supplier. Standards cannot ever be compromised. If they are take immediate action.

19 Speeds and feeds
- Take into account cycle times
- Check the level of bar stock wastage.
- What type and specification of raw material is being used?
- Use your eyes when observing the process.
- Keep a record of your observations.

REMEMBER – You don't need a PhD in space age engineering to check key events at a supplier – good observation should be developed.

20 The blanket order
- It isn't used for ordering blankets for a hospital!
- It can be used for the life of the item/model.
- The schedule is the instrument of the Purchase Order.
- It provides a single record for all items purchased from a supplier.
- Additions can be made simply.
- It is an administrative mechanism which reduces work.

REMEMBER – these blanket orders can be introduced and maintained very easily and they will reduce workload, letting the time be used for other things.

21 Front of purchase order conditions
- They are no substitute for the main terms and conditions.
- They supplement the main terms and conditions.
- Define the detail precisely!
- If in doubt seek a senior manager's advice.
- Make sure they accurately reflect what has been agreed.

REMEMBER – the complete package of purchase order terms and conditions of contract are a critical feature of the deal – make sure you get them right!

22 Savings
- They can always be found!
- The buyer must take the initiative.
- The lowest ultimate cost is a moving target.
- Know your costs through the supply chain.
- Tell someone when you have a success.

REMEMBER – a continuous programme of savings must be a key performance indicator for every buyer!

23 Before you place the order I
- Make sure you know the price
- Check material cost
- Check labour cost

- Check overhead amounts
- Establish the profit
- Find out if tooling costs apply

REMEMBER – you should be controlling price, not only now but in the future.

24 Before you place the order II
- Know the contractual detail from your customers
- Talk to your commercial department
- If your company is paying damages – so should the supplier
- Establish performance criteria on quality
- Check your rights to cancel

REMEMBER – you must not expose your company to unacceptable contractual risk.

25 When you get a price increase notification
- Check what the contract says
- Check cost movements
- Check the original quotation
- Obtain competitive quotations
- Check impact on your business
- If the impact is adverse reject it

REMEMBER – supplier's price increases add to your company's costs and make them more uncompetitive.

26 Knowing intellectual property rights
- If you are buying a new item make the supplier sign a confidentiality agreement
- Brief the design team not to divulge secrets
- Check patent rights when they are claimed
- Check if a supplier's patent can be 'got around' without breaking the law
- Ask if you can use their IPRs and what will it cost

REMEMBER – IPRs are either yours, the supplier's or someone else's – check them out!

27 You need a grasp of detail
- Know your spend per commodity
- Know your spend per supplier
- Know your total spend
- Know if the contracts are being performed
- Know the markets
- Know your suppliers, commercially and technically

REMEMBER – you are accountable for your commodity portfolio, have the detail to hand, you never know when you will be asked.

28 Management of objectives
- You need achievable objectives
- Discuss them with your boss
- If you think they are not achievable – say so but justify it
- Always set tough targets
- Monitor your progress

REMEMBER – you must provide self-motivation for hitting your objectives, the will to succeed must not be sapped!

29 Your training requirements
- Analyse your strengths and weaknesses
- Where can you improve your knowledge?
- Where can you improve your skills?
- What new subjects are developing
- Do I read enough?

REMEMBER – you need continual training and development, never stop learning.

30 Suppliers' contracts
- Find out how many there are in your spend area
- Read them carefully
- Identify the contractual risk
- Establish the expiry date and period of notice
- Check the supplier's performance
- If they are not performing you may cancel

REMEMBER – suppliers generally don't write contracts to help you so – **WRITE YOUR OWN!**

31 When a product is for test
- Ensure you have an agreement whereby it can be returned.
- When does the test end?
- What represents acceptable trials?
- What are you liable to pay?
- Who insures the product on your premises?

REMEMBER – you must control this situation otherwise you will find that the product remains even if it is really unsuitable!

32 Alternative approaches to buying
- Do a make v. buy study
- Do a buy v. make study
- Do a hire v. buy study

- Do a lease v. buy study
- Do a rent v. buy study
- Make sure you establish all the relevant costs

REMEMBER – there are valid alternatives to outright purchase, these must be considered but your costs must be very accurate.

33 Minutes of meetings
- Keep your own notes of the meeting
- Use them to summarize main points at the end
- Make notes of the personalities you meet
- Issue the minutes to the other party

REMEMBER – records of meetings may be required many months after the original discussions and by then your memory has faded; notes are essential.

34 Contractual basics
- Develop your own contractual terms and conditions
- Aim for a retention amount – say 20%
- Develop your logic for damages, liquidated or unliquidated
- Make stage payments (if you must) against milestones

REMEMBER – It is the buyer's job to ensure that the contractual detail has been agreed with the seller and that the risk is minimized.

35 Buying capital equipment
- Always start from a neutral specification
- Never issue one supplier's specification to another supplier
- Ensure buying is involved at a very early stage
- Involve all interested parties

REMEMBER – capital equipment buying involves large sums of money and the buyer must create as much competition as possible.

36 Pricing considerations
- Get the price broken down to at least sub-assembly level
- Price the spares separately
- Get the costs of product support
- Identify 'one-off' costs, such as design

REMEMBER – the price will be a large amount and it is therefore essential that the buyer understands all the constituent elements of the proposed price from the seller.

37 Writing a contract
- Work out a plan before you start
- Prepare the main contract headings
- Draft the main clauses

- Discuss them with legal / commercial experts

REMEMBER – writing contracts is a very serious matter and the detail cannot be left to chance, therefore the planning is critical.

38 Reducing contractual risk
- Don't accept the seller's conditions of sale
- Don't compromise your contractual requirements
- Make the supplier accountable for breaches of contract
- Realize that contractual terms and conditions can cost money if you get it wrong

REMEMBER – the battle of the forms must end with the buyer making sure that the buyer's contractual terms and conditions prevail.

39 Anticipate the seller's objections
- The seller will not want consequential loss in the contract
- The seller will want force majeure
- The seller will want the contract jurisdiction in the country where they are domiciled
- The seller will wish to limit the guarantee period

REMEMBER – the seller will seek to minimize contractual risk – for them! You are paid to protect your business and that you must achieve.

40 Negotiation of terms and conditions of contract
- Make the seller detail any objections they have to your conditions of contract
- Work out the possible cost and risk to you if you deviate from your requirements
- Make the seller responsible for key aspects such as delivery and quality
- Emphasize how important your contract is and why performance is vital

REMEMBER – the negotiation of terms and conditions of contract is very difficult and you must understand the absolute detail in order to be successful.

41 Thinking about negotiation
- It is a tremendous skill
- Many buyers have not worked hard enough to develop the skill
- The seller is usually well trained in negotiation
- You can always improve your skill level

REMEMBER – negotiation skills are vital in the success of a buyer in all sorts of negotiation situations, do everything possible to sharpen your skill!

42 Planning for a negotiation

- Ensure you have allowed enough time
- Decide what are the main features of the impending negotiation
- Think about all the 'angles'
- Try to anticipate the seller's objectives

REMEMBER – you should allocate sufficient planning time to ensure you deal with the detail of each point that requires negotiation.

43 Influencing skills

- There are only six ways to change someone's opinion
- Concentrate on positive behaviour
- Use logic and support it with facts and analysis
- Listen to the seller's points – you may learn something

REMEMBER – it is the buyer's job to influence the other party that you have a point of view which is valid, you must make the running!

44 Bringing it to a conclusion

- Make proposals to the seller for lower prices, etc.
- Make sure you deal with all key points
- Do a summary at the end of the meeting
- Don't let the seller backtrack on what has been agreed

REMEMBER – the buyer must exert the pressure for an agreement, otherwise the seller will close the sale with the buyer not in an advantageous position.

45 Finding world-class suppliers

- Read a good cross section of business journals
- Contact embassies and high commissions
- Interview representatives of existing and potential suppliers
- Visit trade exhibitions

REMEMBER – it is the buyer's job to find new sources of supply who can meet world-class standards.

46 Tooling costs

- Check how the supplier arrived at the price
- Is it full or part cost?
- Check the life of the tool, ideally expressed in quantity
- Get competitive quotations for tooling

REMEMBER – the expenditure on tooling is a critical on-going cost and it must be controlled and negotiated just like everything else.

47 Forecasting skills

- Get the economic city pages in the press

- Seek help from financial colleagues
- Check labour and material cost movements
- Read what the contract says about price movements

REMEMBER – the ability to forecast possible movements in any aspect of cost is a tremendous help with forward planning of selling prices.

48 Open book negotiations
- Use open book to eliminate unnecessary cost
- Permits the seller to make a constructive input
- It may uncover estimating errors
- Imposes an ethical code upon the buyer

REMEMBER – this is a new style of managing a supplier's costs and many are not ready for this dialogue.

49 Issue a professional purchase enquiry
- Supply accurate information
- Send the contractual terms and conditions of contract
- Ask for relevant information such as cost breakdowns
- Identify non-recurring costs, such as design and tooling

REMEMBER – The quality of your purchase enquiry will convince the seller that there is a competent buyer handling the enquiry and that is a help!

50 Visiting suppliers
- Do a commercial audit
- Do a quality audit
- Meet the key people and some of them will not be the directors!
- Have a look around the offices and factory

REMEMBER – the effective buyer will visit key suppliers on a regular basis and will plan for this activity – the truth is at the supplier's premises.

51 Sourcing policy
- Use only qualified suppliers
- Take risk of supply into account when making decisions
- Don't put all your eggs in one basket unless there is good reason
- Think about supplier rationalization programmes

REMEMBER – an effective sourcing policy lies at the heart of a buyer's strategy; the right balance of suppliers is essential.

52 The ideal buyer
- Has integrity and courage
- Deals with queries promptly and efficiently
- Is not a 'clock watcher'
- Believes in satisfying the client's needs

REMEMBER – a dedicated buyer stands out a mile with colleagues and commands respect from suppliers.

53 Going overseas to buy – the minimum you need
- Credit cards, passport, travellers cheques, etc.
- Your terms and conditions of contract
- Understanding of the culture
- Commercial audit documents
- Tooling or other special questionnaires
- Dates of public holidays, religious festivals, etc.

REMEMBER – the conventions of your country are most unlikely to prevail elsewhere and therefore you must take account of this when visiting overseas suppliers.

54 When you are negotiating
- Don't let them pressure you with time or language
- Ask for privacy if you have to do complex calculations
- If you don't understand any phrases, ask for clarification and persist until you do understand
- Don't assume words mean the same in each country
- Maintain your ethical beliefs – no matter what the temptation

REMEMBER – overseas negotiations will be quite different and you must adjust to the different practices, timings, culture, etc.

55 Provisional contractual agreements
- There may be no contract but you can reach agreement in principle
- Dig in on major points – don't feel inferior if you don't understand the language
- Know the difference between letters of intent and instructions to proceed
- Write down the salient points in such a way that you can later understand the detail

REMEMBER – you may wish to reach provisional agreement pending final confirmation of a contract when you return to the office, make that absolutely clear to the other party.

56 Negotiating overseas – more pointers
- Use an interpreter if you need to, don't struggle to the point of no return
- Maintain a pace that you are comfortable with
- Beware of commercial data sent by you to the office, it may be read
- Your timescales are not theirs, so don't be impatient
- Think about the payment methods and know how they work
- Check the political situation

- Be aware of the inflation rate and its history
- Don't accept excessive hospitality
- Observe the customs of the country
- Be sensitive to loss of face when 'winning' a major point
- Do not reveal highly confidential data of other suppliers
- Never sign anything in a meeting
- Recap all major points and make sure there are no misunderstandings

REMEMBER – you cannot return to the country to tie up the points you missed the first time around – get it right first time. That demands high-level planning.

APPENDIX B: STANDARD FORMS FOR PHOTOCOPYING

PURCHASE ORDER

TO: THE SUPPLIER

DATE:...............

PURCHASE ORDER No 1500

FROM: THE COMPANY

CONTACT........................

TELEPHONE....................

FACSIMILE......................

DESCRIPTION

A-165588 BRACKET   £1.00 EACH.

QUANTITY: 500

PACKING: NON RETURNABLE

DELIVERY POINT: NO 6 STORES

DELIVERY REQUIRED BY 21.09.95

TO CONFORM TO SPECIFICATION 99-409/341. COPY ATTACHED.

....

SIGNATURE   COUNTER SIGNATURE

CONFIRMATION SLIP   **PURCHASE ORDER No 1500**

We confirm that we accept the order subject to the terms and conditions overleaf and that delivery will
be as requested.

....(Authorized signature) for supplier.

ENQUIRY

TO: THE SUPPLIER   FROM: THE COMPANY

DATE: ....   CONTACT: ....

                                                 TEL NO: ....

WOULD YOU PLEASE PROVIDE YOUR QUOTATION FOR THE ITEM/S, MATERIAL/S, GOODS OR SERVICES LISTED BELOW:–

3049 Pressing   1000 per annum

2741 Casting   5000 per annum

9024 Clamp   500 per annum

These items are the components for the assembly 304–6150 widget, and are shown on the assembly drawings and specs enclosed. Do not quote for assembly, in line with operation sheets no. 715/137/22 enclosed.

....

SIGNATURE

Notes:

1. Please quote 'DELIVERED OUR WORKS' (Incoterms, 1990).
2. Tool costs are to be shown separate from unit cost and whether part or full tool cost.
3. Samples must be provided off production tools.
4. VAT to be shown separately.
5. Packaging costs must be included in unit cost.
6. Quotation should observe terms and conditions printed overleaf.
7. Period of price stability should be shown.
8. Quotations to be considered must be received not later than four weeks from date of enquiry and remain open for acceptance for a period of 90 days.

QUOTATION ANALYSIS

Part no.	Current price	Supplier price A	Supplier price B	Supplier price C	Current vol.	Supplier A Vol. × price	Supplier B Vol. × price	Supplier C Vol. × price	Current Vol. × price
Totals									

Recommended source

Supplier Code: A = Romeo-Papa; B = Zebra-Foxtrot; C = Lima-Tango.

Component sets to produce 304–6150 widget

EXAMPLE

Part no.	Current price	Supplier price A	Supplier price B	Supplier price C	Current vol.	Supplier A Vol. × price	Supplier B Vol. × price	Supplier C Vol. × price	Current Vol. × price
3049	£0.75	£0.64	£0.79	£0.73	1000	£640	£790	£730	£750
2741	£1.00	£1.05	£1.01	£1.04	5000	£5250	£5050	£5200	£5000
9024	£3.12	£2.95	£3.05	£2.75	500	£1475	£1525	£1375	£1560
Totals						£7365	£7365	£7305	£7310

Recommended source: Supplier C

PURCHASE ORDER AMENDMENT

TO: THE SUPPLIER   FROM: THE COMPANY

DATE: ....   CONTACT: ....

NO 307   TEL NO: ....

WITH EFFECT FROM   ....   (DATE) WOULD YOU PLEASE AMEND ORDER
NO.   ....   FOR THE UNDERMENTIONED ITEM/S, MATERIAL/S, GOODS OR
SERVICES AS SHOWN BELOW:–

....

SIGNATURE

CONFIRMATION SLIP

We confirm receipt of Purchase Order Amendment no.   ....   to Order No.   ....
and confirm that the Purchase Order Amendment will be implemented as requested. Any costs
associated with this change will be advised separately.

....   SIGNATURE (for Supplier)

ORDER

TO: THE SUPPLIER

DATE: 20.10.95

ORDER: 2140

FROM: THE COMPANY

CONTACT:

TEL NO:

7613 Shaft.   £30.00 ea

Price stability until 1/10/96.
Samples submission date 10/1/96.
Quantity p.a. 30 000. Delivery to Schedule.

Finish: Lightly oiled.
Engineering level 30451/22/1.
Specification: 9345/93.

PACKING INSTRUCTIONS.

Both ends are to be protected by plastic caps.

Shafts are to be delivered in 'A' stillages in four layers of 10. Each layer is to be separated from the layers above and below with corrugated cardboard.

SEE PACKING SPEC M 167.

DELIVERY TO NO 10 STORES.

....

SIGNATURE   COUNTER SIGNATURE

....

CONFIRMATION SLIP   ORDER NO 2140

We confirm we accept the order and delivery will be as required.

....   Signature (for supplier).

DRAFT BUYING CARD

Part no 236–002		Description 3″ × ⅛″ bolt 'S' quality steel		Engineering E.I. release no 47493		First release 1/1/93	

Release date	Quantity	Requisition no.	Delivery required	Received	Supplier	Competition	Price delivered
1/1/93	2000	971	7/1/93	9/1/93	Tree Ltd	Smith Ltd Green Inc.	50p each
3/3/93	4000	1050	10/3/93	14/3/93	Smith Ltd	Tree Ltd Green Inc.	45p each
6/6/93	3000	1120	12/6/93	11/6/93	Tree Ltd	Smith Ltd Green Inc.	48p each
9/8/93	4000	1300	19/8/93	21/8/93	Tree Ltd	Smith Ltd Green Inc.	48p each
11/10/93	5000	1720	28/10/93	28/10/93	Green Inc.	Smith Ltd Tree Ltd	43p each
1/2/94	2000	3100	7/2/94	6/2/94	Tree Ltd	Smith Ltd Green Inc.	50p each
1/4/94	5000	3700	20/4/94	18/4/94	Green Inc.	Smith Ltd Tree Ltd	43p each
1/6/94	2000	3800	15/6/94	15/6/94	Smith Ltd	Green Inc. Tree Ltd	45p each
1/8/94	1000	4020	14/8/94	13/8/94	Tree Ltd	Smith Ltd Green Inc.	50p each

PART NUMBER	DESCRIPTION	WHERE USED
236–002	3″ × ⅛ bolt S. Qual	Stores/Product XP

Quantity required		*Delivery frequency*
18 000 p.a.		400/week

Supplier	*Unit price*	*Payment terms*
Tree	£0.39	30 days nett
Green	£0.37	60 days nett
Smith	£0.365	60 days nett

Quality report

Tree	100% quality
Green	100% quality
Smith	98% quality

Financial status

Dun & Bradstreet Reports.
Tree. No adverse reports. Trading satisfactorily.
Green. No adverse reports. Trading satisfactorily.
Smith. Three recent actions on non-payment of bills. £200 credit maximum allowed.

Supplier comments in quotation letters

Tree. Packed in 500 lots.
Green. Packed in 1000 lots.
Smith. Packed in 250 lots.
All three sources state delivery as required.

STATIONERY QUESTIONNAIRE

	Miss A.	Qty.	Miss B.	Qty.	Mrs M.	Qty.	Mr X.	Qty.	Mrs W.	Qty.	Totals
Paper clips	1	70	2	30	3	45	6	48	4	74	267
A4 paper	1	60	2	25	3	19	6	91	4	48	243
Biros	1	50	2	91	3	16	6	48	4	36	241
S/B files	1	48	2	24	3	60		96	4	72	300
Rulers	1	6	2	18	3	12	6	36	4	48	120
Corr. fluid	1	6	2	24	3	12	6	18	4	36	96
Envelopes	1	120	2	60	3	120	6	400	4	240	940
Manilla folders	1	96	2	200	3	68	6	72	4	84	520
Pritt	1	60	2	30	3	12	6	9	4	12	123
F/C seps.	1	24	2	36	3	48	6	12	4	50	170
Erasers	1	12	2	24	3	12	6	11	4	16	75
Typing ribbons	1	24	2	48	3	36	6	48	4	36	192
Comp. discs	1	20	2	30	3	15	6	23	4	21	109
Pencils	1	36	2	96	3	36	6	28	4	24	220
In-trays	1	4	2	8	3	7	6	11	4	3	33
Calendars	1	6	2	8	3	2	6	13	4	5	34
W/bins	1	0	2	3	3	4	6	4	4	1	12
Note-books	1	3	2	5	3	7	6	11	4	6	32

Paper clips: boxes of 100; paper: quires.

Code 1. Alpha Stationers; 2. Orange Stationers; 3. Victor Stationers; 6. Bravo Stationers; 4. Easy Stationers.

BUYER'S JOB DESCRIPTION

1. Job title: BUYER
    Reports to: CHIEF BUYER

2. Organization:

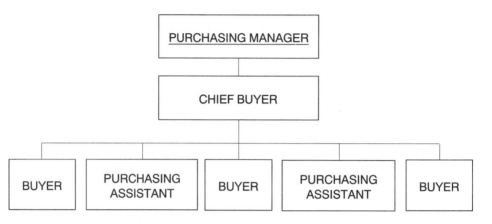

3. Functional reporting lines, other relationships

Each buyer controls an annual turnover approximately £1m minimum (turnovers vary according to complexity and other factors).
   These expenditure responsibilities will cover a range of materials, services and requirements on which the buyer has, or can rapidly develop, speciality market knowledge, both UK and worldwide.
   The objective is to acquire these requirements at the lowest ultimate cost, by identification and establishment of the most effective and cost-efficient suppliers available.
   The work comes from various departments in the shape of requisitions, production releases etc. and the responsibilities include:

(a)   establishing lowest ultimate cost for new projects at the quotation stage;
(b)   acquire materials, goods and services required for current needs at the quotation stage;
(c)   non-production materials required by end-users;
(d)   capital equipment;
(e)   prototype materials required by design engineering, etc.

In addition to the foregoing close contact should be maintained with:

quality control
production engineering
accounting/finance
design engineering
safety department, etc.

   So the buyer has to be 'au fait' with their requirements in order to achieve lowest ultimate cost objectives.

Close links are maintained with suppliers at all levels within their organizations to ensure that the company is obtaining the requirements from the supplier at lowest ultimate cost.

4.   Responsibility for bringing work into the firm

In addition to the prime objective, which is source selection to provide the company with suppliers who meet the company's needs at the lowest ultimate cost, there is a secondary role.

This is to consider where appropriate value analysis, cost analysis, make v. buy can work towards achieving lowest ultimate cost, either with suppliers or **within the company**.

5.   Managerial responsibilities

In certain areas, the buyer will have a small team consisting of an assistant in the form of a junior buyer or a purchasing assistant but apart from this, does not normally have managerial responsibility **within** the company.

Nevertheless, by use of strategic and tactical planning, the buyer manages the efforts of suppliers to meet the prime objective.

Liaison is maintained with internal 'customers' in order to help them manage their own functions by suggesting more cost-effective methods in acquiring, and use of, their material and service requirements.

6.   Undertaking work

By various requisitioning procedures as outlined in (3), work of varying complexity and urgency is undertaken. Considerable discretion must be showed in order that work is dealt with in such a manner as to ensure that materials required by the 'customers' are delivered on time.

In order to obtain these at the lowest ultimate cost, a range of initiatives are created which include:

(a)   study of potential/actual economic movements;
(b)   study of worldwide markets and commodities;
(c)   study of potential suppliers and source selection;
(d)   manipulation of markets in order to create leverage with suppliers giving the company competitive advantage;
(e)   historic data used to forecast likely future demand.

From these processes which go to create market knowledge, enquiries are made in the appropriate market, negotiating price agreements which meet lowest ultimate cost objectives with the most appropriate and efficient suppliers.

In pursuance of these objectives, regular meetings are held with suppliers, sometimes at the buyer's premises, sometimes at the supplier's works in order to further the buyer's projects. In addition, regular meetings must be held internally with production control, manufacturing, sales/marketing, quality control, design engineering, accounting, factory management, as well as meetings within purchasing with the staff and management.

7.   Innovating

It is axiomatic that there are always further cost benefits which are available. Methods include:

•   material substitution;

- component rationalization;
- improved supply/inventory methods such as bond stock, consignment stock etc.;
- inventory reduction;
- improved supplier performance;
- supplier concentration;
- importation skills;
- currency control;
- use of competition;
- make v. buy;
- supplier liaison;
- contract writing;
- joint developments;
- supplier manufacturing methods;
- value analysis.

The buyer will always be reviewing the foregoing against the range of commodities for which responsibility is taken in order to uncover new opportunities.

In this regard, the buyer needs to be at a high level of skill and knowledge which is constantly improved on in the fields of:

- commercial law;
- UK/foreign contracting;
- methods of manufacture;
- labour and overhead rates;
- stores/inventory;
- budgeting/planning/finance;
- procedures/systems;
- market knowledge;
- negotiation psychology;
- best course analysis.

8. Workflow

As has already been alluded to in (6), the buyer must always be able to align the expeditious conversion of requisitions into enquiries and then to completed orders, while creating and sustaining an environment of efficient cost-effective suppliers.

This requires good levels of skill in time management and job prioritization in order that the two separate aspects of the buyer's role are harmonized.

The buyer is often required to work to extremely tight deadlines and thus often works under pressure.

9. Skills

The skills listed in (7) are acquired in the Chartered Institute of Purchasing Diploma, or Higher National (Business Studies), plus the Purchase Specialities or in BA Business Studies, followed (or in parallel) with experience gained in a purchasing working environment.

After training, buyers should be proficient in the first commodity ranges, in 9 to 18 months, then should be rotated on to other commodity ranges, in one year to two year cycles, since the wider the commodity range experience, the more effective they become and the more promotable they become.

QUOTATION ANALYSIS BY MAJOR FEATURE

Feature	Noccini	B & L	S & J	Dartmoor
1	£5000	£4000	£6000	£3000
2	£5000	£4000	£6000	£3000
3	£7000	£8000	£5000	£6000
4	£10 000	N/A	£10 500	N/A
5	£50 000	N/A	£52 000	N/A
6	£15 000	£12 000	£16 000	£14 000
7	£30 000	£30 000	£29 500	£30 500
8	£140 000	£160 000	£120 000	£165 000
9	£40 000	£37 000	£39 000	£42 000
10	£48 000	£50 000	£44 000	£60 000
11	£40 000	N/A	£41 000	N/A
12	£20 000	£18 000	£22 000	£16 000
13	£200 000	£180 000	£180 000	£195 000
14	£90 000	£80 000	£85 000	£79 000
15	£150 000	£140 000	£138 000	£152 000
Totals	**£850 000**	**£723 000**	**£794 000**	**£765 500**

CAPACITY TOOLING QUESTIONNAIRE

In responding to the accompanying enquiry could you please respond to the following questions:

1. Please provide a brief description of the special tooling planned. Also please state if multiple or single unit tooling.

   . . . .

   . . . .

2. What machine/machines will the above special tooling be mounted on?

   . . . .

   . . . .

3. What is the hourly production rate planned?

   . . . .

   . . . .

4. Are there alternative machines that the special tooling can be mounted on, without modification of the special tooling?

   . . . .

   . . . .

5. Does the supplier work a single or double shift?

   . . . .

   . . . .

6. What is the lead time for the acquisition of the special tooling?

   . . . .

   . . . .

6b. Will the special tooling be made in or bought out?

   . . . .

   . . . .

7. What is the lead time for the acquisition of the appropriate raw material?

. . . .

. . . .

8. What is the normal transport you will employ to deliver to this plant?

. . . .

. . . .

9. What is your preferred delivery frequency?   . . . .

10. What is the normal transit time from your plant to ours?

. . . .

. . . .

THE COMMERCIAL AUDIT

1. Supplier name and address	Telephone Number Facsimile Telex
2. Compnay structure	Plc Privately owned etc.
3. Management structure and names	Chairperson Managing Director Sales Director Engineering Director Purchasing Director
4. Number of factories and locations	Brief description
5. Associations with other companies	Ownership Sister companies
6. Founded	History
7. Factory: (a) area of plant (b) extension opportunity (c) structure (d) ownership, i.e. rented	
8. Condition of buildings	Brief description
9. Employees	Staff Hourly paid Production/non-production
10. Processes carried out: (a) state: capacities (b) obtain plant list (c) facilities	
11. Major customers > 2% of supplier's turnover	
12. Quality control approvals AQUAP. BS5750 etc.	
13. Wage review anniversaries	
14. Industrial relations history	
15. Financial status Annual report? Do they accept open book negotiation?	
16. Prepared to hold stock?	

17. Payment terms.	
18. Carriers. Own/other	
19. Toolmakers. Own/other	
20. Internal scheduling system	
21. Internal Purchasing resources	
General notes	

APPENDIX C: INCOTERMS

The International Chamber of Commerce first developed their International Commercial Terms (Incoterms) in 1936, with the aim of defining uniform rules for the interpretation of trading terms. These have subsequently been updated in 1953, 1967, 1976, 1980 and 1990, to take account of new methods of transportation and lately advances in communications technology, e.g. electronic data interchange (EDI).

Function of Incoterms

The prime function of Incoterms is:

> To determine at what point the seller has fulfilled their obligations so that the goods in a legal sense could be said to be delivered to the buyer.

They also have secondary functions to define:

1. the responsibility for providing export and import licences;
2. the responsibility for and the extent of insurance cover;
3. the packing of the goods;
4. the nature and type of documents and responsibility for their own origination;
5. the duties of both parties to notify the other of arrangements made;
6. the duty for any checking operations.

Bills of lading/non-negotiable documents and EDI

The bill of lading has traditionally satisfied three functions:

1. proof of delivery on board nominated vessel;
2. evidence of existence of carriage contract;
3. provide a negotiable document permitting sale of goods in transit.

In recent years the use of non-negotiable documents, e.g. 'sea waybills' and 'liner waybills', has increased. Such documents satisfy the purpose of bills of lading in so far as they provide proof of delivery on board and evidence of the existence of the carriage contract.

Such documents, when agreed between the two parties, may be replaced by an

EDI message. It should be stressed, however, that under current ICC rules the bill of lading cannot be replaced by a non-negotiable document or EDI message for the purposes of selling goods in transit. Their use should thus be restricted to such contracts where there is no intention for the buyer to sell the goods in transit. It is expected, however, that changes will be made in the rules to provide for the use of EDI for all contracts.

Incoterms 1990

The terms have been grouped in four basically different categories.

Group E -- departure
This Incoterm deals with contracts where the intent is for delivery to be effected at the seller's premises.

Group F – main carriage unpaid
Under these Incoterms the seller is obliged to deliver the goods to a carrier as appointed by the buyer.

   FCA – free carrier
   FAS – free alongside ship
   FOB – free on board

Group C – main carriage paid
Under these Incoterms the seller has to contract and pay for the main carriage of the goods. It is important to note that under Group C terms the seller **does not** assume responsibility to risk in the goods or additional costs incurred after shipment or dispatch.

   CFR – cost and freight to port or destination
   CIF – cost insurance and freight port of destination
   CPT – carriage paid to named place of destination
   CIP – carriage and insurance paid to named place of destination

The distinction between port of destination and place of destination is drawn to take account of different modes of transport. The CFR and CIF terms should only be applied for sea and inland waterway transportation.
For transport where the ship's rail bears no practical purpose, e.g. roll-on, roll-off or container transport, the CPT and CIP terms should be used.

Group D – arrival
Under Group D the seller is responsible and assumes risk in the goods and all costs incurred in delivering the goods to the country of destination.

   DAF – delivered at frontier
   DES – delivered ex-ship
   DEQ – delivered ex-quay

FOB – seller's responsibilities

1. Provision of goods and commercial invoice or EDI message in conformance with the contract for sale.
2. Obtain at seller's risk and cost such export licenses and clearance necessary for the export of the goods.
3. Deliver the goods on board the vessel nominated by the buyer at time stipulated by the buyer and in a manner customary at the port of shipment.
4. Bear all risks in the goods up to the point where the goods pass over the ship's rail at the port of shipment.
5. Pay all costs related to the transport of the goods up to the point that they pass over the ship's rail at the port of shipment.
6. Pay all costs related to export/customs clearance and documentation.
7. Give the buyer sufficient notice that the goods have been delivered on board.
8. Provide the buyer with such documentary proof as defined in the contract for sale of delivery at the seller's expense. Where this is agreed with the buyer this may take the form of an EDI message.
9. Pay the costs of all checking operations for delivering the goods to the vessel for shipment.
10. Pack the goods in a manner required for their transport in so much as the mode of transport is known.
11. Mark packaging in appropriate manner.
12. Assist the buyer, at buyer's expense, in obtaining any documents or EDI messages required for importation of the goods or transit through another country.

CIF – buyer's responsibilities

1. Pay the price of the goods as provided for in the contract of sale in accordance with agreed method and credit terms.
2. Obtain at buyer's risk and expense import licence and clearance necessary to import of the goods.
3. Accept delivery of the goods from the time they have been delivered to the nominated vessel at the port of shipment and receive them at port of destination.
4. Bear all risks and costs from the point where the goods have passed over the ship's rail.
5. Pay all costs associated with the carriage of the goods with the exception of main carriage costs, from the point the goods are delivered on board the vessel at the port of shipment. These costs to include unloading costs, lighterage and wharfage costs.
6. Pay all taxes, duties, customs clearance costs and other official charges associated with import of the goods.
7. Give seller sufficient notice of time for shipping the goods and/or port of destination.
8. Accept the documentary proof of delivery as defined in the contract of sale provided by the seller. Where agreed this may take the form of an EDI message.
9. Pay, unless otherwise agreed with the seller, all costs associated with the

pre-shipment inspection unless mandated by the authorities of the country of exportation.
10. Pay all costs incurred by the seller in providing documents or EDI messages required for importation or transit through another country.
11. Provide the seller with information necessary for procuring insurance.
12. Pay all costs incurred by the buyer in rendering assistance in obtaining such documents or EDI messages necessary for the purposes of delivering the goods.

DDP – buyer's responsibilities

1. Pay the price of the goods as provided in the contract of sale in accordance with agreed method and credit terms.
2. When requested by the seller provide, at seller's expense, every assistance in obtaining import licences or other official authorization required for the import of the goods.
3. Take delivery of the goods.
4. Bear all risks and costs in the goods from the point where they have been delivered.
5. Bear risks and costs in the goods should the buyer fail to take delivery at the agreed time and place notified to the seller, providing that such goods have been clearly set aside for the buyer.
6. When entitled so to do by the contract, stipulate the time and place of delivery.
7. Accept delivery documents or EDI messages provided by the seller.
8. Pay, unless otherwise agreed with the seller, all costs associated with pre-shipment inspection unless mandated by the authorities of the country of exportation.
9. Render the seller, at seller's expense, with any assistance requested in obtaining such documents or EDI messages necessary for the purposes of delivering the goods.

We acknowledge the source of Incoterms as ICC Publication Number 460 ISBN 92-842-0087-3.

Even though Incoterms help the transfer of ownership, there are still points of interpretation.

1. the duty to provide export and import licences;
2. the nature and type of documents;
3. the extent of insurance protection;
4. the duty to pack the goods;
5. the duty of paying for checking operations.

The importation of goods has to be preceeded by the negotiation with the overseas source to agree the Incoterm and then who will cover items 1 to 5 above.

All of the costs naturally add to the unit cost and it is to the buyer's advantage to attempt to have CIF or DDP as the term borne by the supplier in order to ensure that the final unit cost is competitive.

In fact, it is wise to request all overseas sources to quote at either CIF or DDP in the enquiry.

APPENDIX D: CODE OF ETHICS

In 1976, the Institute of Purchasing and Supply, as it was then, issued a Code of Ethics (slightly abridged here) which has stood the test of time.

Purchasing personnel shall never use their authority or office for personal gain, and shall seek to uphold the standing of the profession by:

1. maintaining an unimpeachable standard of integrity in all their business relationships both inside and outside the organization in which they are employed;
2. fostering the highest possible standards of professional competence among those for whom they are responsible;
3. optimizing the use of resources for which they are responsible to provide the maximum benefit to their employing organization;
4. complying with both the letter and the spirit of:
   (a) the law of the country in which they practise;
   (b) such guidance on professional practice as may be issued by properly constituted bodies including the Institute of Purchasing and Supply;
   (c) contract obligations;
5. rejecting any business practice which might reasonably be deemed improper.

In applying these precepts, purchasing personnel should follow the guidance set out below.

1. *Declaration of interest*
   Any personal interest which may impinge or might reasonably be deemed by others to impinge on any purchasing personnel's impartiality in any matter relevant to his or her duties should be declared.

2. *Confidentiality and accuracy of information*
   The confidentiality of information received in the course of duty should be respected and should never be used for personal gain. Information given in the course of duty should be fair and true, and never designed to mislead.

3. *Competition*
   While bearing in mind the advantages to the purchasing personnel's employing organization of maintaining a continuing relationship with a supplier, any arrangement which might, in the long term, prevent the effective operation of fair competition should be avoided.

4. *Business gifts*

   Business gifts other than items of very small intrinsic value such as business diaries or calendars should not be accepted.

5. *Hospitality*

   Modest hospitality is an accepted courtesy of a business relationship. However, the recipient should not allow him or herself to reach a position whereby he or she might be or might by others be deemed to have been influenced in making a business decision as a consequence of accepting hospitality; the frequency and scale of hospitality accepted should not be significantly greater than the recipient's employer would be likely to provide in return.

6. When it is not easy to decide what is, and what is not, acceptable in terms of gifts and hospitality the offer should be declined or advice sought from the employee's superior.

APPENDIX E: THE CHARTERED INSTITUTE OF PURCHASING AND SUPPLY PROFESSIONAL QUALIFICATION COURSE OF STUDY

The Professional Qualification can be studied through distance or flexible learning, part-time in local colleges, or full-time in selected higher education institutions.

The Professional Qualification is awarded by the CIPS and entitles the holder to seek corporate membership of the CIPS.

The general course of study follows the areas shown below:

Foundation stage

Economics
Business Law
Quantitative Studies
Business Accounting
Management Principles and Administration
Introduction to Purchasing and Supply Management

Professional stage (compulsory subjects)

Purchasing and Supply Management I
Planning, Policy and Organization
Purchasing and Supply Management II
Provisioning
Purchasing and Supply Management III
Logistics
Purchasing and Supply Management IV
Legal Applications
Case Study

Professional stage (elective subjects)

Materials and Production Management
Marketing
Project and Contracts Management
Public Services
Retail Merchandise Management
International Purchasing
Project

APPENDIX F: MANAGEMENT BY OBJECTIVE – POSITION OF MBO REVIEW PART-WAY THROUGH YEAR

MANAGEMENT BY OBJECTIVE			
NAME:		**SUPERVISOR:**	
PERIOD:		**PURCH.MGR:**	

Objective	Weighting	achievement	
1. Paint, oil and grease Turnover £70 000	10		
2. Electrical requirements Turnover £60 000	8		
3. Cutting tools Turnover £100 000	14		
4. Janitorial services Turnover £50 000	8		
5. Stillages and pallets Turnover £70 000	8		
6. Forklift trucks Turnover £60 000	10		
Items 1–6. Unit prices to be held at or below last years.			
7. Rectify administration. Problem on forklifts and copying machines	10	10	Problem resolved. Over- payments recovered
8. Rectify production administration. Problem with stillages and pallets	12	12	Problem resolved
9. Learn French to intermediate std. (London Chamber of Commerce)	10		
10. Attend Farrington negotiation course	10	10	Course attended
Total possible	100		Score achieved

Objectives agreed.

Signed .... Buyer   .... Chief Buyer

Concurred .... Purchasing Manager

FURTHER READING

Baily, Peter and Farmer, David. (1990) *Purchasing Principles and Techniques.* (6th edition) Pitman for the CIPS.

Berg, A. G. (1991) *Drafting Commercial Agreements.* Butterworth.

BSI Buyers Guide. (1990) BSI Quality Assurance, PO Box 375, Milton Keynes, MK14 6LL.

Dobler, D. W. and Lee, Lamar (1981) *Purchasing and Materials Management,* McGraw-Hill.

Farrington, Dr B. and Waters, Derek (1994) *Managing Purchasing,* Chapman & Hall.

Farrington, Dr B. (1993) *Negotiation Techniques – A Guide to Key Factors,* Brian Farrington Ltd.

Raven, A. D. (1971) *Profit Improvement by Value Analysis, Value Engineering and Purchase Price Analysis,* Cassel Management Studies.

Sutton, C. J. (1980) *Economics and Corporate Strategy,* Cambridge University Press.

INDEX